SAINT DOMINIC'S SUCCESSOR

SAINT DOMINIC'S SUCCESSOR

The Life of Blessed Jordan of Saxony
Master-General of the Dominican Order
1222 - 1237

by
MARGUERITE ARON

INTRODUCTION BY P. MANDONNET, O.P.

MEDIATRIX PRESS
MMXVIII

ISBN: 978-1-953746-29-0

Nihil Obstat:
Patricius Morris, S.T.D., L.S.S. *Censor Deputatus*

Imprimatur:
✠ E. Morrogh Bernard, *Vic. Gen.*
Westmonasterii, die 10a Novembris, 1954

Originally published in French by Desclée de Brouwer under the title '*Un Animateur de la Jeunesse au XIII Siècle*'.
First published in English in 1955 by Black Friars.
This work is in the Public Domain.

Typesetting ©Mediatrix Press, 2018. Reproductions may only be made for educational purposes, quotations in articles or reviews.

Mediatrix Press
607 E. 6th Ave
Ste. 230
Post Falls, ID 83854

CONTENTS

INTRODUCTION.. vii

Chapter I
    AT THE UNIVERSITY OF PARIS..................... 1

Chapter II
    MASTER OF ARTS................................ 21

Chapter III
    AT THE PRIORY OF ST JACQUES................... 33

Chapter IV
    FROM PARIS TO BOLOGNA......................... 47

Chapter V
    BOLOGNA, CITY OF LEARNING..................... 65

Chapter VI
    MASTER GENERAL OF THE FRIARS PREACHERS... 91

Chapter VII
    EN ROUTE...................................... 111

Chapter VIII
    'I AM GOING TO ROME'.......................... 135

Chapter IX
    CREATIONS AND CONQUESTS....................... 153

Chapter X
    FROM OXFORD TO MILAN..................... 173

Chapter XI
    THE LAST YEARS............................ 197

Chapter XII
    THE WORK AND THE MAN..................... 213

INTRODUCTION

FTER ten years of apostolate in Languedoc (1205-1215) St Dominic, with the consent of the Roman Curia, had established and built up the Order of Friars Preachers with an astounding precision and rapidity. With a handful of men, he had accomplished the seemingly impossible. The high aim of the Order and the means proper to attain it were firmly fixed by the time of his death, August 6, 1221, and already the new institution extended throughout Europe.

Meanwhile, so clear was Dominic's idea and so vigorous the strength of the initial impulse given to his work, that only four years had passed since that August 15, 1217, when he had sent out the little group of his first disciples from Toulouse, in the name of Christianity; and although the work was growing well, it was still fragile because of its novelty.

The Founder had aimed to recruit, not only students fitted to lead the apostolic life which he had just established for the first time in Christian Europe, but also, with his characteristic foresight, capable lieutenants to second him in the administration of the Order and, when necessary, to succeed him.

Already, in the appointment of the first and only Abbot of the Friars Preachers, Matthew of France, founder of the Priory of St Jacques in Paris, there is foreseen some thought of investing for the future; but it was chiefly in Reginald, dean of the chapter of St Aignon at Orléans and former professor of the University of Paris, that Dominic believed he had found his counterpart, as much in apostolic ardour as in the art of government and the power of attracting the young men of the schools.

After having done wonders at Bologna, Reginald was about to continue his work at Paris in a field of action long familiar to him; but almost as soon as he arrived there, he died. However, he had had time to take into the new Militia of the Friars Preachers a celebrated Master of the University, whom Dominic had already noticed during his stay at Paris in the preceding year (1219)—Jordan of Saxony.

It was this man, after the loss of its great Founder, who was to be unanimously placed at the head of the whole Order by the General Chapter of the Friars Preachers held in Paris in 1222. Even though he had worn the habit only two years and a few months, it was manifest to all that Jordan of Saxony was predestined to be the successor of St Dominic.

Both of them were endowed with the same apostolic ardour and the same precise knowledge of the needs of the Christian society of their time; Dominic and Jordan had also in common something exceptional among religious founders of that age: a doctrinal culture which allowed them to fulfil literally the programme which the official title of their Order implies.

The *Ordo Praedicatorum*, which ecclesiastical tradition and even canon law from the time of Innocent III identified with the *Ordo Doctorum*, represents the teaching activity and authority of the Church, whether in regard to the Christian layfolk or in regard to clerics themselves deputed to lead the faithful. In imposing these titles and the obligations which they implied on the Dominican Order, to ensure through its means an efficacious doctrinal apostolate, the Roman Church had opened an immense field to the new Friars Preachers and the extent of the task was equalled only by the number and gravity of the obstacles to be overcome.

When Jordan of Saxony was hastily elected Master General of the Order, he already occupied an important place in his government of the Province of Lombardy.

Now, suddenly, an unlimited field was presented to him. Jordan viewed it with serenity and resolution. He could not have been ignorant of the multiplicity and gravity of the obstacles which stood abundantly in his path; but he worked his hardest to face and overcome them. He, like Dominic, had the faith which moves mountains, and also he had hope of great assistance, which was never to fail him, especially and above all that of the Roman Church. Without presumption he could also rely on himself. His experience of men and his previous experience of governing, a persuasive oratory like that of none other, great dexterity in the conduct of business affairs—these things encouraged him; and if the modesty of the new Master General left him in some doubt as to his personal worth, the members of the General Chapter of 1222 who raised him to the dignity of their head could not be mistaken about the gifts which nature and grace had imparted to the former Master of Arts of the University of Paris.

The life of Jordan of Saxony was ruled by the exigencies of his office, the consolidation and promotion with all his power of an institution which, the first of its kind in the passage of the Christian centuries, was especially dedicated to the evangelization of the faithful and of the infidels, and to the teaching of the sacred sciences.

In the Order of Friars Preachers the central point of community life was the annual General Chapter whose business is to legislate, command and correct, while the Master General ensures the execution of what it initiates and of all the measures taken by the sovereign assembly.

Two Most General Chapters were celebrated under the government of Jordan of Saxony, both at Paris, in 1228 and 1236, the only such which the Order has known. They were evidences of the intense activity which pervaded Dominican life at these times; their aim was to hasten the development of the laws which the rapid growth and progress of the Order demanded.

In Jordan's time, the General Chapters were held at Pentecost, alternately at Paris and at Bologna, and they constituted, so to speak, two sources which regulated and controlled the travels of the Master General, since he was obliged, unless absolutely prevented, to preside each year.

Paris and Bologna were, moreover, from the time the Friars Preachers began, the two principal theatres of their activity, because there more than anywhere else were concentrated the Christian schools of the twelfth century, and it was from the world of letters, from the body of cleric students, that the Friars Preachers drew the best part of their recruits. That is why Jordan of Saxony regularly devoted a notable time each year to evangelizing the Universities and to drawing a great number from among them, both masters and students, into the ranks of the Order. And if a scholastic strike took the students away, whether from Bologna or Paris, Jordan went to join them and to win them over in the very places whither they had withdrawn. His contemporaries estimate at a thousand the number of recruits he brought into the Dominican life. It was under his government that the Friars Preachers, incorporated as students of the University of Paris from their first establishment there in 1217, obtained about ten years after two chairs in theology; and it was Jordan himself who instituted at Paris the custom of religious conferences in the evening on Sundays and feast days for the young men of the schools.

To the work of recruiting for his spiritual family the new Master of the Friars Preachers added that of foundations throughout the Christian world. He was probably unable to visit all the houses that were in existence before his election or founded under his generalship; but by his personal relations he had in many cases prepared for the establishment of the Friars Preachers in towns where their preaching had never been previously heard. In many places he had watched over the beginnings, upheld the courage of his sons and removed difficulties. If it had merely depended on him, no Province would have been without the presence of his zeal and his devotion. We know that well enough when we see him perish in a shipwreck near Ptolemais in 1237 because he had wished to bring to his sons in the Holy Land the consolation of a visit from him and the benefit of his wisdom.

Historical documentation relative to the life of Blessed Jordan of Saxony not only lets us know the multiform works he accomplished but also allows us to enter intimately into his personality, a rare thing with the celebrated men of his era. We owe this privilege largely to the important series of letters from him which have been preserved for us. In spite of their relative brevity these letters are rich in historical information, and they reveal to us the profound depths of their author's soul, his qualities and his character. We feel, through his advice and his direction, the intensity and firmness of his religious faith, his detachment from earthly things and his heavenly aspirations and the solid and deep affection which he felt for his spiritual daughters and his friends. Jordan of Saxony has left us the first collection in Christian Europe of letters of spiritual direction addressed to a woman—Blessed Diana d'Andalo. In this respect he marks an epoch.

We would like to know the level of the international culture of this University man who led so many others to the Order of Preachers, but here we run up against a great problem. It is not difficult to judge the literary worth of Jordan of Saxony, to the extent that this expression must be understood relative to the thirteenth century. In his *De Initiis Ordinis Praedicatorum*, devoted to the history of St Dominic and the first luminaries of the Order, Jordan reveals himself as a master of the art of composition. The good arrangement of this work, the sobriety and swift pace of the exposition, the purity of style, the elegance of the wording, all place our author, from the point of view of perfection of form, well above most of his contemporaries and certainly above the many historians who wrote about St Dominic in the century following his death. In the second Master General of the Friars Preachers we meet a remarkable man of letters.

But if Jordan of Saxony is a writer of taste, a master of the Ars Dictaminis, to use a contemporary phrase, is he also the great mathematician of his era? It could not be doubted if Jordan of Saxony is to be identified with Jordan Nemorarius, as historians of the sciences and critics generally, especially in Germany, would do. In that case it would be easier to explain the exceptional development of the Order of Friars Preachers in the thirteenth century not only in the theological and philosophical sciences, which flowed directly from its vocation, but in the sciences properly so called; and we should follow clearly a generation which was to go from Jordan of Saxony to Albert the Great, to St Thomas Aquinas, and to William of Moerbeke, to indicate only the greatest. Useful information concerning this problem of identification will be found in the present work.

The author of this interesting study of Jordan of Saxony has been concerned to make the book worthy of the subject himself. Caught between two possible historical procedures, pure erudition and simple popularization, she has taken the middle road to give satisfaction to the greatest number of readers. She has reduced the amount of references and technical discussions in order not to displease those who are not interested in documentary evidence and who are sometimes unhappy about it; on the other hand, she has allowed to remain a limited critical apparatus to meet the needs of historical science and to permit the initiated to go back to the documentary sources if they are interested and desire to do so. In this way she does not waste the long labour of the research required in undertaking a biography of Jordan of Saxony.

I offer my excuses for having so poorly dealt with the contents of this book. I have the sole merit of having been brief. I trust I may have indicated sufficiently to any hesitating reader what he will find if he continues to read, namely, the knowledge, through a well-informed and agreeably written book, of a beautiful page of history from the most beautiful century of Christian Europe.

P. Mandonnet, O.P.
Le Saulchoir, March 7, 1930.

CHAPTER I
AT THE UNIVERSITY OF PARIS

'He was studying at the University of Paris.'[1]

HE year was 1220. The University was still new, scarcely organized under the statutes recently given to it by a former chancellor of Notre Dame, Robert de Courcon, who had become Cardinal and Papal Legate; the University was the tremendous pride of Paris in the reign of Philip Augustus.

Paris, with its new ramparts, its workmen laying flagstones at great expense, under the admiring gaze of loungers, on the crossing of the two Roman roads cutting one another at right angles on the banks of the Seine, its masons raising with famous speed the white towers of Notre Dame and the heavy round towers of the Louvre; established on the four city bridges covered with gabled houses and shops, and encircled with its cincture of beautiful abbeys, spread out beyond the moats of St Victor and St Germain in the meadows and vineyards—this Paris was itself a very young city.

More than its ancient reputation, more than the dignity of its history, the students during their stay in Paris savoured this newness, which enchanted them. They boasted of its beauties. They scattered in lively groups through its streets, sometimes singing and cocking a snook at the townsfolk, and sometimes escorting in procession the reliquary of St Geneviève, when the Chapter of Notre Dame carried it back with full honours from the sanctuary of the City to the sanctuary of the Mount.

To study at the University of Paris was a joy and it conferred

---

[1] 'Hic eum esset scolaris Parisius, et probus (alias: probatus) in theologia.' *Vitae Fratrum*, note by Humbert Romans.

a cachet. 'A universal association'—as its name says[2]—of masters and scholars studying together in Paris, the University of Paris was a confused agglomeration of divers schools where private initiative played greater part and administrative organization much less than official usages of today would be able to permit. It was not even then, in the early days of its existence, a corporation properly so-called. The only corporative mark of the whole was the privilege by which, in 1200, King Philip had put the masters and scholars of his capital under the sole control of the ecclesiastical authorities. A privilege of this sort was in some sense imposed by the very fact that, in those days, anyone who studied or taught was necessarily a cleric. Thus the youthful collection of professors and pupils, often equal in age, governed themselves according to their own sometimes variable customs.

At a time when books, all of them manuscripts, were rare and costly and public libraries were non-existent, intellectual people could not learn or impart the learning they had acquired except by oral teaching. The master alone owned the texts which he expounded by drawing from them material for his lectures, so much so that to teach and to read were one and the same thing. Thus each student attached himself to a master—or lector (reader)—freely chosen by himself, followed him with his companions to the house where he had established his professional chair and daily received from him knowledge which he in his turn, if later he showed himself capable, communicated to other hearers less advanced than he. Each one who had the talent for it thus passed from the rank of disciple to that of master; and often, while already teaching some subject wherein he had proved himself, he nevertheless pursued instruction as a pupil in some other branch of knowledge.

The universal language was Latin. It was the only one understood by everyone, for this scholastic milieu was an

---

[2] Universitas magistrorum et scholarium Parisiis studentium.

international one. From this time on all Christian Europe sent its young students from all parts to 'the City of Letters and the Mother of the Sciences', as the University of Paris was called. Rome had the Papacy and Germany the Empire, but France had the kingdom of the Schools.

But people of the same nationality found and joined one another in this cosmopolitan territory of the intellect. Affinity of language and customs determined their grouping, and not political frontiers which did not yet exist. Four principal nations were enough for them to divide these clerics of the Paris schools into four groups, offering them local regulations and a closer fraternity. There was the nation of France, which united to the people of the Ile de France the Provençals, who came from south of the Loire or from the valley of the Rhone, and the Lombards from northern Italy; and by itself it equalled in number the three other nations: the Normans, the Picards and the English, the latter numbering also amongst them the Teutonic students.

Masters and pupils of the same nation lived together in hostels, which meant that they lived a communal life in furnished houses which the townspeople rented to them, generally as dearly as possible when the authorities did not impose limited fixed prices on them. There they lived as best they might, with a common exchequer, taking care of one another when they were sick, reprimanding one another and generally acting the policeman according to their own customs, and choosing from among their number 'chiefs', 'rectors' or 'provosts' according to their countries.

Those who were fairly rich lived in grand style; the poor scraped through somehow by selling their old clothes, worming things out of distant relatives by heartrending letters, by whatever subsidies they could obtain, and by going into parishes of the city, for a trifling salary, to give the liturgical responses to the priests who were not often served by any but illiterate acolytes.

Among themselves they spoke their native language, pleasantly intermingled sometimes with the barbarous Latin that served as the usual interpreter between the nations.

In this way, from the evidence of the most ancient chronicles of the Friars Preachers—and better still, from the memories recorded by himself—we can picture Jordan living in a hostel with several students of his own nation, among others Henry of Marbourg and Leo of Germany. Being of noble family he lived in comfort, possessed books, gave alms, and being older and more learned than his companions, as it seems, he exerted a certain authority over them.

The scholastic division among the students of Paris was not that of the four nations but that of the four Faculties: the Liberal Arts, Law, Medicine and Theology.

Each faculty imposed on its schools its customs, its intellectual discipline, and its already established traditions as to the recruiting of students and the granting of the degrees which it conferred. And, something characteristic of the Middle Ages, each had its own territory. The Faculty of Arts and the Faculty of Theology in particular marked out sharply on the map of Paris their respective areas.

From the end of the twelfth century Theology, which had flourished for a short time in the famous abbey schools of St Victor and of St Geneviève, was no longer taught except in the cloister of Notre Dame, under the eye of the Bishop and in the heart of the city; and for a long time the masters of theology were to be forbidden to 'cross the bridges', at least until about 1230 when, with the establishment of schools by the Friars Preachers and the Friars Minor, the domain of theology would extend to the door of St Jacques.

Logic, on the other hand, and the secular sciences, ruled over the slopes of the left bank where the most famous schools of the arts had already caused the name of University to be given to the whole of the new quarter bounded by the rampart of Philip Augustus, from the tower of Nesle to the Porte St Jacques and from the Porte St Bernard to the moats of St Victor and to the banks of the Bièvre.

There, following the courses of teaching bequeathed to the Middle Ages by the Roman Studium, they studied both the *Trivium*, that is grammar, rhetoric and logic—*lingua, tropus, ratio*—*and the Quadrivium*, learning arithmetic and music, geometry and astronomy—*numerus, tonus, angula, astra.*

The interior portal of the narthex vestibule of the Cathedral of Chartres, built in the twelfth century before the schools of Chartres, made famous by master savants, had not yet been gradually eclipsed by the schools of Paris, shows at the feet of the Blessed Virgin Mary—Seat of Wisdom—allegories of the seven liberal arts. These were considered the necessary antechamber through which the mind, at first curious about secular researches, was introduced to the knowledge of divine things. Many clerics especially, and among them the greatest, delayed long in the study of the arts, often also studying medicine or law, and certain theologians, like Jean de St Gilles and Roland of Cremona, did not supplicate until very late for the doctor's hood.

The schools of liberal sciences were established for the most part not far from the banks of the Seine, in the neighbourhood of the Petit-Pont or in the rue du Feurre, or Fouarre, so named because of the hay and straw which were sold there and which provided the students at the schools with the bedding on which they curled up in a huddle. The houses were very small and poorly furnished. Fires destroyed the houses of the Petit-Pont, which were then rebuilt, not of wood, but of good stone.

The heavy mass and sombre arch of the Petit Chatelet at the bottom of the rue St Jacques, guarding the entrance to the bridge, watched over, and if need be housed, the restless population of the students of arts. Not only most of the lodgings of this section of the University, but the narrow and crooked alleys interweaving around the straight, steep rue St Jacques, and the small plots and orchards by which they were broken up, and the very atmosphere which floated above the pointed roofs and vividly coloured tiles punctuated here and there by the grey leaden roof of a chapel—all was theirs, and it was not a good thing to dispute their possession of a particle of it.

They had driven back the 'decretists'[3] to the foot of the St Geneviève mountain, into the enclosure of an old Gallic-Roman villa, called 'le clos Bruneau', which today is represented by the blocks of houses in rue Jean de Beauvais and nearby.

The medical apprentices were still wandering in search of settled quarters. Their masters took them for lectures to the cloisters of hospitable abbeys and even into the churches, especially the church dedicated to St Geneviève, in the western part of the city, under the title of 'St Geneviève des Ardents' because, during the reign of Louis VI, the patron saint of Paris had healed the fever-ridden people who invoked her and had arrested in that city the terrible epidemic of the 'mal des ardents'.[4]

The arts students were actually the most numerous and the most restless of all the students, because they were the youngest.

From the age of fourteen the youths could be admitted to the Faculty of Arts, provided they could read and write and possessed the first rudiments of Latin, which they would learn in the little episcopal schools.

Seven years were usually devoted to the Trivium and the Quadrivium. At twenty-one the student in arts had normally completed this cycle, and if he was reputed to be of good morals and the reports of his masters were unanimously favourable to his capacities, a 'licence to teach' could be given to him, within the territory of their respective jurisdictions, by the chancellor either of the Chapter of Notre Dame or of the abbey of St Geneviève. He was then free to conduct a school if he had the necessary resources. So although the number of masters of arts was large

---

[3] Students in ecclesiastical law, or in decrees.

[4] They soon found shelter in the Friary of the Friars Minor (Cordeliers), near the present location of the School of Medicine and the Dupuytren museum.

enough, the worth of their teaching was diverse in the extreme. For many, however, teaching was a just trial of their powers, or a way to earn a living, rather than a definitive pursuit, a career such as today occupies a man's whole life.

At that time when a determined scholastic hierarchy and routine 'channels' were still unknown, a man could teach while he was still learning under a master, and he could teach geometry after having given lectures in grammar and logic, and could pass from one professorial chair to another.

There is attributed to Jordan of Saxony a commentary on Priscian which shows that he taught grammar. But, far from inferring that because he was a grammarian he was not a geometrician, this evidence of his mastership in arts indicates that after having taught the *Trivium* he could and indeed must also have given lectures to students of the *Quadrivium* and have written commentaries on numbers, angles or weights. Finally, it would be still more rash to deduce that, having been master of arts, he could no longer be a student of theology.

Thus the degrees of one Faculty did not confer any rights in another. Their respective courses of study did not depend in the least on one another, and a man was not led to pass inevitably and rapidly from one course of studies to another. Sacred science did not attract all the clerics. A large number never got that far because they did not persevere in the clerical state but returned to the world to follow a career as a lawyer, a diplomat, a great lord with some learning, perhaps a scribe or a juggler. Others, who were destined for the priesthood but aspired to the highest offices, thought that knowledge of one kind of law or another would be more useful to their future career and more suitable than theology in view of their desire for fat benefices or their ambition for important chancellories or large dioceses.

Jordan separated himself from such types and took another path.

The Faculty of Theology was of another order. It sheltered and united chosen students in the shadow of the buttresses of Notre Dame and if it constituted, as has been said, 'the masterpiece of the University of Paris', if it was and would be the supreme glory and most undeniable speciality, this was due not to the number of its students or its masters, but to their quality.

We know from a Papal Bull that in 1219 there were only nine chairs of theology at Paris. The holders were carefully chosen. They knew personally and watched closely all their students, who were relatively few in number. Very quickly they picked out from among them the ones most fitted to become masters in their turn and entrusted to them a part of the teaching. But it was not until the student had been seen at work for at least two years, after he had been tested by having to give oral expositions, readings with commentary, and had held public disputations with other candidates and with masters of the subject, that the chief Professor finally presented him to the Chancellor of Notre Dame and had him entrusted with a series of lectures.

These lectures bore on the text of the Bible. They were still elementary in character and, above all, impersonal. They were meant to initiate newcomers into the literal sense of the Sacred Books, in such a way as to open out in the minds of the listeners thus predisposed a clearer road to future commentaries by the master himself.

The student who was charged with this duty—we would today call him an assistant teacher—might be prematurely called 'Bachelor' but was more often designated 'biblist' and even more frequently called '*cursor*'—the reader of the current text in abridged form, briefly explanatory of the whole passage.

For himself this reading of Holy Scripture was only a preparation. It did not normally occupy more than a year. If it ended to the satisfaction of the master, the '*cursor*' went up a step. He became '*sententiarius*', that is to say, he was allowed to comment (for two years) upon the great manual of general theology of the time, the classic work of Peter Lombard, the 'Book of the Sentences'.

He had now become a theologian; from day to day becoming more practised in speaking and having behind him at least five years and often more of hard study in sacred science, he was in many cases counted with the acknowledged masters who treated him as an equal.

His position was much more like that of a present-day lecturer or supplementary professor in the Faculty than that of a student. It was at this point that his contemporaries gave him the title of 'bachelor' (*baccelarius*) *and to distinguish it from* '*cursor*' and '*sententiarius*' they often added the word '*formatus*' or '*probatus*', and by contraction or false reading '*probus*'. He is the complete bachelor; if he is over thirty-five years of age (for according to the statute of Robert de Courcon he must be at least thirty-five to become a Master of Theology) he is now ready for that title. He needs now only the formalities of the public disputations and lectures conducted in the presence of the bishop to have imposed solemnly on him the cap of a Doctor in Sacred Theology of the Faculty of Paris.

It was to this stage of Master of Arts and student of sacred science, no doubt, that Jordan of Saxony had reached when Humbert of Romans, his disciple, says of him that 'he was studying in the schools of Paris and was "*probatus*", that is to say, bachelor in theology'. That is the time, then, according to a naïve account in the *Vitae Fratrum*, that we must see him going to Notre Dame to assist at Matins of the Chapter. He had already moved from the mount St Geneviève to the City and had a lodging near the Cathedral. It happened that 'one night, the even of a solemn feast, believing the bell for the Office had already rung, he got up hastily, put on only his cloak and belt, and ran at top speed to the church. He met a poor man who asked alms, and, having nothing else he could part with, gave him the belt. When he reached the church he found the doors closed, for the bell had not rung as he had thought. He waited until the doorkeeper opened them, and as soon as he entered the church he went to pray before a crucifix. As he looked up at it often and with devotion, he suddenly saw that the figure wore around its middle the belt he had just given to the poor beggar for love of the Crucified.'

Piety, then, pervaded his studies; charity crowned them.[5] But we must not let the edifying simplicity of the ancient texts deceive us or lead us to deny to those whose doings they record the high intellectual level shown in their lives and so profoundly marked in their works.

In reading these stories of the Middle Ages, one might generally suppose that they were about children—such is the tone of the narrators. We must not ourselves be misled. These men were men, and sometimes rough men. But they did not analyse themselves and did not explain themselves. One would give much to have some texts of a more precisely historical sort, letting us catch a glimpse of the life of this élite of so many different nations, gathered in the heart of Paris to learn divine things.

Practically nothing contemporary exists of the place where so many wise discourses and so many brilliant disputations took place.

But considerations of a proper hygiene, which have steadily widened streets and squares, and the more contestable aesthetic notions which must at all costs segregate the monuments of the past and isolate them by the clearing away of all evidence of life around them, have, between them, completely disfigured the city of the Middle Ages. Banal avenues, ugly façades and cold spaces replace what was formerly a very hearthstone of life.

---

[5] Jordan of Saxony must have been affiliated to the Confraternity of 'Parisians who get up to say matins'. This 'Confratemitas Beatae Mariae Parisiensis surgentium ad matutinas' had been founded recently, in 1205. (Lebeuf and Cocheris, Hist, de la Ville et de tout le diocese de Paris, 1883.) It was composed of pious men who, in imitation of canons, got up in the middle of the night and came to assist at their matins. It is not too much to suppose that it was recruited from among the students of theology.

The uneven, entangled houses and the green enclosures have disappeared. The most important buildings, like l'Hôtel Dieu, have been reconstructed in a barrack-like style on sites opposite to those which they used to occupy. The cathedral closes, shaved bare and enlarged, have become weary waste spaces in front of the cathedral. The steep banking up of the river has raised the level of the ground and this, together with the narrowing of the quays, has deprived the base of the cathedral of its twelve steps and lowered its height by that much. In those days the City was a low-lying island, with a grassy circumference, connected to the river banks by only four bridges[6]; it bristled, in every direction, with uneven roofings, little steeples and towers; huddled about the scarcely finished Notre Dame were twenty-two churches and a mass of dwelling places of various sorts.

At the left of the great portal of the cathedral, backed against its north flank, St Jean le Rond, former baptistery of the bishops, lifted its Gallic-Roman cupola. Close by, withdrawn somewhat, opened the door of the cloister.

A little city in the big one, the cloister of Notre Dame enclosed its houses, its little gardens, its covered walks where clerks chatted, within the ellipse between the two curves of the north bank of the island and the apse of the cathedral. On the south side the bishop had his palace, and an arched passage led down to his private landing-stage on the little arm of the river: the Port l'Évêque.

The embankments of the quay and the Pont d'Arcole have covered the remains of these, and razed a whole group of river houses where the bishop lodged his guests and servants. Beyond them and off the cathedral close itself opened the merciful gate of the 'Hospital of the Blessed Virgin Mary', l'Hôtel Dieu, which the Chapter, at great expense, had recently substituted for an earlier

---

[6] Le Pont St Michel and le Petit Pont on the south, le Pont Notre-Dame and the Exchange Bridge on the north.

hospital, St Christopher's, which had become too small. Of the latter the oratory alone remained, situated just in front of the new buildings, which were on such a scale that, although they were begun in 1165 and occupied in 1195, they were not completed until toward the end of the reign of St Louis. They stretched between the cathedral close, the rue du Sablon, the *marché palud*, and the Seine which they overhung by means of a closed gallery, whilst down along the river edge were the wash-houses, the laundries and the disinfecting ovens. A covered footbridge linked them to the wide domains on the left bank where soon the church of St Julien le Pauvre was built in an enclosure and reserved as a chapel for the Infirmary Sisters.

There, all sick persons, whoever they were, once they had been to confession and received Holy Communion, were served like lords whom God had sent in order that they might be received in his name and be treated as though it were himself.

Meanwhile in the little square space of the cathedral close surrounded by low walls, stall-keepers held a permanent market-fair. A fountain, ornamented by the enigmatic antique statue which Parisians had perhaps already begun to call 'le grand Jeuneur' ('The Great Faster') or 'Monsieur le Gris' ('The Grey Gentleman'), furnished an abundance of clear water for the inhabitants. An immense crowd of people (say the documents of that time) herded together in these spots which were enlivened by the noise of the oars, the shouts of the boatmen and the songs of the washerwomen at the water's edge.

The little island of Notre Dame, which the Pont Neuf had since connected to the City, showed not far downstream its green patch of pasture-land and its poplars surrounding a little farm belonging to a boatman.

Upstream, the course of the Seine embraced in its windings still more islands of fallow land: the Ile St Louis, the little Ile Louvier which could still be seen, facing the Arsenal, in the days of Charles Nodier; the Ile aux Vaches, and two others which have disappeared under the piles of a modern bridge.

The City remained a world apart. And in this area, limited in size but of right proportions, in which were singularly mingled the animation of the city and the freshness of the country, the grave charm of study and the generous grace of a youthful civilization, permeated throughout with Christianity, the students in theology, isolated by the river from the tumult of the rue du Fouarre and du Clos-Bruneau, strangers to the brawls of the Pré-aux-Clercs, still aloof from the intrigues and ambitions of that century, began a life of most profound thought.

Such is the milieu in which we must look for Master Jordan on the eve of his entrance into the Order of Friars Preachers. There he moved, lived, breathed, thought and prayed, worked and developed in himself the Dominican vocation which was to change his destiny.

There, if we could know it better, we might hope to catch a first glimpse of him among his fellow-disciples and his masters.

Who among them had instructed him in the 'Sentences'? Of whom had he become the cursor and afterwards the sententiarius? Was his teacher the excellent Jean de Barastre, dean of the Chapter of St Quentin, the same who gave his house at the St Jacques' Gate to the first Parisian Friars Preachers and whose professor he was? Was Jordan the disciple or the comrade of Master William of Auvergne, future Bishop of Paris? Both of these men were there, surrounded by students already famous in scholastic disputations and some of them destined to glorious futures: Robert Kilwardby, later archbishop and cardinal, the most celebrated Augustinian doctor of the century; Haymo of Faversham, who was to be Minister of the Franciscan Order; Boniface of Brussels, amiable and eloquent Cistercian, later Regent of the schools of Cologne and at the same time bishop of Lausanne; finally more intimately linked with Jordan, his two compatriots, Leo the German and Henry of Marbourg.

Generous friendship and fraternal confidence were the rule in this select company, more serious than in the Arts circles, probably more mature also. Most students in theology, it seems, had passed their first youth. Henry of Marbourg appears to have been one of the youngest; especially if, at the time of his premature death in 1225, he was 'in the middle of the prime of life', as the text of a letter of Jordan of Saxony[7] would make us think, he was not less than twenty-five or thirty years old in 1220. The others were more advanced in age, some with perhaps fifteen or twenty years of University life behind them.

Because Jordan was *sententiarius* in theology, it is groundless to conclude that he must have been a very young man. How can we reconcile such a baseless hypothesis with the fact of his election, two years later, as Master General of the whole Order of Preachers? We cannot imagine with any likelihood that the preacher companions of St Dominic, already mature in apostolic works and several of them formerly famous masters in the schools, would have unanimously put at their head a very young student.

This very rapid elevation from total obscurity to so much power and responsibility, from being nothing to being everything, makes us think. We know nothing about him as Bachelor of Arts of the City. Nevertheless he took the habit of the Order at the Priory of St Jacques on Ash Wednesday, 1220; and although he had spent—as he himself tells us in De Initiis Ordinis—only two months in the Order, it was he who with two other Parisian Friars was sent to represent Paris at the first General Chapter called by St Dominic at Bologna. As soon as he returned, he was named lecturer in the Priory where he had just been received. The following summer St Dominic and the second General Chapter called him to be head of the Province of Lombardy, the most

---

[7] 'Excellent labourer in the vineyard of the Lord, he was called not at the end of the day, but at about the sixth hour.' The day of the Gospel labourer (Matt. 20) was twelve hours and the normal duration of human life, in Biblical style, would be seventy years; this symbol can be interpreted as giving about 35 years to Henry of Cologne at the time of his death.

important province of the Order. Less than a year later, St Dominic having died in the interval, it was Jordan who was elected as his successor.

It cannot be said that he was a young unknown. He was neither young nor obscure; he was a personality!

It is too ingenuous to rely upon the arithmetic that consists of calculating the hypothetic years of a regular academic course, and to say: at twenty-one, the course of the arts is finished; five years of theology? Let's say he is twenty-six. Or to calculate: If he had just passed as master of theology, he would have been not far from thirty-five; but he was not that old yet; let us say he was thirty-two—not more. He was still only a sub-deacon.

We know, from the evidence of Jordan himself, that he did not receive deacon's orders until after he had seen and consulted St Dominic[8] and had been to confession to him, and that St Dominic did not come to Paris until the summer of 1219. But here, as when it is a question of the degree of bachelor, modern customs lead the imagination astray. However, even in our own time and in our seminaries we see late or retarded vocations. But in the Middle Ages, although all who were at the Universities were either clerics or aspiring to become clerics, they were not all in major orders and many never would be. The taking of ecclesiastical orders never parallels the taking of University degrees. It is not necessary to consecrate oneself to God's service in order to study theology. On the other hand, some priests were such bad scholars, knowing so little Latin and pronouncing it so badly, that a student could one day play on a curé of Paris, whom he was serving, the trick of giving him street-cries as responses, without his noticing it. There were even bishops so little learned that the election to the bishopric of the dean of the Chapter of Chartres, Hugh de la Ferte, was annulled by the Pope because 'the said dean has too little

---

[8] Sanctum magistrum Dominicum ... vidi... ci confessus sum et, ad ipsius voluntatem suscepi diaconatus officium. *(De Initiis Ordinis.)*

learning'.

The clerical life was distinguished from the lay in that while the latter was the life of illiterates, the former was that of the student; and the clerical state signified intellectuality, not inevitably the priesthood. Moreover, there were many important people in the theological world who followed the study of sacred science until far advanced in it, and yet remained sub-deacons indefinitely; for, although the priesthood was not required for teaching theology, the reception of one of the major orders was so required. Master William of Auvergne, renowned professor of the Faculty of Paris, from 1223 Canon of Notre Dame, was no more than a sub-deacon when in 1228 the Pope called him to Rome to confer priestly ordination on him and at the same time to consecrate him bishop. Saint Richard Wych, Master of Canon Law and Chancellor of the University of Oxford, was not ordained to the priesthood until well after that at the Priory of the Friars Preachers of Orléans: he was forty-three years old at that time. Finally, and perhaps the most curious example of all, William of St Amour, that turbulent Master of Theology of the University of Paris, was only a sub-deacon when he began that memorable quarrel against the Dominicans which threw him into conflict with St Thomas Aquinas; but he was then fifty-six years old, and he was never more than sub-deacon.

No; although Jordan of Saxony was not ordained sub-deacon until he had begun to work for the degree of Master of Theology in the cloister of Notre Dame, and although he stayed at that level, not deciding to receive deacon's orders until St Dominic advised him to do so, why should we see him as an adolescent still uncertain of himself? It seems more likely that this decision, delayed until that time, was made by a reflective man who was perhaps well over his youthful illusions.

What future was there for a distinguished man entering the secular clergy? Would he be able to preach and teach, meditate and practise mortification? Deans of chapters, canons, abbots, chancellors, bishops, saw the best part of their activity absorbed by temporal administrations which were the plague of the Church under the feudal system; and all high ecclesiastics, of whatever rank, were obliged to keep up an external state which clashed with the evangelical counsels.

We know well enough that this was one of the profoundest causes of the impotence of the higher clergy in face of the Albigensian and Vaudois heresies, and how the bishop of Osma and his sub-prior Dominic had urged the Cistercian abbots to imitate them by sending back their equipages and walking barefoot on the roads of Languedoc. This was only fourteen years previously. St Dominic himself entered Paris by the Porte d'Orléans, a simple pedestrian coming from Spain, without suite or baggage, having repudiate for himself and for the Brethren of his Order all temporal goods and administrative burdens, setting themselves free from everything except the service of God and work for the salvation of souls. Dominic was a priest—'Sacerdos Dei sanctissime', it is thus that later Jordan invoked him in the prayer which he dedicated to him. For it is by seeing him and hearing him that Jordan finally became conscious of the high and divine mission of the priesthood, which became compatible both with a life of intellectual study and with a life of evangelical renunciation; he felt himself drawn to it both by reason and by charity.

Jordan, who nevertheless did not yet, as it seems, envisage his own entrance into the Order of Preachers, decided to receive major orders. He was made deacon, and then priest.

But how old was he?

The customs of that time were strangely vague from a biographical point of view, and it is extremely rare to find the date of a birth. The best means at hand therein to establish anyone's age is to try to find a text that reveals his years at the time of his death. But so far as Master Jordan is concerned, his contemporaries did not trouble to do even that.

What impression, however, of him was preserved by the friars who witnessed the latter part of his life? What picture of him have they left us? It is that of an old man. The word '*senis*', old, is in fact found in the text of the *Vitae Fratrum*, in the most official text, the one probably revised by Humbert of Romans in his desire for precision. It occurs in an anecdote, prior to Jordan's journey to Palestine and in the very year of his death.

As always in these stories meant for the education of novices, the aim is to edify and to teach by showing how far the Master was detached from exterior things and indifferent to all that was not the love of God and zeal for the salvation of souls.

We are shown Jordan visiting some house of the Order. It was summer. He spent the recreation, as he loved to do, with the youngest friars, and sat down informally on the grass among them; and with this movement his belt showed under his scapular; and what did they see? This belt was not 'in accordance with the rule', for it had ends of silver! There was scandal and shocked whispering among the young men. One of them boldly seized the end of the belt. 'What's this, Master?' The good Jordan was the first to be amazed; never, all the while he had worn this belt, had he noticed that it was not a suitable one for a begging friar.

The narrator tells us, 'that, being already old, or, better, because he was already old', Master Jordan had one day consented to exchange his belt for that of a noble lady.[9] Was it to leave a

---

[9] Caput vigesimum secundum 'De abstraccione ejus ab exterioribus et de cingulo quod non advertit' ... 'Unde contigit semel, quod quaedam magna persona nobilis valde et devota sibi et ordini corrigiam suam pro devotione peteret et obtineret ab eo (cum autem vir sanctus recurreret, aliam non habens, accepit et illius dominae corrigiam). Unde post spacium temporis, cum esset senis, et in quodam pratello in quaedam recreatione sederet cum fratribus, et illa corrigia subtus scapulare penderet, in cujus summitate erat plastes argentea, accepit eam quidam frater et in altum elevans dixit: "Quid est hoc, magister?" Die vero curiosus et diligendus eam intuens et admirans dixit: "Deus meus, quid est hoc? Certe ego numquam nec vidi nec perpendi usque adhuc." *Vitae Fratrum.*

friendly and pious souvenir of the ladies who sometimes gave him lodging at some halting place in his long journey? Or was it the pledge of the official reception of a penitent into the Third Order, which was still indeterminate but perhaps already in existence? We are told nothing.

The fact to note for the moment is that he was old—'*cum esset senis*'.

Who is called old? It is certainly a relative term; and perhaps the thirteenth century called people 'old' whom the twentieth century would judge to be still young. Nevertheless the word was never used of Dominic, who died at about fifty years of age, or of Thomas Aquinas, who died at forty-nine. There is thus reason to think that Jordan had considerable passed the half-century.

Looking elsewhere, the tone of his letters often indicates a mature man, conscious of his authority, sometimes a man who has long fathomed the vanities of life here below. To Stephen of Spain, who had entered the Order at Bologna following the express call of Dominic, a man of importance, then prior of Lombardy, Jordan wrote about 1229 a letter of remonstrance which was singularly firm.[10] To Diana d'Andalo he did not fear to show, in a letter which seems to have been the last of their correspondence, a deep tenderness and a definite detachment from things of this earth.

It is probable that Jordan of Saxony had lived long enough to become an old man; and even supposing, with some truth, that this old man, still an intrepid traveller and tireless preacher, had not passed his sixtieth year when he died, in February 1237, still, seventeen years previously the Bachelor of Theology of the Faculty of Paris could hardly have been less than forty-three years old.

---

[10] 'Your conscience has taken alarm at a rustling of leaves... You must learn that it is not prudent to change your mind every time someone expresses a new opinion.'

CHAPTER II
MASTER OF ARTS

IF Jordan of Saxony had reached his fortieth year before he entered the Order of Preachers, before he had even pursued his study of theology as far as the doctorate, how many years then had he spent in the Faculty of Arts? What had he so long, and doubtless so profoundly, studied and taught in the Trivium and the Quadrivium?

He was a good grammarian, a consummate classical Latinist, and there is attributed to him a Commentary on Priscian, which seems to have been of some repute[1] in the schools of the thirteenth century. But he was not a man to spend so long playing with words and phrases. The course of his life and work shows him to be supremely realistic; we must therefore look for some other interest. Now, just at the same time—at any rate, in the opinion of all historians of mathematics, before 1231[2]—a Master of Arts by the name of Jordan left his mark as an incomparable teacher in the mathematical sciences. He was frequently designated under the name of Jordanus Nemorarius, or Jourdain or Jordan de Nemore; perhaps it was he who was also called Jordanus Weige;[3] and often, most often, simply Master Jordan.

No indication of his origin, no trace of his biography remains to us today; a mystery which makes us suspect that his real identity is mingled with some other. Only his work, even though imperfectly preserved, vigorously attests his existence and stands out as a precious landmark in the history of the sciences in the Middle Ages. It is of sufficient worth to make competent savants,

---

[1] *Notula Super Priscianem minorem*, a unique manuscript kept under number 1291 in the Library of Leipzig.

[2] Daunou: 'Jordanus Nemorarius, or Jordan the Forester, must have begun his work about 1183 or later, and had finished it before 1235.'

[3] Pierre Boutroux, Les principes de l'analyse mathematique, I 1914, II 1919. T. II, p. 467.

like Buoncompagni and Libri in Italy, Moritz Cantor, Treuttlein, Max Curtze in Germany, and in France Chasles, Pierre Duhem, and Pierre Boutroux (to name only the principal ones) hail it as a work of genius and very advanced for a period which did not, as yet, know the Euclidian traditions.

Whether he had already received, by some channel unknown to us, some knowledge of the work of Archimedes and of his infiltration into Arabian science, or whether he was urged on by his genius alone, he worked on the general notion of number, introduced the algebraic language into geometrical demonstrations of the Euclidian type, and caught a glimpse of the solution of problems of the displacement of equilibrium. The author of this work, whoever he was, showed himself to be an accepted master in mathematics and statics and he was a recognized authority up to the Renaissance and even afterwards.

The schools of the *Quadrivium* were growing in importance to such an extent that, in the last years of the twelfth century, the literary studies of the *Trivium* were shortened in order to enable the students to proceed the sooner and with great eagerness to the study of the sciences. In these schools of the *Quadrivium* the Middle Ages already counted some specialists in the science of weights, geometricians interested in the problem of equilibrium. They remained anonymous, however, and in the learned writings of this period, the only name appearing with those of Archimedes and Euclid is that of Master Jordan 'Nemorarius'.

In arithmetic and in geometry, to judge by the treatises 'De Lineis Datis', 'De Triangulis', 'Elementa Arismetice' attributed to him, he shows himself to have been a first-rate expositor, already in advance of his times; but in the 'De Ponderibus' he reveals himself to be an original worker of genius. He widened the horizon and inaugurated a method which enabled the researches in statics to take a great leap forward, starting to build on 'the scanty alluvium of Greek and Mohammedan science' which the scholastics then had at their disposal. He founded a school; indeed, the number of works credited to him is too great to belong to only one man; and, as was done in the Middle Ages, later geometrists, more or less direct disciples of his, elaborated under his name commentaries inspired by him.

The works in which we find the undoubted traces and first movement of a new thought and the proper mark of the master's originality, is the 'De Ponderibus', an introduction to a thesis by a Greek geometrist, named Chariston, on the Roman balance, entitled 'De Canonio', and a 'Philotechnes', in part lost (evidently the fate of Jordan Nemorarius was doomed to be mysterious) but of which the remnants are singularly rich in wise hypotheses and have commanded the attention of modern savants.

With the treatise 'De Lineas Datis', these works enjoyed a classic fame for three centuries; copies were made by the Universities for the use of the Masters; on February 2,1476, Arnauld de Bruxelles, Master of Arts in the University of Naples, accepted delivery of a copy of 'Elementa Jordani Ponderibus'. Ten years later Lefèvre of Etaples printed in a gothic folio the 'Elementa Arismetice' which had a second edition in 1514. The famous Italian geometrist of the Renaissance, Nicolo Tartaglia, edited a part of the 'De Ponderibus', and at almost the same time the master of Gassendi, Regiomontanus, quotes and comments on that excellent work, 'De Lineis Datis', printed at Nuremberg in 1537.

Finally, if genius best recognizes genius, it is not without some interest that we read these notes of Leonardo da Vinci: 'Master Stefano Caponi, Doctor of Medicine, has a "Euclides De Ponderibus" '; and elsewhere: 'Take the "De Ponderibus" '; and finally, in a memorandum in his own handwriting (Coll. Leoni., Windsor), in still clearer words, 'Giordano De Ponderibus'. If it was while reading the 'De Ponderibus' that the astonishing notes of the 'Codice Trivulzio' and of notebook E in the Library of the Institute were put on to paper, the mysterious 'Giordano', the enigmatic Jordanus Nemorarius, was the first of the precursors of

Leonardo da Vinci and his direct inspirer in the most daring and most singularly modern part of his research.

But was this personage really the same as Jordan of Saxony?

This opinion has been accepted by several famous historians of mathematical science. For Pierre Boutroux it is not even a question, it is an understood thing. Father G. Théry[4] was of the same opinion. In Germany it is upheld by erudite scholars, Moritz Cantor, Professor Treuttlein, Maximilian Curtze. It was vigorously denied by Father H. Denifle, whose great authority in matters of medieval history put an abrupt closure on debates as to the identity of Jordan the geometrist with Jordan the Preacher; for the time being there was no further word about it. The question nevertheless goes back to 1887, at a time when information on the University customs of the Middle Ages still showed many gaps and uncertainties; and the objections of Father Denifle rest principally on three sets of arguments which are far from being decisive. According to him,[5] the sources educed by those who maintain the

---

[4] In the Dictionary of Catholic Theology, page 1574.

[5] To judge this controversy, one should read: Moriz Cantor Bd. II, p. 53, in Vorlesungen ub. Geschichte der Mathematik and in T. 14 p. 501, Allgemeine Deutsche Biographie- Treuttlein in Zeitschrifft fur Mathematik u. Physik, 1879... Maxim. Curtze, Jordani Nemorarii de triangulis libri quatuor, in Metteilungen des Copernicus Verein f. Wissenschaft u. Kunst, Thorn 1887 and in Zeitschrist f. Math. u. Phys. XXXVI, 1891. D. Gunther in Monum. Germ. praed. III, 156. H. Finke, in Zeitschrift f. vaterlandische Geschichte und Altherthumskunde, Bd. 46, p. 107 and s. Munster, 1889.

These are in different degrees convinced of the truth of the identity of the two Jordans. The other side is presented in the letter of Father Denifle to Mr Curtze, dated from Rome on January 5, 1887, and inserted, p. IV, as a note, in the Jordani Nem. de triangulis libri quatour of the latter. It is developed in the article of Father Denifle in *Historisches Jahrbuch*, T.X. p. 566 ff. 1889 which replies, not without some asperity, to the article previously quoted of H. Finke, where the latter claimed to draw triumphantly out of the neglect of their own brothers and compatriots the glory of the two Master Generals, Jordan of Saxony and John the Teuton. The great specialist of the Archives of the Order of Preachers was annoyed by it, and his arguments show that it would be

identity of the two Masters Jordan have no real value.

Never in the chronicles of the early days of the Dominican Order was Jordan of Saxony mentioned under the name of Jordan Nemorarius. Also, in a general way it seems inadmissible that he had been for several years a brilliant Master of Arts and yet held, in the Faculty of Theology, only the Bachelor's Degree.

The picture of the customs and manners of the University which we tried to sketch out in the first chapter is sufficient to show that this last assertion can reasonably be doubted. It even surprises us, coming from so authoritative a person as Father Denifle, editor of the Chartularium of the University of Paris. But the fact is that to collate the texts and read them is one thing; to interpret them is another.

As for the question of names in the Middle Ages, that presents to our minds, used to the discipline of the modern civil state, oddities which we find bewildering.

In the modern sense Jordan of Saxony is no more a name than Matthew of France, Stephen of Spain, William of Auvergne, Leo of Germany, John of Paris, Paul of Hungary; being vague denominations from the country of origin of those men, these appellations do not represent anything very definite. Often they vary because of circumstance, because of some happening or legend, from some office or residence.

The greatest decretalist of the schools of Canon Law at Paris, later chancellor of the church of Orléans, then a Dominican, in whose hands Jordan made his profession, was called sometimes Reginald of Orléans, sometimes Reginald of St Aignan, sometimes Reginald of St Giles, and a mystery play of the fifteenth century puts him on the stage under the name of St Renaud. Albert the Great was called Albert the Teuton outside Germany, and in the

---

prudent to go back to the sources put on trial in this argument, for they are far from having equal value, and their apparent contradictions require to be examined before forming a fixed conviction.

scholastic world Albert of Cologne, because he had made himself famous in that city as a theologian; he was almost the only one to remember (and we know it from a seal of his coat-of-arms) that he was called Albert de Lawingen. A certain Preacher named Henry of Germany, appointed in 1228 (as we shall see later on) Provincial of the Holy Land, was from that time on called nothing but Henry-from-beyond-the-Seas. There are amusing instances; for example, a celebrated dialectician of the schools of Paris, Master Adam, taught in a house of the Little Bridge; he became Adam Littlebridge, and his pupils were called 'the Little Bridges' ('Parvi Pontani').

Jordanus Nemorarius—in the fifteenth and sixteenth centuries mathematicians translated it Jourdan or Jourdain de Nemore—cannot have been a name properly speaking. Certain Italians have compared it to the name of the geometrician Giordano de Nemi. But even in scholastic Latin Nemi could never have become Nemorarius; it would have been turned into Jordanus Nemiensis, as Le Fèvre d'Étaples was made into Faber Stapulensis. Nemorarius is good Latin, moreover; it is an adjective and an epithet: the forester, a man of the forests; he whose homeland is a wooded land.

Now according to the most ancient chronicles of the Order of Preachers, Jordan was born in the diocese of Mayence, in a castle called 'Borcberg'. Borcberg was identified by the Bollandists with Borgentreich, near Paderborn, fief of the Counts of Eberstein. Others, among them Father Berthier, are inclined to prefer the reading Padberg, a town situated in Westphalia. Another tradition links Jordan to the family of the von Dach and would have it he was born near Darsel, in the diocese of Hildesheim and near Treves, close to the Black Forest.

The point cannot be settled. The diocese of Mayence was very large. But, whether we wish to cradle his infancy in the Black Forest or whether we lean to the tradition that he saw the light of day in the high forests of the Erzgebirge, it is very possible that

Jordan, whose real patronymic would be difficult for international tongues to pronounce or to latinize easily, was surnamed by the students of Paris 'the Forester', *Nemorarius*.

But once he had become a priest and a Friar Preacher, once he had entered the Order of St Dominic, he could not have retained the surname the students had given him. A surname had to be found which would be the simplest, the widest, the most conformed to the geographical usages of the times, the easiest to put into Latin; Jordanus Nemorarius gave place to Jordanus de Saxonia, and was relegated to a past which the swift present, full of happenings and labours, did not pause to recall, at least in those rare texts which have come down to us.[6]

Concerning the authenticity of the sources on which the wisdom and learning of Father Denifle was brought to bear, we must admit that protagonists of the identification of Jordan the Friar Preacher and Jordan the Master of Arts have not had much good fortune, having almost always chanced upon links between the two at second hand. But whence comes the statement in them that the Preacher was a famous geometrist? From a text which offers the most certain historical guarantees, since it is signed by a notably reliable chronicler, whose prudent information has never been proved wrong. He is Nicholas Trivet, English by birth, student at Paris and professor at Oxford, a shrewd Friar Preacher, attached to the Papal Court. Admittedly he is not a contemporary of Jordan of Saxony, for he writes in the early years of the fourteenth century;[7] but at the convent of St Jacques as well as at

---

[6] It is worth noticing that in the various manuscripts, although we always find the name of Jordan, we do not often find the epithet Nemorarius.

[7] About 1320, after having lived and taught at Paris and at Oxford, Nicholas Trivet went to the Roman Curia, then in Avignon. He undertook a sort of general history of ecclesiastical facts between 1136 and 1307. There are in the pontifical archives records of the encouragement and the gifts of the Sovereign Pontiff addressed to Fr Nicholas Trivet for this work, which is much larger and more European than its title promises. Trivet is not an ordinary annalist. He

the Parisian schools he had found, still alive and very recent, the memory of the Master. He fixes this memory in a few lines of crystal clarity:

'In the year (1222) the third General Chapter of the Friars Preachers, Brother Jordan, by nationality a Teuton of the diocese of Mayence, was made successor to Blessed Dominic in the mastership of the Order of Friars Preachers; who, being held to be great in the secular sciences and particularly in mathematics, is said to have been the author of two very useful books, one De Ponderibus and the other Lineis Datis. Afterwards he transferred to the study of theology.'[8]

Could there be anything more definitely affirmative? Yet no one in the scholastic world, among the masters and students who used those two 'very useful books' here attributed to Jordan, raised the least protest against this statement. 'Dicitur edidisse', Nicholas Trivet wrote; people said it, it was a known fact. But there is nothing that cannot be wiped out of men's memories. Eighty years after the death of Jordan of Saxony, it was not without value to record his titles, not only to sanctity, but to science. But seeing that this exact witness comes just eighty years after the death of the Master, why should we see in it only an unfounded legend, arisen suddenly without any living tradition to justify it?

It has taken the arguments of learned moderns to throw doubt on this quite definite statement.

---

has the critical qualities of a historian and his work is very superior to all contemporary chronicles.

[8] Fr Nicholai Triveti, annales sex regum Angliae qui a comitibus andegavensibus originem traxerunt (ed. Hog. p. 211): 'Hoc anno (1222) in capitulo fratrum praedicatorum generali tertio quod Parisiis celebratum est suicessor beati Dominici in magisterio ordinis fratrum praedicatorum factus est frater Jordanus, natione Teutonicus diocesis Maguntinae; qui cum Parisiis in scientiis saeculoribus et praecipue in mathematicis magnus haberetur, libros duos admodum utiles unum De Ponderibus et alium Lineis datis, dicitur edidisse. Postea ad studium theologiae se transferens.'

Why not accept it? Or, at least, refrain from rejecting it?

If we do not accept it, there is something inexplicable about the personality of Master Jordan and his prestige among the students of his time.

No other, not even St Dominic, ever put the scholastic world into such a ferment. The oldest and most official records of the Friars Preachers show us Priories buzzing with activity 'like beehives' at the approach of Friar Jordan 'of blessed memory'. And if the house of the Friars was in a University city, they hastily cut out and stitched an abundance of tunics, hoods and cappas, so much did they fear to run short in view of the number of novices that the word of Master Jordan would draw from among the students with lightning speed.

Where had Jordan gained his understanding of the youthful student, which often went so far as to divine the secret debates within their souls and made one student of Padua (Albert the Great, perhaps) ask: 'Master, who revealed my heart to you?' Where had he gained this combined good-nature and authority, which permitted him to let the novices laugh lightheartedly even at Compline without taking exception to it, give them the most affecting and intimate spiritual instruction and at the same time remaining in their eyes the firmest of masters?

Why from the time of his arrival in a convent did he surround himself always with the youngest of the novices, and follow them up in their studies, their progress, their difficulties, with so much wisdom?

Finally, why did he particularly take to the students in arts and have a strange and attractive affection for them?

It was among the arts students especially that he effected innumerable conversions, to such an extent that he was reproached for bringing into the Order too many young students and too few learned ones.

It was among the same students that the appearance in the rostrum of the illustrious Master of Arts, clothed in the humble habit of a Friar Preacher, where he spoke of nothing but God and the works of God, produced the most extraordinary effect. And he was not surprised at this.

To some question that was asked of him one day on the subject he replied, according to an account in the *Vitae Fratrum*: 'Haven't you noticed that peasants used to drinking water get drunk when wine is poured for them more quickly and easily than nobles and townsmen who are accustomed to wine? It is the same with dialecticians. All the week they drink the water of Aristotle. Then when on Sunday they come to drink the word of the Gospel, they succumb more easily than others into a holy intoxication. The theologian accustomed to feed his soul with the divine sublimities does not always appreciate at its true worth the gift he has received. Too often he is like the sacristan who is so used to passing before the altar that he no longer makes a reverence to it.' This passage is full of wisdom and very significant.

Master Jordan had known the two Faculties, Theology and Arts, and it was for the students in arts that he continued to have the preference of a professor who had been listened to by keen, though sometimes hot-headed, students. He preferred them to the theologians, and delicately indicates why: the latter 'did not appreciate the gift which they had received'; they were learned men already become too self-assured; they paraded their knowledge pridefully and, in their debating and quibbling about the divine sublimities, they sometimes forgot God.

We begin to understand why he preached by preference to the arts students and why he pursued them from city to city, from Bologna to Padua, from Vercelli to Paris, from Oxford to Naples.

Amongst them the great geometrist found himself in his home country; he knew their circumstances and the obstacles which beset them, their inclinations and their resources. He had himself learned by personal experience and could teach them to their comfort long before Pascal that 'the knowledge of worldly things will not make up for the ignorance of things moral in time of affliction'.

He had commented brilliantly on Euclid and the Arabs, Archimedes and Charistion; he did not wish or know how to comment on anything now except the Gospel and the Word crucified. Formerly he had expounded with genius the principles of Greek statics; now he had accepted the mission of extending as far as possible the consequences of another discovery—the discovery of the Order of Friars Preachers—which had the power to revolutionize not just the world of numbers, measures and weights, but the world of souls; to bring about progress, no longer in the science of equilibrium, but in the science of salvation.

He brought to it a special grace, assuredly, but also a proved talent, and even more, that personal kind of attraction which makes intellectual young men hasten to flock around accepted masters.

The Friars Preachers would soon recognize in him a value arising from his singular realism, a power of effective propaganda in university circles among those whom, above all others, it was necessary to reach and to win for the sake of the Order.

Everything is thus easily explained, both the sudden election of Jordan to be Master of the whole Order and his prodigious faculty of recruiting among the students. Compared one with the other, the two portraits, undefined and vague at first, of Master Jordan the learned mathematician and Master Jordan the Friar Preacher, superimposed and aligned with one another, show at last the features of a great personality which begins to stand out clearly.

Chapter III
AT THE PRIORY OF ST JACQUES

THE year was 1220. For the three previous years Master Jordan had been making the acquaintance of the Friars Preachers and getting to know them.

All we need to do here is listen to Jordan himself speaking. Being the historian of the early days of the Order, he was obliged to be his own historian at the same time. He relates what he had seen. He saw the arrival at Paris of the first Friars Preachers assigned there by St Dominic, in accord with the Roman Curia, to study Sacred Science at its most pure source.

He was there himself, learning theology under the shadow of Notre Dame. His memory is precise about names and persons, dates and places. It was part of his own life, and we have only to follow the text.

The first Dominicans arrived in Paris on September 12, 1217. Their Order had been solemnly established by the papal Bull of December 22, 1216, and in a confirmatory letter delivered on the same day, Honorius had declared that he would himself take in hand the government of the new Order whose aim he definitely expressed in the famous formula: 'Champions of the Faith, lights of the world.' The Friars Preachers were to fight for the Faith, against error and against heresy, and to illuminate the Church by the teaching of doctrine. They had to be finely trained athletes, always ready to give their lives, and they had to be men of proved learning. Their place was among the students; they themselves would have to apply themselves to study and learn in order to teach.

On January 21 of the next year, at the beginning of 1217, the Sovereign Pontiff addressed a new letter of exhortation and encouragement to the Friars Preachers gathered in the first house of their Order at St Romain in Toulouse. And this letter had been preceded, on January 19, by a message to the University of Paris 'inviting masters and students to come and establish schools at Toulouse'. The Pope seems to have wished, by this means, to bring a scholastic body to St Dominic so that he could find recruits in it.

But it was not the right time. The people of Toulouse were about to rebel against the Count de Montfort, and a period of bloodshed was about to begin for Languedoc.

According to Jordan, St Dominic, who had come back from Rome to Toulouse and was there at St Romain with his brethren, had a prophetic vision of the death of the Count de Montfort and the events which were to follow it. Toulouse would for some time cease to be a place of study and meditation. Moreover, it was the method of St Dominic, in line with his apostolic policy, to send his sons out and, leaving them to the guidance of the Holy Spirit, to throw them boldly into the world for the saving of souls. 'I know what I am doing', he answered those who were amazed at such a temerity as seemed to endanger the work he had begun. 'Let me alone; I know quite well what I want. Hoarded up the grain rots; cast to the winds it bears fruit.'

They celebrated together at St Romain the feast of the Assumption of the Blessed Virgin. But it was a feast-day of separation and farewells. St Dominic made them elect from among themselves an abbot—that was the usual title of an ecclesiastical superior in the regular clergy[1]—who could take his place if need be. This was Matthew of France, who had come to the Midi as chaplain to the Count de Montfort and had entered the Order at St Romain. He became the immediate superior of the Friars Preachers designated to begin the journey to Paris at once. While four friars went to Spain, seven were directed to Paris; the latter made the journey in two groups.

First to arrive, having travelled swiftly, were St Dominic's own

---

[1] It was quickly abandoned by the Friars Preachers, whose constitutions broke with the ancient customs of monks. The titles of Master of the Order and Prior replaced it.

brother Mannes and Michael of Spain, with a Norman named Oderic whom they had converted. Then three weeks later they were joined by Matthew of France and Bertrand of Garrigua, with two other friends, John of Navarre and Lawrence of England. We may well believe that their arrival caused something of a sensation. Their mode of life introduced an entirely new fusion of monasticism, poverty, and the intellectual life, and 'the new-born University found in them a support in its effort towards autonomy, which it sought to establish along the lines of the communes'.[2]

They had letters of credence to the bishop issued by the Roman Curia. Therefore they were lodged in a little house situated in front of the bishop's palace, just opposite the Hotel Dieu.

Jordan knew this house. It and its twin (still to be seen on a municipal plan of the time of Charles IX, in which one of them bears the image of St Christopher, patron of travellers) belonged of right to the bishop and he gave shelter there to his transient guests. It was there that Jordan, whose lodging could not have been far away, saw the Friars Preachers established. He had some contact with them. This may have been at the lectures of Master John de Barastre, dean of St Quentin and an excellent Professor of Theology, to whose teaching, as we know by the letters of Honorius III, the friars remained especially attached.[3] Or it may have been at Notre Dame, where they went, no doubt, to chant the canonical hours with the chapter.

At any rate Master Jordan saw in these newly-arrived students, some of whom were distinguished men, the mixture of apostolic zeal and interior asceticism which distinguished the sons of St Dominic. Bertrand of Garrigua impressed him especially, and he has left us this brief and vigorous portrait of him: 'Brother Bertrand, later Provincial of Provence, a man of great holiness,

---

[2] Mandonnet.

[3] The Pope's letter of May 4, 1221, recalls that it was at his own insistence that Master John de Barastre consented to give lectures to the Friars Preachers.

inflexibly strict toward himself, had rudely mortified his flesh and in many ways was patterned entirely after the image of St Dominic whose travelling companion he often was.'

In Brother Bertrand he saw Dominic. With what holy curiosity he must have made Matthew of France and Bertrand of Garrigua tell him of the fight against the terrible Albigensian heresy, of the foundation at Prouille, of the life led at St Romain in Toulouse, of the prophecies and the miracles of the Master of the Friars Preachers! How many times the name of St Dominic must have crossed their lips, while together they paced up and down the walks in the cloister of Notre Dame or chatted in the cathedral close, between the hours of study and the hours of prayer!

The news which came periodically to the group of Parisian Friars Preacher, by pilgrims or students from Rome, could not fail to be singularly interesting to a man like Master Jordan. As St Dominic said, the grain thrown to the winds bore fruit, and precisely in the domains which were specifically those of doctrine and knowledge. After this establishment at Toulouse, centre of heresy, and at the same time as they moved into Paris, centre of theology and dialectics, the Friars Preacher went to Rome, fountain-head of Christianity, and to Bologna, centre of juridical studies. One after another came messages which increased the confidence and the heartfelt joy of the Dominican students in the University of Paris. Their founder, having journeyed from Toulouse to Viterbo and to Rome, had just received from the Pope the monastery of St Sixtus in Rome, near the Colosseum, and established there a house of the Friars Preachers. Then, having obtained information and reassured himself about the missions in Spain and in France, he recalled several friars from Paris, in particular John of Navarre, whom in the spring of 1218 he sent together with a certain Brother Bernard, soon to be joined by Brother Christian and a laybrother, to undertake a foundation at Bologna and to implant the preaching of the Order there among the schools.

Finally, the most impressive thing yet and a matter of strange wonder, it was reported that Master Reginald, former professor of the University of Paris, dean of St Aignan at Orléans, had made profession into the hands of St Dominic and had been clothed in the habit of his Order. This was the same Reginald who was soon to draw Jordan definitely into the Order of Preachers.

Meanwhile at Paris also the seed was germinating; the friars made recruits among the students, and the house in the cathedral square of Notre Dame had become too small. At the request of Pope Honorius, John de Barastre made them a gift of a chapel and a hospice adjoining it, situated at the Orléans Gate. A large watchtower containing the assembly room of the aldermen, the 'parlour of the townsmen', separated them from the rampart. The chapel bore the name of St Jacques (St James), because it was located beside the road which led out of Paris by the south and took pilgrims to Spain and to St James of Compostello.

It was by this very route[4] that, in the spring of 1219, St Dominic, coming back from Spain, entered Paris. He found thirty friars in the house of St Jacques, where they had been established in August, 1218. These men, become a radiating centre, had meanwhile already founded the priory of Orléans several months before.

St Dominic spent several weeks in Paris. There among the notable students and Masters of the University who, frequenting the Preachers' house, had become their friends and now crowded around him, he saw Jordan, talked with him, heard his confession and advised him to receive the diaconate and to go on to the priesthood. Why did he not try to call him into his Order? Judging by Jordan's brief but clear record, there does not seem to have

---

[4] The Orléans Gate was then at the end of a straight extension of the rue St Jacques, that is not in its present location but at the end of the rue de la Tombe-Issoire. St Dominic's Church is thus built on ground where the Patriarch of the Preachers trod when he entered Paris.

been any question of such a proposal between them. We do not know. Perhaps the wise insight of St Dominic foresaw the development which would take place in the soul of the Master of Arts, and he knew it would be useless to try to hasten it. When it was a question of young men, still undecided, he did not hesitate to hasten matters, so that he once went out at the supper hour to seek such a young student, taught him to prostrate himself, clothed him forthwith in the habit and admitted him to the choir,[5] but he seems to have respected Master Jordan's strong personality which could never be gained but by its own gift. Perhaps Jordan, on his own side, still felt himself held by some ties to the secular world, attached to his study of the sciences, and wished to give himself time to think it over. These things we can never know.

St Dominic was called back to Italy by other cares. The season was advanced. He took the road by Burgogne and the Alps. Paris never saw him again. But he would send Reginald there.

It may be that Jordan already knew Reginald personally. It was not so many years since the latter taught canon law with such renown here in the schools of Paris, namely from about 1206 to about 1212.

If Jordan had completed four or five years of theology in 1220 he would not have left Arts until about 1215, and it was therefore before 1215 that he had studied the Quadrivium and taught it so majestically. It is thus by no means impossible that he might have known and been in personal touch with Master Reginald; and even if he did not attend the latter's lectures, at least he must have heard praise not only of his learning and personality but also of his university sermons.

Chief amongst the Parisian jurists, Reginald would not have gone unnoticed. He was in the schools and was a person of importance among the lawyers whose talents kings, bishops and

---

[5] Stephen of Spain entered the Order in this way, at Bologna, according to the account of the *Vitae Fratrum*.

communes were beginning to esteem highly.

The canons of the College of St Aignan, at Orléans, had begged him to take the place of their dean who had died and to help them end an already long-standing argument which had brought them into legal dispute with their bishop. King Philip Augustus, who, for motives of territorial suzerainty, followed such litigation with interest, had nominated Reginald as dean of St Aignan.

Reginald had shown himself equal to all that was expected of him. By a proper appeal to the arbitration of the Sovereign Pontiff, he had speedily eased the current situation, re-established peace between the contending parties, and gained at the same time the esteem of the Pope, the favour of the King, the gratitude of the Chapter of St Aignan, and the friendship of the Bishop. Some of the chancellery documents, sealed with his arms and dictated by him, are still preserved in the departmental archives of the Loiret. In them we can see something of Reginald's spirit of justice and detachment, of his high conscientiousness and his penetrating mind, in fine, of his talents. But we also see in them with what affairs the dean of St Aignan had to occupy himself: territorial or agricultural disputes to settle between the abbeys; revenues, fiefs, contracts of sale or purchase to revise; donations to legalize and legacies to examine; serfs to set free 'amore Dei'. There were incessant audiences where he had to be, at the same time, advocate-counsel, appraiser, and judge; there were diplomatic proceedings and treasurer's calculations.

What time was there left for prayer, the priestly ministry, preaching, and pursuit of the assured means of salvation which, at this time, Master Jordan ardently wished to find? Was it to join in this perpetual business of feudal procedure that one embraced God's service?

We can imagine the distaste with which, after seven years of chancellorship and administration, this chosen soul was seized. We can understand the sense of deliverance with which he left Orléans in 1218 and accompanied his bishop, Manasses de Seignelay, on a pilgrimage to the Holy Land.

The pilgrims stopped at Rome. They were the guests there of Cardinal Ugolino, who was himself a university man and a canonist and knew Reginald. Their conversation can easily be imagined: Reginald's admission of weariness and his hopes not to have to return to the deanship of St Aignan, but to find a way of life which, without taking him away from his intellectual equals, would free him from the current servitude and restore him fully to his true vocation, the life of prayer and preaching.

Cardinal Ugolino was bound to St Dominic by ties of profound and wholly supernatural friendship. He had known him in Rome, he knew his difficulties and his aspirations; he knew what would happen if he brought the two men together; he brought St Dominic and Reginald together.

It was one of those meetings which seem to satisfy, on both sides, an hitherto unexplained yet very real expectation. Reginald saw in the new Order the apostolic ideal to which he was to devote himself body and soul. St Dominic found in Reginald the help which the hour required and at first sight he placed at the head of the Friars Preachers of Bologna this Master practised in the spoken word, this jurist proved in the schools of law. Their understanding was immediate and perfect, as if the Blessed Virgin herself had predestined it. Reginald had succumbed to a fever. He was miraculously cured and miraculously confirmed in his vocation as a Friar Preacher.

He fulfilled his vow and made the pilgrimage to the Holy Land; and returning to Italy he reached Bologna on Christmas Eve, 1218, endowed with full powers by Dominic.

The little group of Friars Preachers was marking time there, far from the centre of the town, at the Mascarella, in poverty and discouragement. The arrival of their new Prior changed everything. Reginald was the man who was needed there. In learning he equalled the best jurists of the schools where perhaps he himself, before teaching in Paris, had taken his degree; in eloquence he surpassed them all. By his preaching, according to Jordan, he kindled the whole city with the fire of his eloquence.

The students hastened to his sermons and many begged for the habit of the Order. The conquest of one of the greatest masters of the University, Master Moneta of Cremona, produced an immediate and contagious effect. Guala of Bergamo, Clair-Sextius of Florence, Ventura of Verona and finally Roland of Cremona followed him, as did many others. To lodge his recruits and organize the new priory, Reginald obtained from the d'Andalo family the church and grounds of St Nicholas of the Vineyards, right in the district of the law schools. The rector of the church, Master Rudolph of Faenza, took the habit of the Friars Preachers and stayed with them.

It was in this active ferment that St Dominic, coming from Paris in the summer of 1219, found the new priory of St Nicholas. And immediately, with the promptness characteristic of him, taking Reginald from Bologna in spite of the prayers and tears of all those new sons of the Order who lived by his teachings, Dominic sent him to Paris to effect there what he had just accomplished at Bologna.

He himself stayed in Lombardy. Cardinal Ugolino was established there as a legate. The work which was begun went on, and the harvest continued.

Reginald reached the brethren at St Jacques in the last days of December, 1219. Too few weeks of life remained for him to accomplish in Paris a work as complete as that of Bologna; for early in February he became gravely ill and fell asleep in the Lord. But he had made a conquest which was worth many others, perhaps the very one which St Dominic, with his power of reading the secrets of the heart, foresaw to be ready and for which he had sent Reginald to Paris; Master Jordan made profession in January into Reginald's hands.

He could not resist this eloquence which was able to give

assurance of heaven conquered and already opened.⁶ More especially he could not resist such an example. Intellectual? Reginald was as much so as Jordan. Devoted to learning and to study? He was that too. Accustomed to the ease of secular life? Still more so was he who had occupied such a high position and had received so many honours. Yet he had given himself entirely to poverty, to humility, and he had found there the fulness which nothing before had given him.

Those who had known him at the University of Paris in his secular glory saw him as 'a man come down from heaven'. Matthew of France was one of these; he could not refrain from asking Reginald, in the presence of Jordan who made a note of it, whether this change of life had not been very hard for him. And he, humble of mien and eyes downcast, replied that 'nothing of all that he could ever have dreamed to merit, nothing could be so sweet to him'.

The Order of Preachers offered the certain way, the narrow gate through which to pass and to lead all those whom distinction of learning, zeal for souls and love of the Church made strangers to feudal ambition and ripe for the new apostolic labours.

For Master Jordan hesitation became blameworthy, delay was no longer possible. He gave his promise to Reginald.

Reginald could soon die in peace; he would be replaced by a man of the same culture, the same eloquence and the same prestige in the University world. Jordan himself understood his

---

⁶ This is the phrase used by Moneta of Cremona. Although this master of the schools of Bologna had been to hear Mass at St Procul on St Stephen's day to avoid Reginald's sermon, he was nevertheless taken by his students to the cathedral of San Petronio. Reginald was still in the pulpit, but the crowd was so great that they could not enter. He stayed at the door listening. 'Now I see the heavens open', said the preacher. 'Now they are open for all those who wish to go in. O my beloved, why are you still waiting? Now the heavens are opened.' Last part, chapter X, *Vitae Fratrum*.

entrance into the Order in this way[7] since, having seen in a dream a limpid fountain of water drying up and immediately two other fountains spout up by it, he dared, in spite of his humble 'consciousness of his own sterility', to interpret this vision as the sign of the reception into the Order of Friars Preachers of Henry of Marbourg and himself.

If Jordan requested of Reginald some delay it was not because he was in the least undecided himself. His way was chosen, his mind firm, his will set to enter this assured way of salvation which the new Order offered to him. It was undoubtedly the same way which he had dreamed of in his heart before he had ever known the Friars. There was nothing more to stop him, except that he did not wish to leave behind in the world his young and brilliant companion Henry of Marbourg.

The fire would burn anew in him, his emotion be roused again, sobered only by the premature death of Henry, when he remembered the story of this first conquest, the nearest to his heart.

To Henry, his dearest friend in life, Master Jordan has devoted pages of such tender expression that they reveal, in this masculine nature which seemed to be dominated by the love of learning, a sensitiveness almost feminine and a wonderful childlikeness of spirit which the heart no longer pours out easily in these modern times.

The blighting wind which critical individualism, born of humanism and the Reformation, caused to blow across the human

---

[7] Reported by Jordan himself in *De Initiis Ordinis* XL i, and *cf. Vitae Fratrum* part 3a, chapter IV, where we find a variant with commentary of this vision attributed to an anonymous religious: 'He saw a clear fountain run dry in the cloister of St Jacques, and surging up after it, in the same spot, a great river. In fact at the death of the Blessed Reginald Father Jordan appeared and was raised up; he was first a lector at Paris... he left and travelled the world preaching for more than twenty years... and drawing more than a thousand subjects into the Order.

spirit in later days had not touched the masters of the Middle Ages. Whether they were intellectuals or mystics, their friendships were at once frank and warm.

At first Jordan could not conceive that anyone could give himself to God and to the Order of Friars Preachers without taking with him his most intimate friends. Woe to the isolated solitary, who hides and guards like a miser the riches of the spiritual life! A man does not go into Paradise alone.

Master Jordan was not to enter the door of St Jacques alone. His joy would not have been complete if he had had to leave his dearest companion on the doorstep. Henry of Marbourg—later Brother Henry, Prior of Cologne—had doubtless been born in the village of that name in Thuringia, and his family was perhaps known to Jordan. He had completed his studies in arts and his first studies in theology in the schools of the Chapter of Maestricht, under the direction of a holy and wise canon. He was handsome, reverent and virtuous, of a mind to grasp everything and with a rare faculty for expressing himself.[8] So, as was the way in those times with men on whom great hopes centred, he was sent to Paris to study theology.

Master Jordan welcomed him there, found room for him in his own lodgings and interested himself in him, so much so that on his side the young man developed an affection for Jordan, and Jordan began 'to work hard to lead his friend and companion to make a vow like his own', because, as he said, 'I saw in him a natural disposition and a very special grace for the ministry of preaching'.

He believed that he had succeeded on the day when Henry, having decided to make his confession to Brother Reginald and coming back to Jordan all shaken, opened the book of Isaiah which lay there, and chanced upon the verses: 'The Lord hath given me a learned tongue, that I should know how to uphold by word him that is weary. He wakeneth me in the morning, in the morning he

---

[8] '*Erat enim linguae facundissimae*'—*De Initiis Ordinis*.

wakeneth my ear, that I may hear him as a master. The Lord God hath opened my ear, and I do not resist; I have not gone back.' (Is. 50, v. 4-5.)

It was like the voice of heaven replying to his secret yearnings; and Jordan exhorted Henry even more to deliver 'his youth to the yoke of obedience' when, reading a little further on, their eyes rested on the words '*stemus simul*', which they translated 'Let us stay together, let us never separate'.

But if the young man's reason and his heart consented, his will, says Jordan, remained recalcitrant. The great obstacle was the life of poverty that he must embrace. The Friars Preachers were mendicants; and this new conception of religious life upset all the accepted notions of the clergy of those times. As Master Jordan knew already, and was to verify later, that was the stumbling block which would trip up the pride of the young men called to the vocation of the Friar Preacher. He waited patiently. Henry argued with himself, meditated, prayed, stayed at the cathedral after Matins until dawn, at the feet of the Blessed Virgin, begging her to make him see himself clearly. His soul remained dry and withdrawn. No, he was decidedly not worthy to enter into the society of Christ's poor. Nevertheless, while he thus fought he saw himself suddenly called to the Last Judgment. He was not conscious of any crime; he was innocent. But a voice cried to him: 'You there, say, what have you given up for the Lord?' His heart softened. He now longed for that same poverty which had seemed to him so hard. He hurried to Master Reginald and made profession into his hands; then, when he went back to Jordan, and the latter, seeing traces of tears on his face, asked what had happened, he replied: 'I have just made my vow to the Lord, and I will keep it.'

As soon as he entered the Order, he must have astonished his former fellow-students by an eloquence so lively and so efficacious that he penetrated their hearts; no one of them remembered, among the clerics of Paris, having heard anything like it. For

Jordan this was undoubtedly the most perfect type of preaching for students, for he seems to have retained the memory of it and to have sought to imitate it. He said in fact later to the Brethren that when he went up into the pulpit it was Henry to whom he inwardly appealed for help and whose blessing he asked in spirit.

In 1221, the Priory of Cologne having been established, Henry became its Prior and left Paris at about the same time that Jordan was called into Lombardy. This was the separation of those who had never wished to be separated. The two friends nevertheless must have seen one another again. Meanwhile Jordan and Henry addressed many letters to one another from Lombardy and Cologne, but not one has come down to us—no more than the letters that the good canon of Maestricht, at first hostile to the Order of Friars Preachers but later won over, wrote to Henry; Jordan read them and found them 'pleasant and full of piety'.

Jordan and Henry delayed taking the habit until the beginning of Lent, to give themselves time to convert and take with them another of their companions, Leo the German, the same who in his turn succeeded Henry as Prior of Cologne.

Having finally set their temporal affairs in order, all three went to the Orléans Gate on the morning of Ash Wednesday, February 12th, 1220. They entered unexpectedly but at an opportune time into the poor chapel where the Friars were just intoning the anthem for the imposition of the ashes: '*Immutemur habitu*', and literally changed their dress; putting off their secular garments in order to receive the habit of the Friars Preachers, they put off the 'old man', in Jordan's words, and what the Friars sang they accomplished in putting on the new man. Reginald had died a few days before, and his body rested not far from there in the cemetery of the Benedictine abbey of Notre Dame des Champs. But his heroic apostolic spirit had passed ablaze into the recruits of his last hour.

Jordanus Nemorarius, Master Jordan, had died, and for always it was now to be Brother Jordan, Preacher.

CHAPTER IV
FROM PARIS TO BOLOGNA

DURING the spring of the year 1220 the Dominicans began the final organization of the Constitutions of the Order of Friars Preachers.

Born out of St Dominic's wide and inspired vision and influenced by the pressing needs of the Church which was then faced by the Albigensian heresy and the general ignorance of the people, it had from the first followed experience more than theory.

For four years the Friars Preachers had been increasing and spreading across Italy, France and Spain.

Originally Canons Regular following the rule of St Augustine, what distinguished them from all other Orders was the apostolic mission signified by their name of Friars Preachers, to which they added a life of study and voluntary poverty. Their written legislation since 1216, under the title of customs, included nothing except what related to conventual life. The Friars recited or chanted the Office according to the custom of the places where they habitually lived and had no liturgy of their own at all as yet.

The legislation of the Friars Preachers from 1216 had a character of expectancy in the original organization of the Order; they waited upon actuality which would show what could and should be accomplished.

But in 1220 Dominic saw clearly what his Order of Friars Preachers needed. The time had come to complete its legislation.

He had spent the year between Bologna, Viterbo and Rome, in close intimacy with the Curia and Cardinal Ugolino. The Pope, the Legate and the Master of the Preachers were in agreement as to the opportuneness of a definitive Constitution. By letters sent to all the houses of the Friars Preachers, Dominic summoned a General Chapter to meet at Bologna.

Each Priory had to send representatives. The Priory of St

Jacques delegated four. We do not know the names of three; but the fourth was Brother Jordan of Saxony.

These 'definitors', as they are called, must have started on their way in the early days of April[1] since the Chapter must have been celebrated on Pentecost Day, May 17, 1220. The season was too little advanced to allow them to take the Alpine road. The Priories of Lyons, Narbonne, and Montpellier, in process of foundation that very year, sent delegates to Bologna, and these joined the Parisian definitors, showing them the ancient Roman road.

Whether, having met at Montpellier, they went to Cette to proceed by sea, or whether, crossing the Rhone and traversing Provence by the Aurelian Way as far as Frejus, they reached Genoa by the road of the Corniche, from there the sure track of the Aemelian Way led the travellers across the Lombardy Plain to Bologna.

Master Jordan has left us only a few lines on the Chapter of 1220; it is probable that he was, nevertheless, one of its principal workers. His character and his past gave him a high place among the masters and the students who had gathered around St Dominic.

Since Reginald's stay there, the Priory of Bologna was peopled with University men and especially with jurists. Their influence dominated the assembly; we see it in the Constitutions which were established there: 'They are in their formulation a pure work of law', said Mandonnet. But they are also vigorously realistic and marked, as it were, with that spirit of scientific clarity which reflects a Master of Arts of Jordan's stature. Nothing could have been more novel than this sober precision. Until then the statutes of religious orders contained outlines of ethics and edifying

---

[1] At the latest. Jordan says himself that he was sent even though it was only two months since he had entered the Order. 'Sed cum mitterer, necdum in Ordine adhuc duos menses peregeram.'

considerations; they left vague the end sought and the means of attaining it; the custom must have been to crystallize those little by little. Here it was the opposite. There was no need at all of preliminary discourses. The Order existed; it knew very well what its own ends were. Its legislation was concerned uniquely to regulate its efforts by defining its organic form and, if we dare say so, its practical specification.

The Friars Preachers were monks by reason of their regular community life, their asceticism and silence; canons by their penitential celebration of the choral office; but they were above all else students and apostles, for, according to the text of the Constitutions issued by the General Chapter of 1220 which defined in its opening words the end of its foundation, the Order since its first days had been especially instituted for preaching and for the salvation of souls. '...and the efforts of its members must tend principally, ardently, and supremely to those things which are useful to our neighbour's soul'.

But they must be scholars as well as apostles, for the tragedy of the Albigensian heresy and the helplessness of the episcopate in the presence of the mounting superstitions among the people had shown that the chief instrument for the salvation of souls is the knowledge and the teaching of doctrine. Positively abandoning the ancient monastic usage of manual labour, which is confined to the Lay brothers, the Friars Preachers set up study as the characteristic law of their Order. The canonical Office was to be recited devoutly but '*breviter et succincte*' so it would not too much diminish the hours of study. The practice of private devotion, meditation, celebration of Mass were left to the discretion of each religious. (This was the general custom in the Church during the thirteenth century.) Assuredly contemplation held a major place in the life of these men who searched deeply into the knowledge of God; but it must in its turn ripen into apostolic action and give to others its best fruits.

The Friars Preachers were scholars in order to be apostles.

They were mendicants, too, in order to be apostles. It was at the Chapter of 1220 at Bologna that the Friars renounced, definitely and absolutely, temporal possessions and even revenues in common, prohibited the carrying of money and travelling on horse-back, abolished, for all Friars Preachers of whatever rank, the rochet of the canons, which was so impractical for journeys, and replaced it by the scapular with a hood or cowl of the same white wool as the robe.

The title of Abbot, which Matthew of France was the only one to bear and that for only a short while, disappeared. They substituted for it the title of Prior—Prior Conventual for the head of a Priory, Prior Provincial for the head of a Province. Dominic himself remained 'the Master of the Preachers', nothing more. Legislative power was given entirely to the General Chapter. It was decided that at each Pentecost the Chapter should meet, one year at Bologna and the next year at Paris alternately. Nevertheless the Chapter of 1221 was held at Bologna. Paris and Bologna, the two greatest University centres of Christianity, the most powerful commune of France and one of the principal ones of Lombardy—it was there that the Friars Preachers felt themselves to be and knew themselves to be especially in their rightful place.

Close to the townsfolk by their rule of life, they were still closer to the students by their culture. The celebration of each Chapter was accompanied by religious ceremonies and sermons which drew crowds of students from the schools; and some let themselves be won over and, first interested, themselves became recruits.

Recruitment was the preoccupation of the Friars in 1220; it was also that of the Papacy which, if not officially represented, was certainly not absent from the first Chapter of the Friars Preachers. In this very spring of 1220 the Pope sent out many appeals to accelerate their recruiting. What the Pope urgently required, in fact, was not the lay preachers, unlettered improvisors who, since the end of the twelfth century, had offered themselves so often to him with as much enthusiasm as imprudence and so often fell into error,² but learned preachers, instructed in doctrine, masters of eloquence, sons of the Church by their culture and their vows. With a man like Dominic at their head, with the chosen circle already formed around him, surely the hour had come to raise the army of missionaries to whom, all along its frontiers, Christian Europe was calling so pitifully for help.

By personal letters of April 1220, the Sovereign Pontiff requested that the archbishops and bishops, particularly those on the military frontiers of Europe, should find in their dioceses 'four, three or even two men of good will, no matter of what religious Order, who are ready to work by preaching in the vineyards of the Lord'. Honorius III went so far as to order the same bishops to take no notice of resistance or opposition on the part of the superiors of religious leaving the cloister to give themselves to the ministry of the Friars Preachers; and these were called to Rome, in haste, for St Martin's feast, November 11, 1220.

On May 12 of the same year, the Pope wrote again, nominally to six individual religious of different monasteries of Italy.³ He declared to them that having learned from Brother Dominic, Prior of the Order of Friars Preachers, that the grace of preaching which they had received could be very useful for the salvation of their

---

² This is the history of the Vaudois movement and that of the singular fanatic Gherardino Segalelli, founder of the so-called Order of the Apostles, condemned by the Council of Lyons. (Salimbene.)

³ These were the Colleges of Canons, like St Victor in Lombardy, Benedictine and Cistercian abbeys like Flore in Calabria. It was an eclectic method; it is unlikely to suppose that the recruits, in the Pope's mind, should abandon their Order to join the Order of Preachers. Analogous facts were already to hand, at the instance of the Roman Curia—there is a question in the Vitae Fratrum of two brothers, Theobald of Sicuna and Nicholas of Campania, who, discouraged by the extreme poverty and small success of the colony of Friars Preachers in Bologna, at the time of Reginald's arrival in 1218, had asked the Pope for permission to return to the Cistercians. The striking entrance of Roland of Cremona had kept them. (Vit. Frat., 1a, c. V, p. 26.)

fellow-men, he ordered them, while retaining the habits of their respective Orders, to put themselves under the guidance of Brother Dominic and to co-operate with him in the ministry of the word of God.

These facts were too recent and too specific to fail to light up one aspect of the General Chapter of May 27, 1220.

To the watchful eyes of Jordan were revealed, as he faced the immense needs of Christianity, the necessary breadth of the Dominican apostolate, its special missionary vocation, and the pressing tactics needed in its recruiting. Recourse to the bishops was slow and distant, and how many men would it give them? As for the religious themselves, learned monks or canons gifted in oratory, how many of them would decide to leave the peace of their cloisters for the wandering life of an apostle? and how many men of mature intellect and already versed in various branches of learning would lend themselves to the rude formation of the Friar Preacher?

No, it was to youth that they must go, and in its turn youth called imperatively to youth. The Dominican recruiting ground must be in the schools.

From the Chapter of Bologna and his renewed and more intimate fraternal contact with Dominic, Jordan came back into France with a will more determined than ever to serve the Order. When it ended, the Chapter had sent him to the Priory of St Jacques with the duty of lecturing. There, during the scholastic year 1220-1221, he interpreted to the Friars the Gospel of St Luke. This teaching, which was limited to novice preachers, was the continuation of the Commentary of St Matthew given by Michel de Fabra, and that on St Mark given the preceding year by Matthew of France. But, like Henry of Marbourg, he must have begun to preach to the secular students of the Parisian schools, for that year he gained many for the Order, though it is difficult to determine who they were.

A vague tradition gives the names of William Perault, who

entered St Jacques in 1221, author of a Compendium of Virtues and Vices, and Robert Kilwardby, but there is no solid foundation for it. Kilwardby was Master of Arts of Paris; he certainly studied theology there before going to teach at Oxford from 1248 to 1261. There is much probability that he did not take the religious habit until he was at Oxford, between 1240 and 1245. But maybe he had known and seen much of Jordan at Paris, and had already made him a promise which was to mature long afterwards.

The only acquisition which is not doubtful, because Jordan himself fixes it for 1221, is that of Master Everard de Langres. He was by no means a young student, but a man of ripe years and in the first rank of the higher clergy.

First canon, then dean of the Chapter of Langres, and finally archdeacon of the diocese, he had shouldered great responsibilities, dealt with a large budget, created a hospital, and continued the building of the cathedral of Langres whose architects were then called to build the cathedral of Rheims; so widely was he esteemed that when the episcopal see of Lausanne fell vacant in July, 1220, the canons elected him as their bishop. But Everard recoiled from the honour. In July, 1220, Brother Jordan came back from the Chapter of Bologna; he and his companions travelled by way of Burgundy and the Ile de France; and he may have followed the direct Roman road that crosses the diocese of Langres in the south. Master Everard must have known him at the schools of Paris, may have shown him hospitality, come to him for advice, and Jordan may well have had a part in Everard's decision to renounce the great functions of secular authority in order to assume the voluntary poverty of a Friar Preacher.

In any event, Everard was soon to give the same example as that given by Reginald of Orléans and by Jordan himself. In his case it was more than just one more recruit; it was a reinforcement to the Order of Friars Preachers—Everard was to bequeath his influence and his connections in the episcopal world to the new

Prior of Lombardy.

The second General Chapter, convened in Bologna on May 30, 1221, had just named Brother Jordan Provincial of the Lombardy Province.

Taking up once more the work of organization embarked upon in the preceding year and in the same spirit of realism, this Chapter divided the Order into eight provinces: Spain, Provence, France, Lombardy, the Roman Province,[4] Germany, Hungary, and England.

Already Master Paul of Hungary, the learned jurist of the Bologna schools, had returned to his native land to establish Dominican preaching there. Already Gerard de Fraxinetus had set out for Oxford and its new-born University. Already Solomon of Aarhus, sailing before the wind to Denmark, his homeland, had been driven by a storm to the coast of Norway, disembarked there and founded the Priory of Oslo. These were the outposts of the Dominican front.

In the interior, Conrad of Huxter was called to govern in Germany, Matthew in France, Bertrand of Garrigua in Provence, Nicholas de Giovanazzo in the Roman Province, and Mannes in Spain. Jordan of Saxony had the duty of taking over the province of Lombardy.

The other nominations seem to have been determined by a certain seniority in the Order and especially by aptness of nationality: the Hungarian was sent into Hungary, the Spaniard to Spain, the Provençal to Provence. Lombards were not lacking in Dominic's company, but it was not to a Lombard that the Lombardy province fell; still more, it was to a man who had entered the Order only a year ago. But the capital of Lombardy was Bologna, the city of the Schools, the centre of a University crowded with students of all tongues, in arts, medicine and law.

---

[4] Provence included all the Languedoc, with Montpellier and Toulouse. The Roman Province comprised Tuscany.

What was needed was a complete understanding of scholastic circles, so readily aroused, so quick to cool off again, and also a measure of prestige that would ensure conquests. There can be no doubt that when Jordan was in Bologna in 1220 he would have made himself well remembered, that he had made contacts and formed friendships. He would be welcome there and that was the important thing.

Of all the recently established provinces, Lombardy was the most important and the most difficult to administer. About ten houses of Friars Preachers had been established there. Their immediate task was to fight against the Vaudois heresy, which was still alive and still multiplying its proselytes and followers; while the stormy birth and rapid growth of the Lombard communes, struggling against the imperial suzerainty and often against the feudal rights of the bishops, created amid the dense population violent eddies of opinion and tumultuous conflicts.

The Provincial of Lombardy needed a firm impartiality which would supersede party strife, a high culture which would allow him to view the world beyond the horizon of the plains of the Po and to embrace the whole of Christendom. The great Master of Arts who had become Brother Jordan was undoubtedly the international personality who could take over such a role.

Perhaps Dominic had already had the secret thought of making Jordan first his delegate and then his successor. The Master of the Friars Preachers hoped, we know, that when his main work was on a sure footing he could take up the missionary's staff and go toward the pagan frontiers between Europe and Asia to seek the conversion of the legendary Cumans and find martyrdom for himself.

The return to Paris of the definitors of St Jacques, with the acts of the Chapter of Bologna, must have coincided with the end of the academic year, June 1221.

Jordan had to leave without delay, not without tearing up

roots and not without uneasiness. 'This office was imposed on me', writes Jordan, 'when, having spent only one year in the Order, I had hardly begun to take root in it; before I had learned how to deal with my own imperfections, here was I sent to govern others.' (*De Initiis Ordinis*, LIV.)

He made his farewells to the Priory of St Jacques, to the studious and meditative life, to obedient silence, to the sweet fraternity of the first year he had spent in the Order. He had to take farewell of his first and sole companion, of the gentle daily intimacy with Brother Henry. This farewell was not made without emotion, kept in restraint until on a morning in July, on foot no doubt, as we see him on the predilla of a Dominican fresco, his rolled cappa slung over his shoulder and his staff in his hand, Jordan went down the rue St Jacques and passed under the arch of the Petit Chatelet, crossed the bridges of the City, saluted Notre Dame and, by the St Antoine gate, came to the road which followed the course of the Seine.

He did not go alone; Everard de Langres accompanied him.

Everard de Langres had received the Friar Preacher's habit in the Priory of St Jacques. Being very much attached to Jordan he did not wish to leave him; he also desired to see Dominic; he seized upon the occasion of this departure for Lombardy[5] and offered himself enthusiastically as the companion of the new Provincial. Jordan, on his part, liked him and knew that he could have no better guide for the journey.

In July the shortest route to Italy was by way of the Alps through Burgundy, and this route, at least for the most part,

---

[5] *De Init. Ord.* LV: 'Hic mecum ituro in Lombardiam, quem tenero diligere videbatur affectu, iter arripuit, desiderans videre magistrum Dominicum; et per omnes partis Galliae et Burgundiae quas mecum pertransibat, in quibus fuerat ipse aliquando notus, Christum egenum et pauperem in corde suo circumferens praedicabat...'

Everard knew and was himself known by everyone along it. 'Through all the land of France and Burgundy which he crossed with me', says Jordan, 'Everard was esteemed by everyone, and bearing the poor and naked Christ in his heart Everard went preaching...' The archdeacon who had become a Friar Preacher seemed to take a delight in exhibiting himself as a beggar where he had presented himself not long before as a great lord. Thus it was that to him the journey became a mission. Each stopping-place opened to him, in bishops' palaces, in monasteries and in Chapters was transformed into a preaching station where men wondered and paid heed. Everard preached, said Jordan; but undoubtedly he did not preach alone, and he did not preach in a desert.

This route through France and Burgundy, whose twists and resting-places he knew, wound like a serpent across a countryside in which were dotted Benedictine abbeys and Cistercian monasteries housing the flower of the regular clergy. Towards this nucleus of monastic reserves, it will be remembered, as toward a strategic point to strengthen himself before entering upon his campaign, the Bishop of Osma and his sub-prior Dominic had been directed by Innocent III in 1204, when having left Rome supplied with the plan of their mission in Languedoc they came first to Burgundy to seek for collaborators among the Cistercian monks.

It cannot be doubted but that the rural isolation and the cares resulting from terrestrial possessions had already deprived these great religious foundations of some of their subjects. Strict discipline was no longer to be found anywhere in its first purity. The monasteries tended to attract fewer men. The Canons Regular were more suited, perhaps, to contemporary social evolution and became in their turn the centres of prayer. Nevertheless these vast monastic communities, so hospitable, so sheltered in their immense enclosures of fields, vineyards and woods, remained attractive.

Everard knew at which doors to knock, which minds he could

convince, which hearts he could touch, which souls he could win. If we take the trouble to reconstruct the most probable itinerary of the two travellers, according to the brief hints given by Jordan himself, we find that everywhere they were received by prelates known to Everard and that Jordan must have taken out of these cloisters the choicest men for the houses of the Dominican Order. If we note the stopping places on their journey, we shall find in them the landmarks of future Dominican foundations in those same districts; and we begin to understand how every subsequent journey of the untiring traveller that Master Jordan later became, must have been patterned on this experience.

The fatigues of the journey, the hazards of the way, the poverty of the lodging-places, the uncertainty of arrival, were for him so many exercises of asceticism and mortification. Looking at Nature, seeing the work in the fields, would have helped his soul to rise in joyful prayer. Always prepared for ministry of the word, he directed his path in such a way as to make of the journey a mission of salvation for the souls he met and a means of the extension and, if possible, the increase of his Order. As Don Diego Acébès, the holy bishop of Osma, was the first one to train St Dominic, so too the good Everard de Langres was the first to introduce Master Jordan to the itinerant method of preaching which was one of his most fruitful innovations.

They left Paris by the route which cuts across the wood of Vincennes and goes through Villeneuve St Georges. It was the time-honoured way which follows the course of the Seine toward the east.

These Roman roads, so solidly laid that parts of them still exist after two thousand years, were then in such a state of preservation as made them the only great highways for traffic. The barbarians had followed them, taking good care not to destroy the only roads that brought them to the countries they were conquering. The great pilgrimages of the Middle Ages frequented no other ways; near each famous sanctuary, or bordering upon it, we find an ancient Roman road, and the abbots or priors who built alongside these pious highways never moved away from them.

Straight, and generally paved, dotted with the occasional landmarks and with mounting blocks for riders, striking through the forests, climbing over the mountains, throwing viaducts across valleys and bridges across rivers, conquering swamps with ditches, or enclosed in the embankments which they dug out in the flanks of the hills, these long sure rigid ribbons stretched across the countryside and bound together by the shortest route towns and cities, churches and fortresses.

This Burgundy road was one of the best and most frequented. Dominic had taken it two years before when he was returning from Paris to Bologna. Everard and Jordan followed joyfully in his steps. It was full summer. The days were long. They provided themselves with satisfactory halts, leaving before dawn in the freshness, taking a monastic siesta during the warm hours, doubling their pace toward nightfall to reach before dark a refuge where Everard knew they would find hospitality.

Above Villeneuve St-Georges, avoiding the dense forest of Sénart to the north and the marshy thickets of the forest of Bière to the south—the remnant of which is today called the forest of Fontainebleu—the road departed a little from the Seine and made use of the valley of the Yerres. It crossed Provins where the Comte de Champagne had built a hospital, then rejoined the river at Pont-sur-Seine with its massive stone arch built by the Romans leading over to the left bank. The Augustinian monks of Val-des-Ecoliers, well known to Everard because their mother-house had been established for twenty years a few leagues from Chaumont in the diocese of Langres, were building the church of St James at Pont-sur-Seine and would certainly have given hospitality to the two Friars Preachers. Passing through the neighbouring town of Nogent-sur-Seine, they reached the episcopal city of Troyes, where Bishop Hervé would have offered hospitality to Master Everard and his companion. A few years later the Friars Preachers were established at Troyes in modest fashion, but in 1223 they received from Nicholas de Brie, the successor of Hervé in the episcopal see, a church and a priory for their use.

At Bar-sur-Seine the travellers entered the diocese of Langres. There Everard knew the map of the country still better and his friends were even more numerous. At Mussy—then called Mussy l'Évêque because the Bishop of Langres, William de Joinville, had his country house there—the Canons Regular had just been established; they would certainly be reliable hosts.

As for William de Joinville, he had already left the see of Langres for that of Rheims; but in that same year he would make to the Friars Preachers of Rheims the generous gift of the church of St Stephen and its dependencies.

After Mussy their route followed the curve described by the Seine at the foot of Mount Lassois, at the point where stands the majestic abbey of Pothières. Its ancient fame and legendary prestige attracted and held pilgrims on their way to Rome. Founded by the Benedictine monks in virtue of the same charter as the abbey of Vezelay, Pothières had around its high altar, so it was said, the coffins in which rested the bodies of Gerard de Roussillon, Bertha his saintly wife, and their son who was butchered in accordance with the pathetic and notorious procedure which had sprung up in that region around the cult of St Mary Magdalene.[6]

Courteous hospitality is the tradition of the Benedictines; Everard and Jordan would certainly have rested at Pothières and perhaps preached there.

A little way beyond Pothières is Chatillon-sur-Seine. According to Thierry d'Apolda it was in this place that St Dominic

---

[6] The relics of St Mary Magdalene had, according to tradition, been taken there from Provence and Vezelay, to protect them from the Saracen invasions. As to Gerard de Roussillon and his wife, we can still see their medallions carved in the portal of the church of Saint-Père-sous-Vézelay.

had obtained by his ardent prayer the restoration to life of a young boy who had fallen from a high balcony and had given him back to his mother. The white habit and black cappa of the Friars Preachers could not but have been well received there.

On leaving Chatillon the road forks into two branches which are still to be seen; one, continuing to follow the Seine, leads towards the Côte d'Or, and the other, threading its way through the valley of the Ource and twisting around the plateau of Langres, passes over the watershed of the Saône. That was the direct way for our travellers. Very probably they made a stop near Recey-sur-Ource, the future homeland of Henri Lacordaire, at the Chartreuse de Lugny whose new church had been consecrated in 1207. The Commanderie of the Templars at Bure might have been the next halt. By the castle of Grancey, then Lux, they would finally have reached Thil-Châtel and the abbey of St Pierre de Bèze.

A significant fact bears witness to the memory left by Brother Jordan. The great Benedictine abbey, six centuries old, was then in a state of decline. It was to Jordan, Master General of the Friars Preachers, that in 1223 the episcopal authority made an appeal to reform the community of St Pierre de Bèze and to give it a new start by leaving a colony of Friars Preachers there.

Such an undertaking was contrary to the Constitutions of the Friars Preachers, which forbade all territorial possessions. Moreover Dominican activity had by then turned not towards rural solitudes, notwithstanding that they were so well suited to contemplation and study, but towards preaching in urban communities and universities. The offer was declined by Jordan; but nevertheless it had been made.

Mirebeau, Pontailler-sur-Saône where the Augustinians of Val-des-Ecoliers still had a house, brought Everard and Jordan on their way by the low-lying valley of Ognon to Besançon, capital of the Franche Comté.

The bishop, who had been recently installed there, was Gerard de Rougemont. He was a man of great reputation who had been elected at the same time to two sees, Lausanne and Besançon. That could not be; the canons of Lausanne had to make another choice, and it was probably on the recommendation of Gerard de Rougemont that their votes were cast in favour of Everard de Langres. Everard did not accept, and we know why. But a reciprocal esteem, a friendly and holy regard for each other, certainly linked these two-men. Gerard de Rougemont could not but have followed with a pious interest the conversion of Everard de Langres. Great were his curiosity and his admiration with regard to this Master Jordan who was now taking Everard into Lombardy. We have proof of it in the foundation, rapidly following upon this visit of the two Friars Preachers to the episcopal palace, of a Dominican Priory at Besançon. It was opened in the following year and in 1224 officially recognized and given privileges by a document sealed with Gerard's coat of arms. It was to visit the Friars there that Jordan came back in 1223 to Besançon and made a visit prolonged by illness and marked by the care that was then lavished on him by Gerard de Rougemont. Between the two must have existed, in their common appreciation of Everard, a moving and affectionate memory.

This stop at Besançon, which he desired and designed for the great good of the Order, was in fact one of the last halts made by the good Brother Everard upon this earth.

He accompanied Jordan courageously along the rough ascent of the route followed by Julius Caesar, who crossed the Jura by Pontarlier and the Jougne. He went with him down the gentler slopes of the Vaudois side and reached Lausanne. But the effort of the long marches, the fatigue of travel and of preaching, had been too much for this generous heart. As soon as he reached Lausanne he fell ill. They wished to hide his true state from him. 'If the doctors are of the opinion that I am going to die', he said to Jordan, who has preserved his words for us, 'why don't they tell me so? It is from those to whom the thought of death is bitter that it must be hidden. As for me, I have no fear of death. There is nothing to fear in death for those who, at the moment when this miserable abode which is the flesh falls into ruins, have the hope of finding an eternal home.'

Jordan adds: 'Of his blessed death I have a consoling token.

At the moment when he breathed his last sigh, instead of the trouble and sorrow which would naturally have shaken me, I felt my soul flooded with devotion and gladness. I was warned by the inner witness of my conscience that I ought not to weep over a man who has gone to eternal joy.'

This must have been during the first days of August. In the Divine Office proper to the diocese of Langres the feast of Blessed Everard is celebrated on August 5.

Alone henceforth, Jordan hastened to cross the Alps.

The most common pass for one coming from the borders of Leman, and the easiest because of its hospitable refuge, was the Great St Bernard. By the valley of Aosta, Ivrée and Vercelli, Jordan reached the great plain of the Po. Without stopping to look at the Lombardy peasants in the monastic fields, turning the flow of muddy water into narrow ditches bordered with little willows or dressing the vines on the dry sticks which supported them, he crossed the river and its wide bed of rolling pebbles by the Roman Bridge of Plaisance.

At the end of the plain and before the first sharp risings of the Apennines, he looked to see, outlined against the blue of the sky, the battlements of red earth and the innumerable brick towers of Bologna where his work awaited him. It was to be more pressing and heavier than he could have foreseen.

A few days before his arrival, and almost at the same moment that Everard who 'desired so much to see St Dominic' had breathed his last in Lausanne, the Friars had slowly gone down, with infinite care, by the rugged path of the Osservanza, carring the dying Dominic. The pure, fresh air, the clear water and the peace of Santa Maria dei Monte could not lessen the pernicious fever with which he had returned from Venice a few weeks before.

Seeing that he was about to die, and well knowing that if he died in the abbey the Abbot of Santa Maria would wish to keep his remains there, he had ordered his Friars to carry him back to St Nicholas.

The sixth of August, early in the morning, the vine-dressers of the coast had seen the litter passing by surrounded by Friars Preachers tearful under their lowered hoods; and towards the middle of the day the Father had left nothing in the arms of his sons but mortal remains.

He was laid to rest under a simple slab behind the altar of St Nicholas, at the entrance of the cloister, 'under the feet of his brethren' as he had asked.

There was an end to the preaching that penetrated into the very souls, to those counsels full of supernatural prudence, to that authority so tender and at the same time so firm, to that luminous mind. The papal legate presided at the funeral ceremonies among a crowd of students. Crowds of students continued to flow into the cloister of the Friars Preachers. The whole city of Bologna claimed the patronage of St Dominic. He himself in dying had promised his sons that after his death he would help them by his prayers before God.

The hour was a sorrowful one, yet vibrant; the emptiness was frightening, but the apostolate a living one; nothing of it must be let go. The circumstances were favourable; they must centre them somehow around the Priory of Bologna, and make it the doctrinal citadel of northern Italy.

Chapter V
BOLOGNA, CITY OF LEARNING

OLOGNA, Jordan was to write a few years later, 'of all the cities of Lombardy, Tuscany, France, England, Provence and even Germany, is to me a very special city, and the dearest inheritance of my heart.'

We tend to attach ourselves to places where we have given the most of ourselves, and given the most deeply. Jordan knew this joy at Bologna. There he had truly chosen souls under him. There he began the convent of St Agnes and watched gathering around him a chosen group of women, noble and pious women, the nucleus of what was to be the Third Order of St Dominic. There he preached to most attentive listeners. There he found spiritual affection which came to mingle its gentleness with the energetic austerity of his life.

There, from the first, his activities extended not only, as in Paris, into the clerical world, but also into the lay society of the city, which had already been set on fire by the preaching of Reginald and remained singularly alive to the attractions of learning, of eloquence and of sanctity.

At Bologna the organization of the schools preceded that of the Commune, and the city, proud of its famous University, was pleased to call itself 'Bologna, the learned'. But if Paris was the studium of theology par excellence, Bologna's glory was the almost exclusive study of Law. Its University was the most ancient of all. A legendary tradition attributed its foundation to the Emperor Theodosius. From the end of the eleventh century Bologna was the home of juridical science, the focal point of interest to all of Lombardy, fought over as it was by the Holy See and the Empire, and violently divided between feudal customs and the memories of Roman legislation.

It was said that the celebrated Imerio—Imerius in Latin, Master Werner to the Germans—had opened at that time a school where he taught, with a freedom unknown before then, the interpretations of the imperial Decretals and the Roman Code. His fame had spread through Bologna and all Lombardy. He was said to have been called into consultation by the Emperor Henry V and Countess Matilda. One of his successors, the Florentine Francesco de Accorse, codified the Roman Law with so much success that the township of Bologna made him a gift, for himself and his sons after him, of the *Palais au Blé*, where he could install in comfort the numerous students of his school. He was still living when Jordan came, since his death did not take place until 1229, and his chair was kept famous after him by the advocate Odofredo, one of the great political influences of Bologna.

But in the Middle Ages one could not study civil law without joining canon law to it. Moreover in the twelfth century the Benedictine Abbey of San Felice had opened at Bologna its school of canon law, soon made famous by the great jurist and monk Gratian.[1] The school multiplied rapidly, as fast as qualified masters were forthcoming from among the more brilliant students. On the other hand, to come to the study of law, it was necessary to have passed through the liberal arts; the schools of the Trivium and the *Quadrivium*, and the schools of medicine were organized. Bologna, at the beginning of the thirteenth century, swarmed with students in their hundreds, and soon in their thousands.[2]

Among them, students of arts and medicine were always the least, both in number and in quality. Lawyers held the highest place, and as Bologna had no faculty of theology until after 1352, they constituted there the elite of high culture which the school of

---

[1] The Decretals of Gratian is the first official collection of the decretals of the Roman Pontifical See. It dates from 1151.

[2] According to a text by Odofredo, there were 13,000 of them. It is not very probable. The statistics of the Middle Ages are problematical, but the whole of Bologna does not seem to have included more than 15,000 souls. Paris at this same time counted about 4,000 students in the whole University; Bologna could not have had more.

theology represented at Paris.

They had a privileged position; in those days of charters and treaties, pacts and confederacies, the public authority, whatever it might be, as well as influential individuals, were obliged to reckon with the lawyers. The communes could not grow and organize themselves without their assistance. The Pope and the Emperor treated them with respect and favoured them, striving to influence them and make them support their policies.

Frederick Barbarossa had conferred on them a privilege, '*Authentica habita*', which placed them solely under imperial jurisdiction. But Bologna having adhered to the first Lombard league, masters and students followed the Guelf movement; soon Innocent III gave them his legate as magistrate, and finally Honorius, regularizing matters, placed all the schools of Bologna under the jurisdiction of the Archdeacon of Bologna, whom he appointed Chancellor of the University. The Roman Curia attached great importance from then on to what happened among these learned young men who were being initiated into one or other kind of law at Bologna. It was one of the places, there can be no doubt whatever about it, which had attracted Dominic's attention as a centre of teaching for the Friars Preachers. And when Jordan arrived there, its eyes were fixed on him.

The first texts in the cartulary of the University of Bologna do not go back beyond 1265. We must get an idea of this clerical world by analogy. As at Paris, the teaching was oral and gave to the masters a great personal authority. As at Paris, the Faculties of Arts, of Medicine and of Law were divided into 'nations'. But the diversity of origin was such that they were multiplied here to thirteen. The first great distinction was between Cismontans and Ultramontans. In Jordan's time, the Cismontans meant only the lawful citizens of Bologna and the Lombards. Tuscans, those from the Campagna and Romans formed another group. Among the Ultramontans, Spaniards, Franks, Provençals and English were equal in number to the eight other nations, among which

Hungary, Poland, Flanders and a few others were well represented.

Each nation elected its Rector, and a Universal Rector was elected alternately either by the four or by the eight Ultramontan nations. These elections were tumultuous and knifeplay was not unknown during them. Therefore the Chancellor and the Commune tried to make them hold their meetings in a safe and closely guarded spot.

For the jurists there was at first the church which they habitually frequented, the ancient San Procolo; then, after the Friars Preachers were established at St Nicholas of the Vineyards, they adopted the Dominican cloister.[3]

Members of the arts and medical schools made themselves at home in the cloister of the Franciscans, in the apse of the church of San Francesco. Today we can still see their tombs there. The cloister of St Dominic has the tombstones of the masters and students of law.

The students in arts and in medicine were nearly all Cismontans. The law students on the contrary, who had come from all parts of Christian Europe to be instructed in law at the famous schools of Bologna, had a great Ultramontan majority. Moreover they were jealous of their respective privileges, mad about freedom, and were often at odds with the Bologna townspeople who, as previously, made them pay raised rents and exaggerated prices. The Commune took the precaution of making the Masters and the Rectors take an oath and endeavoured to retain the Masters by offering them large salaries. But some incident would occur, nothing would be done about it, and it would cause a mass exodus of students and their masters. Accepting the offers of some neighbouring city, they would

---

[3] According to Cavazza, the Friars Preachers received as a deposit on trust the seal of the legists. A text of May 25, 1301, says that the Cismontans were come together to elect their rector 'more solito in domo Santi Dominici'. In 1306 and 1317, the Ultramontans did the same and they first assisted at the Mass of the Holy Ghost 'cantata dai Fratri Dominicani'.

emigrate to Modena, to Padua, to Sienna or to Verona—most often it was to Padua—and would not return to Bologna until they had been formally guaranteed certain advantageous privileges.

Nearly always the authority of the Holy See intervened and its influence predominated in these essentially clerical circles.

The emperors nevertheless tried to counterbalance this power which was a check to them in the Lombard cities. Soon, in 1224, Frederick II brought into being the University of Naples, which he tried to make his own and to which he sought to give a great scientific fame the better to combat the schools of Bologna with their zeal for jurisprudence, their Guelf leanings and their Roman spirit.

For many years Bologna had been emancipated from the suzerainty of Ravenna. Caesarian Ravenna, little by little, had fallen asleep between its sand-blocked harbour and its sombre *pineta*, and notwithstanding the nobility of its past and the splendour of its basilica, it was abandoned by the students who formed its schools. They settled themselves in Bologna, which was more modern, more alive, and they attracted thither numerous craftsmen who, living on their custom, followed the fortunes of the students.

Still growing, proud of its University, conscious of its rights, one of the capital cities of the Lombard League, Bologna had become a sovereign republic. Nevertheless, its sovereignty had nothing democratic about it. The common people had not the least part in it; all the effective power was in the hands of an aristocratic and privileged group. Citizenship was held in Bologna only by the heads of families who maintained in their properties a fortified palace and the means to defend it.

Uniting their resources, the citizens of Bologna had dealt with the Count whom the Emperor had imposed on them as podestà to keep some authority in Bologna, attacked his castello, obtained a charter, and finally at the peace of Constance freed themselves from the yoke of the Hohenstaufen.

They did not readily suffer any meddling in their affairs by a power which they themselves had not chosen. Even their bishop was suspect, at least in that he did not allow Commune delegates to be introduced into his tribunal of temporal jurisdiction, and he resigned himself to a measure of neutrality between the parties in the exercise of his feudal power.

This city of lords was hard to control. Pope Urban II had addressed directly to it his call to the Crusades in 1196. Proud to have responded to this call, they fashioned a coat of arms on which they inscribed the cross and opposite the cross the word: *'Libertas'*. It is easily understood that the city's great resource and support were in the Law schools of the University. Thus to do honour to the Masters and in the attempt to attach them to it by privileges, the city gave them a preponderant voice in its councils, and made them its representatives to diets of the Empire, its negotiators and signers of treaties.[4] No city ever gave more political importance to worthy University men or counted more doctors among the chiefs of its government.

But here, as elsewhere, the conditions of economic life reacted upon the slow and still confused political regime. Material welfare was assured to the city by its corporations, which grew in numbers and riches, and by its merchants and craftsmen. These demanded citizenship and access to public offices. Since the end of the twelfth century, when Bologna introduced a coinage, money-changers and merchants had the privilege of coining and issuing money. A little later there appeared before Imola, alongside the knights of Bologna, a bourgeois militia divided into four corps corresponding to the four quarters of the city.

Little by little, craftsmen and merchants effectively entered the city councils. They had their palace from which, on the 'loggia dei Mercanti', they could harangue the common people, stir them up

---

[4] At the Diet of Roncaglia, Bologna which controlled the fourteen communes of its territory sent to it twenty-eight counsellors, four being doctors of law.

or pacify them. Next to the families of the 'nobili', they had their private chapels in the periphery of the vast nave of San Petronio, the basilica of the Commune.

This development was not effected without strife. At one time or another, conflicts arose, involved and violent conflicts. Arbitration was then asked of some peacemaker who was a stranger to local quarrels, generally a churchman, and every year they altered the statute defining the communal powers. It took half a century of civic disturbance and legislative trials to reach, in 1245, a more balanced constitution and one destined to last more than a single year.

It was in the middle of this feverish period that the mendicant Orders, Franciscans and Dominicans, sent their first missioners to Bologna. Tradition says that St Francis came there before St Dominic and preached publicly in the San Petronio Square. In 1222, the Friars Minor had already established a church on the spot where San Francesco stands today, that is to say, near where the medical schools were then established. Since Reginald's arrival (1218-1219) the Friars Preachers were installed near the law schools at St Nicholas of the Vineyards.

By the logic of things, both Orders presented themselves to the great Lombard commune under the Guelf colours. After all, they were vowed to and supported by and under the patronage of the Roman Curia. They had broken with the feudal usage of the landed monastic Orders. They had replaced the suzerain abbots by Priors and Guardians whose humble woollen hood could be mistaken for that of the least of their brothers. They had restored the apostolic life of freedom and poverty.

The more a sense and love of the common weal developed in Bologna, the more the liberal spirit of the apostolic and Roman Church was seen to be in opposition to the narrower spirit of the Ghibellines who were attached to the Germanic Caesar, and the more Catholic loyalty and the desire to draw closer to the Holy See were strengthened in the families of at least the most famous among them. Thus the mendicant religious had found a welcome from the most influential citizens in Bologna, and the favour of the people.

Reginald and Dominic had aroused veneration, confidence and friendship there, and Jordan succeeded to this heritage.

He already knew what the city and its affairs were like; he knew what fire of ambition, what spirit of juridical pride and tricky greed, what fanatical enthusiasm for the cause of freedom, animated this newborn union.

It was already late summer. Soon, on the feast of the Holy Cross,[5] the students would be crowding in to resume their courses and to give the town its characteristic appearance. City of scholars, if we may so style it, Bologna's streets stretched between two lines of arcades paved with flagstones like cloisters and raised several steps higher than the narrow, deep carriage-ways. Sheltered from rain and sun and saved the mud, the clerics walked about disputing or dissertating under the colonnades made for them, intersected by the little squares with their low shops, yawning cellars and murmuring fountains, and sometimes by the sombre walls, pierced high up with barred windows, of the turretted palaces.

Outside the city gates, in the bright, gentle countryside dotted with steep hillocks, the monasteries raised their little bell-towers.

The priory of the Friars Preachers had its modest enclosure and its little Romanesque church not far from the San Mamolo gate near the law schools, in the highest quarter of Bologna. Its situation was a privileged one. For the past two years its influence had been growing and making itself felt by its teaching, ministry and preaching. Thanks to the University recruits, it had become a home of study. Its Prior was Ventura of Verona, a master of

---

[5] September 14. The scholastic year of the Middle Ages was from the feast of the Holy Cross to the feast of St Peter and St Paul, that is, from September 14 to June 29.

spirituality, the same who had heard the last confession of St Dominic; his Procurator was the wise Rudolph of Faenza, whom Jordan soon sent, in 1225, to govern the Priory of Santa Maria de Gradiis at Viterbo; his Subprior was the Master of Civil Law and Regent of Canon Law, Chiaro Sesto da Firenze; Moneta of Cremona, famous Master of Arts; Roland of Cremona, still more famous Regent in Arts and a skilled physician, and in a fair way to become one of the leading theologians of his time; Bernard the Teuton, who was later to accompany Jordan on his travels: Stephen of Spain, an authority chosen by Dominic, who was soon to become Prior of Bologna and later the successor of Jordan as Provincial of Lombardy; John of Vicenza, a soul burning with love, future peace-maker and wonder-worker of Lombardy; and finally, among the young friars in the novitiate, Peter of Verona, a sublime figure of heroism and humility, destined for martyrdom; Bartholomew of Breganza, already a savant, since 1224 lector at St Nicholas of the Vineyards, destined later for diplomatic missions and for a bishopric—such were the chosen ones of the Priory of Bologna.

Moreover, men of high worth had already been sent out from it: Paul of Hungary, placed at the head of the Danube mission; Conrad of Hoxter, sent to the Province of Germany; Nicholas of Giovanazzo, Provincial of Rome and of Tuscany; Guala of Bergamo, founder of the Priory of Friars Preachers at Brescia, later bishop and legate of the Apostolic See; Philip of Vercelli, chosen Prior of the house at Rheims, before he succeeded Matthew of France as Prior of St Jacques at Paris.

No small prestige had this house which Jordan was called to rule in Lombardy. Nevertheless he found in it certain friars in great trouble of mind, some giving themselves to excessive mortification, others to feverish preoccupations.

Cruel loss though the death of Dominic had been, it was a most holy death that did not leave his sons forsaken. It was not, in fact, this loss or this grief which unbalanced these religious already firmly settled in their vocation; it seems to have been rather the intoxication arising out of the rapid success of their Order and the aura of glory which already surrounded it.

Proud imaginings seize upon the weakest; strange obsessions then arise, which attack even the strongest. A certain Brother Bernard, a very simple man, little instructed in sacred learning, still less in theology, suddenly began to preach with a mesmeric energy, producing sentences worthy of St Augustine, delivered with such religious power that he drew tears from his hearers. His fanatical tirades turned the whole house upside down. At times an extraordinary perfume, a sort of odour of sanctity, pervaded the house, a delight to some, unendurable to others, which followed Jordan himself to the very altar. He resisted these contagious disorders, but he could not escape being affected by them. Were these signs from on high, or rather assaults from below?

Those around him asked anxiously what these strange happenings portended. If the excitement of preaching was to upset the Friars to the point of destroying their peace and lessening their hope of salvation, would it not be better to give it up, at least for a while?

Jordan himself, on his arrival at Bologna, had begun to make his voice heard most fruitfully. But the unfortunate Brother Bernard, in his delirium, suggested one day that, if Jordan ceased to preach, the temptations which tortured the Friars body and soul would instantly leave them. Then the Master, coming to himself, saw the fraud and unmasked the deceit: 'I will make no treaty with death; I will not make peace with hell. It is to preach that we are sent out. Temptations cannot prevent the Friars Preachers from making spiritual progress, from believing in the life of grace. We shall be tempted; very well, are we not soldiers of Christ? and should we not hear what was said to the soldiers of Christ: "Our wrestling is not against flesh and blood, but against the rulers of the world of this darkness, against the spirits of wickedness in the high places."⁶ We shall emerge from these combats, and we shall still be on our feet. Temptation? That is man's life here below.'

His clearsighted and virile energy restored general calm. These obsessions of the senses vanished. Brother Bernard, restored to his senses and to the stolid placidity natural to him, began to speak again as stupidly as before, and nobody troubled any longer to listen to him.

But this strange passage doubtless provided for Jordan the first occasion to exercise his prudence and authority.

It is to him at this time that we owe the origin of one of the most beautiful liturgical traditions of the Order of Friars Preachers. At the height of the temptations which beset the Friars, Jordan ordered them to add to the end of the Office the singing of the response, 'Te Sanctum Dominum', to invoke against the evil spirits the help of the good angels. Since this practice was not efficacious enough and the nights of the Friars were still troubled, he directed them to sing the *Salve Regina* at the end of Compline. This anthem has always since then been chanted at the end of the liturgical day. According to the custom of the times, this was done in procession, by candle-light; and was followed by the sprinkling of holy water by the officiating priest over each one of the Friars.

'A pious and salutary custom', said Jordan, who speaks of its origin in the *De Initiis Ordinis*. There was no heart but was soothed, no conscience but did not find peace, no movement of the flesh that was not subdued and sanctified by the rhythm of this trustful prayer effected by the procession, the genuflections and the inclinations of the body, as much as by the voices raised in unison towards the Mother of Mercy. After it, they could compose themselves to sleep without fear. They could rest. The shadows no longer held any terrors. There were no phantoms to fear, no more demons to dread. This peace was so sweet that all the Friars, say the first chronicles of the Order, 'hastened to Compline as if to a

---

⁶ Eph. 6, 12.

wedding-feast' and it soon caused to be established in the Order the custom of chanting the *Salve* round the bedside of the Friars Preachers in the hour of their death, so that they could end their life in the same ineffable and tender security with which they ended their day.

He who designed this ceremony was a great artist in religious life, so short and so simple and so moving a ceremony which, every evening, placed the Friars Preachers, prostrate at her feet, under the special protection of their advocate and sovereign Queen, the Blessed Virgin Mary. This dedication to our Lady became one of the characteristics of the Order. All the Lombard convents imitated Bologna; and, probably after the General Chapter of 1228, their example was followed by all the houses of Friars Preachers throughout Europe.

Finally, after Raymond of Pennafort, chaplain and confessor to Pope Gregory IX in 1228, had carried this liturgical custom into the Curia, in 1229 Gregory ordered that the *Salve Regina* should be sung every Saturday evening, after Compline, in all the churches of Rome. At almost the same time, according to the account attributed to William of Nangis, who died in 1302, it is reported that St Louis the King assisted every day at Compline with his sons and that at the end of the Office he chanted an antiphon, always the same, to the Blessed Virgin, a gracious custom which spread from the Sainte Chapelle into all the churches of Paris.

The historical importance of this institution is clear. Notwithstanding the diverse legends which have sprung up about it, it is not to Dominic that this custom goes back, but to Jordan.

Within a few months after these events, the priory of the Friars Preachers at Bologna had fully expanded its religious life of study and preaching. Proof of this is given in the account of the visit that James of Vitry made there in the autumn of 1222 on his return from Palestine.⁷

The good French cardinal, whose character shows, along with notable traits of learning and piety, something of the curiosity of a Froissart, took pleasure in describing the 'new religion', that is to say the new rule of religious life, and the preaching of those whom he calls the canons of Bologna. He remarks with admiration that, contrary to the established custom in those times for all chapters and communities, they had no possessions and lived on alms, leading a life of voluntary poverty. A novelty still more striking— they studied and they thought; they mingled with the students who were at Bologna to study and, moreover, they had each day profound lectures in the Holy Scriptures given by one of their own number.⁸ They formed a 'holy and learned congregation of Christ's scholars' (sancta et honesta Christi scholarium congregatio). Finally, the chief characteristic recorded by James of Vitry to describe the religious of St Nicholas of the Vineyards is that they were, above all else, vowed to preaching. The noble chronicler notes also that 'their example inspires and inflames a

---

⁷ Jacobus de Vitriaco: *Historia Orientalis*, Chapter XXVII. Quoted by Fr Mandonnet, Arch. de la Ste d'Histoire du canton de Fribourg, T. VIII, 1903. The term 'canons' has misled certain historians. Fr Mandonnet has shown that it means, not the canons of Reno, but the Friars Preachers of Bologna, who in fact formed, under the Rule of St Augustin, a chapter of canons regular. J. de Vitry indicates that they lived near a city gate and in the middle of the schools; and all their special characteristics which impressed him so much could apply only to the Friars Preachers. J. de Vitry, curé of Argenteuil in France, but canon regular of Ste Marie d'Oignies, legate against the Albigensians, bishop of St Jean d'Acre, later Cardinal-Bishop of Frascati, knew Jordan of Saxony and Cardinal Ugolino, and shared many of their ideas on the reform of the regular clergy.

⁸ Reading of Holy Scripture was, we know, the principal object of theological teaching in the thirteenth century. The 'reader' of the Priory of Friars Preachers at Bologna was in fact a professor of theology. His lectures were followed not only by his confreres but by secular clerics, canonists for the most part, who wished to study theology, since—and the bishop complained about it—there was no other school of theology at Bologna.

great number to imitate them and each day this worthy college of Christ's students increases in number and grows in charity'.

Better than a full recital, these precise notes of a contemporary show what the house of the Friars Preachers at Bologna was like. Jordan knew how to adapt and strengthen there the tradition of Reginald and of Dominic. Fruitful nursery of men of study and of preachers, the great Lombard Priory had not degenerated, and it was to go on developing from day to day.

Its first buildings and its church had become inadequate since the fruitful Priorship of Reginald, and building projects had been envisaged by the first General Chapter of Pentecost 1220; but they had evidently not been able to begin immediately to realize them. The work of enlarging was doubtless gradually undertaken according as donations were given to this end by the rich people of Bologna. The presence and soon the influence of Jordan must have hastened this expansion.

To the clamour of the students in the cloister and the garden was soon added the clatter of workmen. It seems certain that between the years 1221-22 and 1233 (the date of the first translation of the relics of St Dominic and date of the building of his first tomb) the most important part of the work was finished at St Nicholas.

A parchment recently discovered at Bologna, and bought by the Archiginnasio, casts some light on one of these periods of construction and illustrates the conditions under which it was undertaken, not without great financial difficulties. The learned Dr Albano Sorbelli attributes it to the year 1228. It is a letter from Eberhard of Regensburg, Archbishop of Salzburg from 1220 to 1246, who was then returning from Rome to his diocese; it is known that he had obtained for his church certain privileges from the Curia; and, probably with Jordan's knowledge, he must have charged himself, while he was with Gregory IX, with the most pressing interests of the Friars Preachers. As the legate of the Apostolic See he writes in terms of affectionate esteem 'to the

Prior and Religious of the Priory of Friars Preachers at Bologna'[9] and that he delivers to them 'the power of absolving from the sin of usury all creditors, whether Siennese or Bolognese, who have usuriously extorted from them any money under the cover of a loan at interest, provided that these, moved by voluntary repentance, make restitution of this money, in whole or in part, for the fabric of the church of the Preachers.'

This is interesting, because it tells us of the loans that the Friars Preachers of Bologna must have contracted for the good of their work and brings us, as it were, into the midst of their active life; it also emphasizes a delicate point of canon law. It was then forbidden by the Church to make loans at interest; whoever was guilty of 'mutuum' was excommunicated. It was this precise regulation which made the Jews the pawnbrokers and the moneylenders of all Europe in the Middle Ages, because, except for the Mohammedan Arabians, they were the only ones who could give themselves with impunity to such financial negotiations. This power to absolve usurers is an extraordinary power, not usually given to the ranks of the clergy. It was, therefore, a great favour which was bestowed on the Preachers.

It is thus clear what progress they had made in a few years, in

---

[9] Original text: E. Dei gratia Salburgensis archiepiscopus apostolice sedis legatus dilectis in Christo fratribus priori et conventui fratrum Predicatorum domus bononiensis salutem in auctore salutis.

Cum vos et ordinem vestrum semper hactenus speciali dileximus vinculo charitatis, non immerito petitionem nobis ex parte vestra porrectam duximus liberaliter admittendam. Concedimus igitur vobis potestatem ut vice et auctoritate nostra possitis absolvere omnes creditores sive Bononienses sive Senenses qui a vobis aliquam pecuniam nomine mutui per pravitatem usurarum extorserunt, dummodo ipsi, penitentia voluntaria ducti, eandem pecuniam vel partem ipsius restituant ad fabricam ecclesie domus vestre seu ad alias necessitates aut etiam utilitates domus eiusdem et ut eisdem de predicto secundum discretionem a Domino vobis datam iniungatis penitentiam competentem. Ad majorem autem huius rei evidentiam presentem cartam nostri sigilli munimine roboramur.— A. Sorbelli.

public opinion, in the goodwill of the bishops, in the solicitude of Rome. The Priory of Bologna could thereafter expand without undue anxiety and could open its doors to students in still greater numbers.

If Dominic had deferred the work of enlarging St Nicholas, it was because another foundation seemed even more turgent to him: that of a convent of women, after the style of Prouille and of St Sixtus.

This new foundation, however, was reserved for his successor. She who first inspired it, who above all others worked for it unremittingly, was to become Jordan's spiritual daughter. Thanks to the letters that Jordan addressed, between the years 1222 and 1237, to Diana d'Andalo, letters piously copied by the nuns of the convent of St Agnes at Bologna, we can best rediscover the stages of the history of Diana d'Andalo and of the building of the convent of St Agnes at Bologna.

In 1221 Diana d'Andalo was but a young woman of eighteen or twenty years, but an indomitable energy lay hid in her shapely body and in her small aristocratic head.

Diana was born of one of the most noble and richest families of Bologna, the family of the Carbonesi. Her parents possessed land around Bologna; and in the city their palace raised its proud walls near the San Procolo gate, not far from the communal square. Her grandfather, Pietro Lovello, was the landlord and patron of the Church of St Nicholas of the Vineyards and its dependencies; it was at the prayers of his granddaughter that he had conceded them to Reginald by legal transfer on March 14, 1219.

Diana's father, Andalo or Andreolo, was a man of considerable importance in Bologna. He exercised the office of 'pretore della montagna', that is to say, the prefect of all the suburban communes of the Appenines which were dependent on Bologna. Her older brother, the nearest to her in age, earned, notwithstanding his premature death, a great military and juridical reputation; he was a magistrate of Genoa. Another younger brother, a pious and idealistic type, was the founder and first Prior of a Guelf confraternity at once religious and chivalrous, the Congregation of the Glorious Virgin, popularly called the Frati Gaudenti. Diana's mother, Lady Otha or Otta (diminutive of Octavia), seems to have been a very distinguished woman. Her young sister, also named Otha, who died young, was her 'sweet and faithful friend' and merited the regrets of Jordan who had 'so much wished to see her again'.

They all had gifts of the highest order, and all had a great charm of manner. All were of an ardent nature, and when they gave themselves to something or someone, did not give by halves. Diana, who is said to have been beautiful, learned and eloquent, at first loved the world with all her heart and was no less warmly loved and welcomed by it.

According to tradition, it was from a sermon of Reginald's that she first received the sudden movement of grace. On his arrival at Bologna, as we know, he drew not only the students of the University but also the great ladies of the city to his sermons. They came to hear him in all their finery and not always clothed as modesty demands. One day Reginald took for his text the animadversions of the Apostles SS. Peter and Paul on women's attire. Diana was there and was much moved. She sought out Reginald, made her confession to him and promised to change her life; and she kept her promise with the fine integrity which characterized her. Henceforth she turned to God and to God alone, began to seek another glory than that of the world and to desire the self-denial of the religious life.

This was in the winter of 1218-1219. Under Reginald's direction she could hardly fail to become Dominican, at least in mind and heart. She was intelligent enough and well-educated enough to understand what the Order of Preachers was, and generous enough to be fired with zeal to serve it.

She was instrumental in effecting the transfer of the Friars Preachers from their distant and precarious situation at Mascarella to St Nicholas. But that material service was not enough for her to render. She knew how the Order of Friars Preachers had been born and on what Dominic had based its earliest efforts, namely, on the cloistered prayer of the Dominican nuns of Prouille. When the Friars had received from the Pope the church and cloister of St Sabina at Rome in which to establish their new home, St Dominic gathered at St Sixtus the nuns of Sta Maria de Transtevere and arranged for them to be instructed by Sister Blanche and six religious detached from Prouille in the rule and the contemplative spirituality of the Friars Preachers.

To establish at Bologna a convent whose unceasing prayers, offered close by the studium of the Friars Preachers in the midst of the University, should become the firm support of Dominican preaching, that was her vocation; of that she had no doubt at all. She invited her most faithful friends to join her, the daughters of Bologna's noblemen, and already some of them were won over.

It was thus that Dominic, arriving at Bologna in August of 1219, found Diana d'Andalo. He recognized in her a strength that came from God and he encouraged her in her plans. The hour had not yet come for her to carry them out. But before the departure of Reginald Diana dared to ask for permission to take her vows, courageously undertaking to lead the religious life without changing her dress or her dwelling, in spite of the obstacles which she would have to overcome within her family and outside in the world. It was a conflict to be feared; but she was of warrior mould and she had a will of her own. Dominic consented. He received her vows at St Nicholas in the presence of Reginald, of Rudolph de Faenza, the former chaplain of St Nicholas, an old friend who had known her since infancy, and of Guala of Bergamo.

From then on Diana wore an iron chain under her worldly clothing. Rising during the night or at the dawn, in the silence of the palace, she found a way to consecrate three hours a day to prayer and the study of Holy Scripture. So well did she persevere that, after the first General Chapter, Pentecost 1220, the commission to find a piece of land suitable for building a convent and making its foundation possible was entrusted to Rudolph of Faenza, to Ventura of Verona, to Guala of Bergamo and to the great jurist Master Paul of Hungary. It came to nothing; the bishop considered that the land was too near the town and showed himself indifferent to the project; the d'Andalo family was unwilling to furnish the necessary funds and showed itself hostile. The project had to be deferred.

In spite of her steadfastness, Diana's situation became intolerable. She saw the time corning when the paradoxical compromises by which she struggled between the life of the world and the religious life could no longer endure.

In default of the Dominican cloister which she still dreamed of creating, she looked around for a religious house which would accept her and take her in. There is a record of an application which was made in her name to the abbess of the Benedictine convent of St Gregory. The abbess refused to accept within the cloister a recruit who, she felt, must be only a transient one and whose entrance would not fail to lead her into serious difficulties with the d'Andalo family.

Diana then turned to a great friend of Dominic's, Brother Alberto Spinola.[10] This saintly man had founded the chapter of

---

[10] Alberto Spinola, dean of St Mark's at Mantua, must then have been an elderly man. He died shortly after St Dominic. According to the *Vitae Fratrum*, part 2, c. XXIX, he was one of the most intimate friends of the Blessed Father; he was present in the church of St Nicholas at the funeral watch over the body of St Dominic, and it is then that, after he had kissed his dead friend he stood up joyfully and said to Brother Ventura, 'Good news, Father Prior! Master Dominic has told me that this very year I shall join him in Christ.' He was very eloquent and had preached the Lent at Bologna in 1204, easing the conflict then going on between Modena and Bologna and converting many sinners.

Canons Regular of San Marco at Mantua. This institution, whose rule was that of St Augustine and who, in certain ways, tended somewhat to the Friars Preachers' way of life, had daughter houses, one at Bologna, at Santa Catarina di Quarto, the other at Ronzano, a rustic site on one of the first spurs of the Apennines, some distance from Bologna. On this mountain plateau were two convents, one for men and the other for women, both dedicated to the Holy Trinity and under the rule of the Canons of Mantua. Alberto Spinola frequently spent time in retirement there. According to a legend told in the *Chronica di Ronzano*, he took Dominic there and the saint planted two cypress trees with his own hands near the sisters' chapel. Fra Alberto could refuse nothing to 'Master Dominic'. It was secretly agreed that Diana should enter the nuns' convent there; it remained only to put the plan into execution.

Doing violence to her proud integrity, Diana sometimes still played a comedy role; and seeming to take up her former diversions again, she organized a pleasure ride into the mountains, on the feast of Mary Magdalene, July 22, 1220. She led her companions to Ronzano and there dismounting went into the convent. They were expecting her. She was taken to the dormitorium, put on the religious habit then and there, and remained in the cloister.

This caused an uproar. Andalo gathered his friends and relations and, at the head of an armed troop, came to take his daughter home by force. Diana refused to take off the religious habit; she fought those who attacked her and was wounded. Taken back to Bologna with a bruised side and for a long time immobilized and in pain, she yielded, yet without giving up entirely, and resigned herself to the hope of obtaining by patience and waiting what she had not been able to gain by audacity.

Dominic corresponded with her, and without doubt also Brothers Rudolph and Ventura; a letter from the former still exists, addressed later to Diana and to the sisters of St Agnes. She perfected herself in the knowledge of Latin, in the practice of prayer and in the exercise of the virtue of her fortitude. The death of Dominic did nothing to change her attitude. The legate of the Holy See in Lombardy, Cardinal Ugolino, was won over to her cause and that meant a great deal; the Bologna commune was growing and its newborn constitution leant on the protective liberality of the Roman Curia. Ideas were changing all around Diana.

Jordan of Saxony was able to inspire in her a renewal of confidence and hope, while constraining her to temper the hot fighting blood of her race which boiled up in her all too often. He also undoubtedly knew how to conciliate the autocratic Andalo; it was in this year 1221 that, Pietro Lovallo having probably died, an act was drawn up by Pasquale di Saragozza, notary of the Sacred Palace, by which Andalo solemnly confirmed his father's donation to the Friars Preachers. (Melloni, Appendix, p. 205.) From this moment Jordan became the director of Diana's conscience and her spiritual father. Like herself he was a child of Reginald and of Dominic. But more than Reginald, more perhaps still than Dominic, the Master of Arts who had become a Friar Preacher knew the world, the business of human life, the characters of men, their passions, their motives and their weaknesses. She could not but give herself up to his prudent guidance.

Advised by him, she eventually triumphed over the resistance of her family and it was without any violent battle that on the Vigil of All Saints she returned to Ronzano, and was this time able to stay there peacefully in a long retreat that, according to Melloni, was prolonged until the Octave of the Ascension, which fell that year on May 12.[11]

---

[11] Should this second journey to Ronzano be assigned to All Saints' Day, 1221, or All Saints' Day, 1222? Melloni, followed by Cormier, indicates 1221. I have found reason, in my edition of the letters, to opt for 1222. But if Diana had only made a sort of retreat of probation lasting six months with the Canonesses, we can suppose with probability that she returned to Ronzano,

There was no longer any opposition to her vocation. At least she was allowed a chance to test it in these six months in the cloister, and to make a trial of religious life and observance. Without any doubt, Diana found herself again at Ronzano, and after the actual purchase of the lands destined for the convent of St Agnes[12] she was officially domiciled there.

But if Ronzano offered her silence and solitude, it did not appease her ardent desire to consecrate herself to the Order of Preachers. She heard no more preaching there, she did not find the spiritual resources manifested to her by Reginald, Dominic, Ventura, Rudolph and finally Master Jordan, for which she had developed a taste. 'I know', Jordan wrote to her, 'that if your spirit is not refreshed with spiritual honey, it will die; for it is delicate and disdains to use coarse nourishment.'

It was also at this time that there began a correspondence between Diana d'Andalo and Jordan of Saxony which lasted fifteen years and of which fifty letters from Jordan have come down to us. The first of these letters, which can be attributed probably to the summer or autumn of 1222, reflects so clearly the state of Diana's spirit and gives so good an idea of Jordan's direction and the ascetic but tender counsels by which he sustained and consoled his daughter, that it must be read in its entirety. Its form of address is noteworthy.

Diana was not yet Sister Diana, but Lady Diana; it was thus that she is designated in the deed of purchase signed at Ronzano; and to the canonesses of Ronzano she was certainly also 'Lady Diana'. But with great delicacy Jordan softens the pain this name gave to her impatience by calling her his daughter, his sister, and

---

in the winter of 1222, when the purchase of lands was in negotiation, and she was preparing to take the Dominican habit, which suggests a reasonable conciliation between the two hypotheses. It was actually in 1222 that Ascension Day fell on May 12.

[12] Melloni, Appendice agli Atti, vol. 1, p. 376, V. Date of the contract, May 13, 1223. '*Actum in Ecclesia ubi stat Domina Diana*'.

above all his associate in the same rule of religious life. (*In participatione religionis sociae.*)

'To the Lady Diana, his daughter in the filial fear of the Father, his sister in the adoption of the Son (Rom. 8, 15), his well-beloved in the charity of the Holy Spirit, his associate in the religious life, Brother Jordan, useless servant of the Order of Preachers, greetings, speedy freedom from present sadness, and the enjoyment of future happiness.'[13]

'It is your great desire which has urged you to write the letters you have sent me. I shall therefore say something to you on the subject of this heavenly desire. Most dear sister, it was the desire of the Patriarchs[14] which invited your Spouse, Christ the Son of God, to come to suffering, and he came. Invited to joy[15] by your desire, why should he not come? Direct all your desires toward heaven. He who does not wish to link himself with hell, attaches himself wholly to heaven; the dweller on the plain is not at peace, for he is exposed to all his enemies; but he who is established in an entrenched fortress and behind towers, such a one is secure. Do not set your dwelling place, my dear, upon the plains, but after the example of David before Saul flee into a fortified place and,

---

[13] Prayer from the Mass '*Salve sancta Parens*'.

[14] The allusion to the Patriarchs may assign this letter to Advent. Diana is not yet a religious because she is elsewhere called 'Lady'. On the other hand, since Jordan styles himself 'servant of the Order of Preachers', he has already been elected Master General and this letter is dated after the Chapter of May 22, 1222. In the symbolism of the times, the fortified place and the opposition of the mountain and the plain could very well refer to Ronzano. Finally, Jordan had not known Diana long, since he says, 'I believe that you do not know German'. This letter is thus probably the first of their correspondence and must be put between May 22, 1222, and the beginning of Lent 1223, when Jordan came back to Bologna.

[15] of union with souls: *Jesu, amator nostris zelator animarum...*

like him, by your desire dwell in the shelter of heavenly ramparts.

'I believe that you do not know German; there is nothing surprising in that, since you have never been in Germany. We use in this world only worldly idioms, for he who is of this world speaks of this world. (John 3, 21.) So, my dear, if you wish to learn another language, dwell by desire in the heavenly regions and when you come back from them take up a book which will give you spiritual help or try to hear spiritual things preached, so that you may have knowledge of them. One who has never been in the spiritual regions does not understand them.[16]

'You must not forget that in man there are two principles, soul and body. The body, as you know, does not cease hunting for its food in the world of corporal things, so as not to die of hunger. But the soul is worth more than the body. Do not then, my dear one, put your body before your spirit; but when you are in quest of nourishment for your spirit, it is into the region of spiritual things you must send it to find there this food which is not to be found on earth and which we buy with devoted desire and not with money.

'What wretched being would let himself die of hunger for lack of some good thing that can be obtained by desire alone? Say with the Prophet: My eyes are ever towards the Lord, as the eyes of the poor towards the rich from whom they await alms with great desire.

'Bees collect from earthly flowers an earthly honey, carrying it into their hives and keeping it carefully there for the future. If your spirit is not refreshed by spiritual honey, it will die; for I know it is very delicate and disdains to use the

---

[16] Correction of the translation which I gave previously in Jordan's Letter, 1924, and taking into account the variant readings between Reichert's text and Altaner's.

grosser foods. Send your spirit then, my dear, towards the flowers of the celestial meadows which never fade, so that it may there gather honey on which to live. This honey is not destined to be consumed at only one meal; we keep a part of it in the hive of the heart, so that when we come to a failing of desire, we can find in ourselves and in this storehouse which we carry in our hearts something to delight in. My dear one, when this good to which all your great desires tend shall be yours, do not forget your needy correspondent.'

Thus, while Diana d'Andalo sighed for the foundation of the Dominican convent which she held so dear to her heart, and she was left without adequate direction, reduced to spiritual reading without any longer hearing its meaning explained, she called from her spiritual isolation to her father and master and Jordan attempted in his answers to turn all her aspirations toward God, and God alone. She must know how to wait, she must know how to hope, she must nourish her hope at the divine source of charity.

Like Dominic and Reginald, Jordan also discerned in her the sovereign flame of the contemplative vocation, the thirst for a transforming union, for a life hidden in God and with God. He wished to help this soul, so exalted but at the same time so realist, if one may so phrase it, in all that she sought, to climb step by step the mystical mountain.

His doctrine is here the pure doctrine of divine love, such as was expounded by the great doctor of the Church in the twelfth century, St Bernard. God is sweet to those who seek him. To desire him with the holy desire of a purified soul is, if not yet to possess him, at least already to touch him. This was granted to the unwearying desire of the Patriarchs. This is granted to the fervent appeals of hearts which are really his. But the ineffable moments of this blessed meeting are brief. It is the memory of them, piously guarded in spite of weakness and dryness of the soul left solitary again, ceaselessly renewed by suppliant prayers, which supports and continually inspires the spiritual life.

In his letter Jordan showed his daughter how to buy the supreme good, the sole necessity. He gave her the secret of union with God. He gave her, in this simple manner, which was above all concrete and alive, something of his own, the fruit of long and rich meditation. This teaching was of the clearest and most concise, most profound and most opportune, since they were then and for a long time separated from one another.

Chapter VI
MASTER GENERAL OF THE FRIARS PREACHERS

ORDAN must have left Bologna at the beginning of April for the General Chapter of the Friars Preachers convened at Paris for Pentecost, May 22, 1222.

What had he done as Provincial of Lombardy, what part had he played in the destiny of the Order since the day when, in company with Everard de Langres, he had left the convent of St Jacques whither he was now summoned back for the General Chapter? At Bologna he had strengthened, enlarged and at the same time wisely consolidated Dominican action. At the time of St Dominic's death, four priories were being founded: in the valley of the Po, at Brescia, where Guala of Bergamo was now in charge; at Parma; at Plaisance; and at Venice, the last of those intended by St Dominic.

Jordan did what was necessary to establish these houses. But already he was hopeful of making a foundation as yet still uncertain in a place which, according to him, was still more qualified to have a house of Friars Preachers, namely, Padua. Padua, whither doctors and lawyers who found themselves in disaccord with the citizens of Bologna so often emigrated, was the most urgently needed of Lombard foundations. Without doubt Jordan had already been there to ascertain the intentions of the Commune and had worked to instal the Friars Preachers there, for in 1223 the Padua Priory was established.

But we get the impression, hard to prove from definite texts but deduced from general facts, that in this first year of his administrative work the influence of Jordan must have gone beyond the Lombard province. His correspondence with Henry of Marbourg, Prior of Cologne, now unfortunately lost but spoken of by himself in *De Initiis Ordinis*; his relations with the Universities of Paris and Oxford; his collaboration with the legate of the Apostolic See in Lombardy, Cardinal Ugolino, an all-powerful personage at the Roman Curia, in all that concerned the fight against heresy and the extension of the preaching of the Church; all this allows us to think, not without foundation, that he must have already been mixed up in the general affairs of the entire Order; the more so as the absolute unanimity of his election, on May 22, 1222, made it appear to be the solemn ratification of an established fact.

According to a tradition in early Dominican writings at this chapter he must already, by an act of supreme authority, have decided to send two missionary Preachers to the Holy Land, Burchart of Strasbourg and a brother called Xyronius of Milan.

When Jordan was put at the head of the eight provinces and the forty Priories that the Order had established between 1217 and 1222, he courageously foresaw how they should increase from then on.

In the University of Paris, in the same St Jacques where two years before he had taken the habit of the Friars Preachers, Jordan received the highest office of the whole Order.

It was neither the time nor the place to look back. The Priory itself was already being rebuilt; under the impetus of the new Master, the work increased and so, as at St Nicholas of the Vineyards, the noise of carts unloading materials, the clatter of tools, the shouts of masons, mingled with the psalms of the Office and the coming and going of curious students. The Friars Preachers of St Jacques—the Jacobins, as they were called by the people of Paris, whose number in 1219 was not more than thirty, were one hundred and twenty in 1223. They were probably near to a hundred in 1222, and it is certain that the first buildings were no longer large enough for them. Steven of Bourbon, contemporary Friar Preacher who received the habit at Lyons in 1223 but who had been studying theology at Paris before that date, had known and frequented the Priory of St Jacques and speaks of the work of construction which was then going on. The little chapel of Jean de Barastre was already giving place to a much larger church, very simple in style, with two naves, one for friars and clerics, the other for laymen. At the same time they began to build the cloister, a large refectory, and an infirmary. This work was so urgent that it was completed with a speed not common at those times. This explains the relatively short duration of the buildings of St Jacques, and their complete disappearance when so many other buildings of the same period have left vestiges still standing today. After Jean de Barastre, dean of St Quentin, their first benefactor, it was the University of Paris and its Commune which became benefactors of the Friars Preachers. The University had just conceded to them all rights not only to the hospice of St Jacques but also to the adjoining houses belonging to it; and at the time of the election of Jordan, at least within the month following it—since the gift was ratified by Philip Augustus, who died in 1223—the Commune of Paris gave the Friars Preachers a building large enough for them, enclosed in the ramparts between the St Michael Gate and the St James Gate, and the close adjoining it outside the walls, formerly the 'Clos du Bourgeois', which now became the 'Clos des Jacobins'.[1]

Such considerable additions were not made without great expense. As at Bologna, the Friars Preachers knew financial difficulties. As at Bologna, these were cleared up; not by a bishop-legate but, at the request of the Bishop of Paris, by the Queen, Blanche of Castile.

This fact is attested by Stephen of Bourbon. Blanche of Castile

---

[1] The plan carved on the marble slab in the Church of St Stephen of the Mountain shows the places then covered by the priory of St Jacques on the hill of St Geneviève. It extended to the St Michael Gate (Boulevard St Michael, corner of the M. le Prince) to the St James Gate (corner of rue S. Jacques and rue Soufflot). The cellars of rue Cujas and rue Victor Cousin are the former crypt of the church.

was about to make a pilgrimage to St James of Compostello and was ready to devote to it 'a marvellous outlay'. The bishop, William of Auvergne, her confessor, who knew that the Parisian Friars Preachers were completely unable to pay off a debt of about 1,500 livres, said to her: 'Madame, do you not think that you could do something better than spend so much money for the glory of the world and to make a great display in your native land?'

And she, who knew very well in her heart that this pretentious pilgrimage was more a parade than an act of piety, replied: 'Give me your advice; I am ready to follow it.'

'The Friars Preachers', said William, 'who are called the Friars of St Jacques, are in debt more than 1,500 livres. Take your pilgrim's staff and go to St Jacques, their house, and pay their debt; and since I have commuted your vow, I promise you that I will answer for you at the Day of Judgment; for you could not do better than to use in this way the money which would otherwise have served only for useless pomp.' And 'the woman of wise heart followed the advice of the holy man'.

This holy man was William of Auvergne, who was consecrated Bishop in 1228, and if he was already a bishop at the time of this incident, this puts it between 1228 and 1230. This must indeed have been a difficult time for the Friars to have large debts falling due in the work, which was begun in 1221 or 1222, seems to have been finished in 1231,[2] and judging by the size of the buildings the cost must have exceeded first estimates.

We can see the hand of Jordan in those events whose material shapes we can grasp. Already in 1222 the future Regent of France, soon to be Queen by the accession of Louis VIII, gave ear to the advice of the Master General and showed herself to be a faithful

---

[2] 'I have learned that all are united under the same roof.' (Letter to the Brethren of St Jacques.)

friend of the Friars Preachers.[3] Taken as a child to France to be married when she was scarcely sixteen years old, perhaps she had in the first place loved in Dominic de Guzman and in his first sons something of her own native Castile. She must have seen Blessed Mannes arrive in Paris in 1217. She must have seen St Dominic in 1219. We can scarcely believe that, coming back just then from Spain, St Dominic could have gone through Paris without greeting the daughter of King Alphonso there, without, perhaps, taking to her—in those times when it was the custom to entrust letters to travellers—some message from her homeland.

However that may be, Blanche had confidence in and a constant veneration for the Preachers. It was apparently she who, already near to becoming Queen, obtained from the dying Philip Augustus the grants of land for the enlargement of St Jacques. It was she who urged her husband, Louis VIII, after his accession to the throne, to take up the crusade against the Albigensian heresy in accordance with the wishes of the papal legate, Cardinal Romain de St Ange, and by reason of the information which the Friars Preachers would have given her about the district of Toulouse.

An event which occurred only fifteen days after the election of Jordan as Master General confirmed the interest which Blanche of Castile had in the Friars Preachers and in the extension of their Order in the kingdom of France; and in this event it is impossible not to see Jordan's own work and influence.

A day's ride from Paris, on the wooded plateau which dominates the valley of the Eure, the episcopal city of Chartres, although deprived of its former scholastic prestige by the recent growth of the University of Paris, still remained a city of schools and scholars. Peter the Lombard had taught the Sentences there, great masters had come out of it, subtle dialecticians, recognized

---

[3] A little later Jordan wrote: 'The Queen loves the Friars Preachers so dearly that she has discussed her business affairs intimately with me.'

mathematicians, Guillaume de Couches, Gilbert de la Porrée, who had drawn to their lectures students of all nations. In spite of its decline, at about 1222 Chartres still had illustrious canonists: the Chancellor Robert de Brou, the Dean Bartholomy, soon to be bishop of Paris, the de Grey brothers, Aubry Cornut, Constantine of Sicily.

If a breath of discord arose between students and townsfolk in Paris, just as those of Bologna went to Padua, Verona and Sienna, so Parisian students would make their way to Chartres. No one knew and foresaw this better than Master Jordan.

But there was yet another motive that turned his thoughts toward Chartres. Chartres, a privileged home of devotion to our Lady, had its first cathedral destroyed by fire in 1194, and afterwards, by an unusual co-operation of benefactors of all ranks, benevolent workmen of all conditions and anonymous pilgrims of every social class, raised the triumphant edifice which still stands. A fervour of pious generosity animated a whole army of workmen and craftsmen, stone-masons, master workmen and glass-makers, whose encampment obeyed the discipline, not of bugles and military commands, but of prayers and church bells. Blanche of Castile had taken upon herself the cost of building the north door, especially the famous rose window with the arms of France and of Castile which rises above it, where her son is delineated as a young blond King Solomon; nor was this work finished without her arriving from time to time to see the progress that was being made on it.

She was at Chartres on the Sunday after the Octave of Pentecost in the year 1222, on June 16, fifteen days after the Chapter of St Jacques and the election of the Master General. And there she presided at a ceremony at which Jordan, if he was not there in person, as was probable, was certainly present in spirit.

Before the Bishop Gautier of Chartres,[4] the dean of his chapter, Hugues de la Ferté, and a great gathering of magistrates, nobles, and clerics whose names are unfortunately not recorded in the text which has come down to us, she solemnly confirmed the gift of a house made to the Friars Preachers by Hugues de la Ferté. This house, according to tradition, was against the rampart near the Clos Muret. A little old chapel adjoined it, but it needed to be rebuilt.

We do not know who the first Friars Preachers were whom the priory of St Jacques sent to Chartres. But we do know that their installation there was not without difficulties, for, though they had the bishop and the dean on their side, they had the majority of the canons against them; and the sequence of events allows us to understand very well why Jordan had asked Blanche of Castile to give so much help by her presence and that of her court in respect of the donation of Hugues de la Ferté. He had to establish the Friars Preachers in Chartes in such an emphatic way that hostility would be forced to withdraw, but it was not to be finally overcome for eight years and that not without conflict.

The place ceded to the Friars Preachers remained, in accordance with the jurisdiction proper to such places, under the patronage of the Chapter. The Friars could not change anything or build anything without its consent. But a small house was not sufficient to allow the Preachers to have a regular priory and church, and in particular the thing that was essential to their purpose and certainly of greater moment to the bishop, namely, a

---

[4] Bishop from 1218 to 1234, a Cistercian; Hugues de la Ferté, dean of the Chapter, succeeded him as bishop. It was he who seems to have been the advocate of the establishment of the Friars Preachers at Chartres; he gave their priory an illuminated Bible in sixteen volumes. He was buried in the Friars' cloister. He was nevertheless not a learned man, if we can credit a bull of Honorius III of Jan. 8, 1219, taking away the right of election from the members of the chapter, who had twice chosen him for bishop, because he was 'indignum ob defectum litteraturae'.

school.⁵

But the canons were firm in their refusal to allow the Friars Preachers the right to arrange as they wished the place which had been conceded to them and to celebrate the Divine Office there. Quibbling and wrangling, the dissident canons managed by invoking particular laws and usages of the district of Chartres to delay matters from year to year until 1230. It required a fulminating bull from Pope Gregory IX to overcome their stubbornness.

This papal document, sealed as from Anagni on November 9, 1230, was not drawn up without the intermediation of Jordan, as we shall see later; and again it was Blanche of Castile who lent confirmation to its effects by assisting at the first Mass celebrated in the new church of the convent of St Jacques at Chartres on the octave day of the Ascension.⁶ She offered to the friars chasubles, copes and dalmatics of silk, and a great silver cross, gilded, ornamented with a fleur-de-lis, containing a relic of the wood of the true Cross.⁷

The first Prior was Nicholas of Sienna, later Provincial of the Holy Land; he came to Chartres from Orléans, where he was a teacher, and was elected in chapter on St Michael's day, September 29, 1231, in the presence of Pierre de Reims, Provincial of France, and soon to be preacher and advisor to St Louis. The following year, at the Provincial Chapter of France, he and his definitors

---

⁵ 'In isto Conventu Camutensi liberalium artium et sacrae theologicae studia a prima ipsius institutione diutissime floruerunt.' According to Clerval, the 'little schools' of the Jacobins of Chartres later had several lectors and sub-lectors besides the principal lector, and they counted between 200 and 300 students.

⁶ An inscription giving witness to it was still visible in the 16th century in the church of the Preachers.

⁷ Father Le Febvre (Praedic. Camut.) saw these ornaments in 1637 and said that this cross was carried in his time in processions of the Holy Name of Jesus on the second Sunday of the month.

made a proposition, we do not know what, which was accepted and confirmed by Jordan in a circular letter which has disappeared but the text of which the historian of the Priory of Chartres, Father Le Febvre (*Praedicator Carnutens*), had seen at the beginning of the seventeenth century, and he had copied a passage which interested him.[8]

From then on the house of the Friars Preachers at Chartres greatly extended its scope. Their lectures in theology were open to students from outside. Some of their masters, like Friar William d'Autun, went to the Sorbonne; two others, Brother Thomas d'Epeautrolles and Brother John d'Anet, were respectively chaplain to St Louis and his confessor for twenty years, and both were his historians.

Blanche of Castile and her son seem to have preserved a warm regard for Chartres. As for Jordan, this was his first foundation in the Province of France and one that he held dearest to his heart. But he had to visit the other priories of the Order and Lombardy called him back. It is probable that, if he preached in Advent to the students of Paris, he would return to Bologna to preach the Lent there, because it was his almost invariable custom to spend Lent where the General Chapter was held. Thus the Chapter became the occasion for the Master to give the habit to the novices who had been converted during Lent. Moreover, he must have preached at Bologna for Pentecost, June 11, 1223, at the General Chapter.

Another matter, which for some months he had followed attentively from afar, claimed his presence and his authority. Diana d'Andalo had gradually overcome the resistance of her family and the scruples of the bishop of Bologna. Ronzano was to her only a temporary refuge; her wish was to live, under the rule

---

[8] '...et insuper a.d. 1232 ut constat ex quodam scripto B. Jordanus Magistri Ordinis, sub his verbis: "Universis praesentes litteras inspecturis Fr Jordanus Ord. Praed. servus inutilis. Noverit universitas vestra quod nos et ratam habemus gratam, firmam et stabilem promissionem quam F. Nicolaus Prior domus nostrae Camutensis et fratres ejusdem loci fecerant... etc." '

of the Friars Preachers and under their direction, a life of contemplation and mortification for the benefit of their Order. Jordan also wished to see a house of Dominican nuns built at Bologna; he could foresee its social value and the supernatural help it would provide.

It must have been his arrival which finally decided matters, for they were hurried through; the contract of sale of the land bought by 'the Lady Diana' to build her convent on was drawn up by a notary in the church of Ronzano on May 13, 1223. Evidently both buyer and seller were already in agreement, for she had only been waiting for that moment to begin the layout of the spot, the cloister and the construction of the little house, low and poor as it was, which received the first Sisters; three weeks afterwards, on the Octave of the Ascension, June 8, 1223, Diana and the four young women of Bologna whom she brought with her came down from Ronzano again and received the Dominican habit in this humble dwelling which had been prepared for them: a robe of white wool with a capuce[9] of the same material, a leather belt, white veil, cappa of coarse serge of black or brown. Finally, on June 29, the feast of St Peter and St Paul, the new Sisters made their solemn vows before Brother Rudolph and Brother Ventura, Brother Bernard the Teuton and Brother Guala of Bergamo, who served as witnesses.

Thus the convent of St Agnes was founded. It was situated outside the city, between the San Mandalo Gate and the Gate of Saragozza, on a little hill not far from St Nicholas of the Vineyards, at a place called Volsampero.[10] Diana's desire was fully satisfied.

It was Jordan who had brought this to pass, and who had attached enough importance to the consecration of the nuns of St

---

[9] The capuce was a scapular of medium length to which the hood was sewn. It is the first scapular of the Order. A hood was also sewn to the cappa. The material of the cappa was wool of natural colour, neither bleached nor dyed.

[10] Present location of the Villa Casalini.

Agnes to delay his departure several days. But a strange impatience possessed him. Not all the students of Bologna had attended the Lenten preaching. Several groups of Ultramontans, after one of their frequent quarrels with the Lombard townsfolk and the Cismontan clerics, had left Bologna before Jordan's arrival. Jordan, who had got to know them the previous year, was aware of the value there was in them, what advances some of them had made to him and what hopes they had raised in him. He went back in mind to a certain sixteen-year-old student at Padua, a lively and delicate lad, son of a great German family. He knew this youth's fancy to enter the Order, and how this was opposed by his uncle, who lived with him and who had made him promise not to listen to the Friars Preachers' sermons any more. He could not forget his fervour, his assurance. Above all, at a glance the Master of Arts, the great mathematician, Nemorarius, had seen in this young man a precocious and assured scientific genius. Such an intelligence, in a soul already sanctified, would radiate a great light. By bringing him into the sound and vigorous Dominican way of life and learning, he would be saved from the current dissipation of mind, from the attraction of useless ambitions, he would be consecrated to truth. Jordan had no wish to make him abandon the sciences. On the contrary, he encouraged him to pursue those researches of which ignorant people were afraid, which frightened timid people; they alone could build a bridge between routine theology, too far removed from rational and experimental methods, and a liberal culture that was without restraint, dangerous to subtle imaginations and to consciences not balanced by a sufficiently strong faith. Albert of Lawingen would be a great man. Master Jordan must find him again and win him over.

Meanwhile, the final establishment of the Priory at Venice, of which the preliminary plans had been drawn up by St Dominic two years before, urgently demanded the presence of the Master General, and to go first to Venice was to travel toward Padua. He did not let Diana d'Andalo keep him. Admittedly, for so young and new a religious as she to undertake alone the formation in the religious life of companions yet more inexperienced than herself was well-nigh impractical; difficulties were already appearing. But provision could be made. 'Be patient', Jordan would write to his daughter. These are the letters which, after seven hundred years, provide us with the landmarks of his journeying and bring his travels and his preaching to life again.

So he set forth with long strides, along the dusty road, under the harsh July sun. Two friars accompanied him, Brother Archangelus and Brother John. Archangelus was a man of Bologna, known to Diana to whom he is attached and whose prayers he requests.[11] John and he were to accompany the Master to Paris; their names, which appear again and again, enable us to locate the letters where they are mentioned in the postscripts and to reconstruct their trip with certainty. There are reasons to suppose that these two young Friars Preachers of good family were taken by Jordan to St Jacques so that they could study theology there.

They travelled at his side. The Master sometimes spoke to them of the things of God and of the Order, sometimes remained silent and recollected, inviting them to silence and to prayer, sometimes chanted aloud with them the Psalms of the Office and anthems he loved, such as *nostra redemptio*, and especially the *Salve Regina*. They walked quickly and with light step. The two Brothers were scarcely able to keep up with this smiling, robust man, whose temples were already beginning to grow grey, whose head was bowed sometimes by the weight of so much thought.

The first stop on the route must have been Faenza, where still

---

[11] Letter II, A, XXXV, B. 'The brothers who go with me, Brother Archangelus and Brother John, greet you. Archangelus regrets very much not having seen you before leaving Bologna. He meant to see you, but obstacles prevented him. I think that, although he appears to have shown himself neglectful, he is attached to you in his heart; be indulgent to him, then, and remember him in your prayers.'

today the road from Bologna forks to Florence at the south-east and to Ravenna toward the west. One of the first Lombard Priories had been established there three or four years before. From there it was not far to Ravenna, where they could take ship to Venice, thus saving considerable time. Jordan was in a great hurry; doubtless this is the route he took[12] and stayed only a very short time at Venice; the letter in which he informs Diana of his happy arrival in that city announces at the same time his departure for Padua.

This short letter had two objects: Jordan did not forget the spiritual needs of his daughter; he urges her to strengthen herself and her sisters in charity. 'Soon will come the wedding-feast of the Lamb', he wrote. 'He will give the sweet wine of the date-palm to those whose soul is bitter with the thirst of love.' A mystic exhortation which is meant to help the nuns of St Agnes to live in the love and in the hope of God. But at the same time he assigns a precise object to their prayers: that they beg Jesus Christ to bless the preaching that he is about to undertake at Padua, that they obtain 'for his voice the power of the Word, so that it may bring forth fruit to the honour of God'.

That was his great preoccupation and also his hope. While he went along the road from Venice to Padua, meditating on his sermons, his memory turned back, tender and confiding, towards the humble cloister where he knew they prayed unceasingly for him; dear little house, not in vain has its foundation already cost so much trouble; it is the holy reservoir upon which he relies for his preaching; it will not be either his talent or his prestige, but the unremitting sacrifices and valiant faith of this handful of religious women that will bring down divine grace and win the victory.

Meanwhile these matters were to be long drawn out. The next letter asks again for prayers: 'The students of Padua are terribly cold; so far only one of them has allowed himself to be won over...

---

[12] A very probable hypothesis which I borrow from Dr B. Altaner.

I recommend to you to pray assiduously to our Lord that he may deign to move their hearts and to draw them to him for their own salvation, for the glory of God and the Church, and for the growth of our Order.'

On her part, Diana doubtless implored direction and words of consolation. Jordan excused himself for having no leisure to write at length to her; he gives her over to the care of the Holy Spirit, 'whose consolations are unmixed, and infuse into the soul truth in its entirety. Rest in him, and wait patiently in him for the time of my return.'

The weeks went by, the month of August came, and Jordan, a prey to discouragement, was thinking of returning. But no; suddenly grace flooded into the closed hearts of these students hitherto indifferent; ten of them entered the Order, 'and among them two sons of two great German lords; one was a provost-marshal, loaded with many honours and possessed of great riches; the other has resigned rich benefices and is truly noble in body and mind.' This was Albert de Lawingen; he had triumphed over temptation and the artifices of the world, over his uncle, and over his own hesitations; later, among the tribulations of life, it was enough for him to remember the words of Master Jordan at this decisive moment to regain strength and certainty.

He was bound to the Order for ever. Jordan's letter is a canticle of thanksgiving, a song of praise. He addressed it not to Diana alone, but to 'his sisters of St Agnes, very dear in Christ'. All had shared in the labour, all must share in the honour and all must be thanked.

Another letter to Diana followed soon after. Twenty-three others had come to join the first ten recruits, 'all clerics eminent in letters, except two layman who would be Lay-brothers; several are of the high nobility'. Six others, 'quite notable', had made a promise binding them in conscience to enter the Order later, and many still were expected. Overwhelmed, Jordan had sent for Brother Ventura, his successor in the office of Prior Provincial of

Lombardy, and probably also with him Rudolph de Faenza and several friars formerly at the Priory at Bologna.

It became urgent to open a house of Friars Preachers at Padua: they must profit by the enthusiasm of the University world and by the good dispositions of the town, which was anxious to have the students and masters start this house without delay. Jordan could not wait any longer at Padua; Brother Ventura had the necessary authority and experience to take his place, to begin the education of the novices and, if need be, while waiting for the foundation of the new convent, to take them to the 'studium' of Bologna.

Diana was alarmed at the abrupt departure of Brother Ventura, her Superior, her spiritual father, her adviser in Jordan's absence and her support since the departure of the Master. There was far from unanimity in the house of the Friars Preachers of Bologna on the subject of the foundation of St Agnes; several of them disapproved of the expenses and the anxieties generally involved in looking after monasteries of women; they felt great repugnance for this new charge, not having grasped its value for the Order. Therefore Diana must have felt very strongly about Brother Ventura's departure.

Jordan reassured her. 'Do not have any uneasiness on the subject of Brother Ventura', he wrote, 'for it is not with the intention of making him Prior of Padua that I have called him here.' He did more. How could she have thought that he would lose sight of St Agnes, that he was not concerned to organize its life and regularize its administration? Negotiations were under way at Rome to arrange for the transfer to Bologna of a little nucleus of those Sisters of St Sixtus which had been founded not long ago by St Dominic himself. The Prior of the Roman province[13] was charged with this duty. 'He has written to me', said Jordan to Diana, 'about the matter of the Sisters of St Sixtus, and as far as

---

[13] Nicholas Palea, of Giovenazza, first Prior of the Roman province, an important man.

they are concerned, all goes well and they are well disposed towards it.' The difficulties and the delays in this matter must have come, not from the nuns themselves, but from Honorius III who, proud of his convent of St Sixtus, could not bring himself to denude it in this way.

Jordan wrote in paternal fashion to calm his too ardent daughter: 'I beseech you in God of your charity that your heart be neither troubled nor afraid... Endure sadness, be patient in humility.' Perhaps to this message of the Master, Brother Ventura, in collaboration with Rudolph de Faenza, had added the letter of exhortation, the text of which has come down to us.[14] It is a consolation in the allegorical style of the times, addressed to Diana, their Prioress, and to the Sisters and to all in the convent of St Agnes, by Brothers Ventura, Prior, and Rudolph, of the Order of Preachers.

> 'We exhort you', it says, 'to go forward towards the City which is above... let neither covetousness nor toil stop you: the strong castle which allows itself to be captured as soon as it suffers assault by the engines of war is reputed of little value... If sometimes your hearts are troubled by the song of deceiving sirens or the hissing of other monsters whose prey you might easily become, because you do not know their language, do as the nobles do to ensure the education of their sons, for they send them to the court of the great in France or

---

[14] Reichert attributes this letter to the years between 1225 and 1228, because at that time Rudolph de Faenza was at Florence; but was he there with Brother Ventura? On the other hand, since in this letter Diana is called Prioress, a title that she never officially bore, but whose office she exercised in the early days of the building of the St Agnes convent, this document must have been before 1225, as an act of June 12, 1225, mentions as Prioress a certain Sister Agnes Romaine. This letter dates then probably from the summer of 1223 when Diana was so forlorn and Fr Ventura was away from Bologna, and also Fr Rudolph who must have followed him.

Germany, so that equipped in every way and instructed in languages, they know how to avoid the snares. So, direct your thoughts towards the heavenly court, so that if you hear some horrible monster, you may be warned to flee the peril by the angelic tongues which resound about you.'

This text, with its clear significance delicately dressed, recalls the first letter sent to Ronzano by Jordan—so much so that it seems to reflect something of Jordan himself.

Meanwhile the Master had taken the road again.

The Priory of Padua was founded. It was the first Lombard creation of the Master General, as Chartres had been his first French creation, and both marked the progress of the Friars Preachers in the University world. Now Jordan was awaited at Brescia.

Located on the highway from Milan to the Adriatic, near Verona and Padua, Brescia had one of the first houses of Friars Preachers established in northern Italy by St Dominic. It was in existence in 1220, and from that time Guala of Bergamo was its Prior. But the original establishment in one of the churches of the town, Saint Afre, was inadequate. By an official act of May 24, 1221, Cardinal Ugolino, papal legate in Lombardy, had invested in Guala of Bergamo the possession of the church of the holy martyrs Faustinus and Jovitus, patrons of the city, with its dependencies, houses and vineyards, on condition that they paid the revenue of these dependencies to the former Canons of the place for four years more.

From then on, Guala of Bergamo was held to have the confidence of the Cardinal-Legate. He might have been forty years old. Born of a noble family, a distinguished canonist of the schools of Padua, he was already a priest when he entered the Order and was sacristan at the Priory of St Nicholas of the Vineyards from the time that Moneta of Cremona entered in 1219. He had been a witness, with Reginald and Rudolph, at the profession of Diana d'Andalo made into the hands of St Dominic, and, with Ventura, Rudolph and Bernard, at her clothing. He was one of the best business men among the Friars Preachers, one of those whose signature most often appears in official acts. In the near future he was to become a familiar of the Roman Curia, which entrusted him with very important diplomatic missions and delicate negotiations with the Lombard League and the Emperor Frederick II. He was to be bishop of Brescia from 1230 and to introduce into the communal statutes new legislation against heresy. Jordan would on many occasions have recourse to him as a negotiator and to gather information. Now he hastened to Brescia at his invitation.

The year had been full of trouble for the city. An earthquake and a flood followed by an epidemic had severely tried it. To avert these evils and in the hope that they would not come again, a solemn translation of relics of the holy patrons of Brescia had been decided upon by the bishop. The relics were exposed and carried with great pomp in procession throughout the city. The Friars Preachers, guardians of the holy bodies, must have led the procession among the higher clergy and the magistrates. It was good to see the Master General in their midst and maybe he spoke in the course of the ceremony. Such demonstrations did much to confirm the prestige of the Order and to establish its authority in Lombardy which was so much disturbed by heresies, and nevertheless so rich in its religious elements. Jordan was well acquainted with the communal spirit and its passionate unreasonableness, and he knew the importance of such demonstrations. He was present at the translation on August 23.[15]

---

[15] Bayonne and Kuczynski give August 8, Altaner August 23. The latter date seems the more probable. However fast Jordan travelled, since he did not leave Bologna until after June 29, was at Venice and preached 'during a long enough period' as he says himself, to the students at Padua, he could hardly have reached Brescia before August 15 or 20.

Doubtless he expected to leave Brescia the next day to return to Bologna. But the air of Brescia was charged with the germs of marsh-fever. Jordan fell a victim to it, and attacks were to torment him repeatedly thereafter. He had to give up the return to Bologna and, as soon as he was convalescent, to go to Milan. Jordan was committed to preach the Advent to the students of Paris and to spend all the winter at St Jacques until the General Chapter which would meet at Paris, at Pentecost, 1225. The season was already advanced. To take the road over the Alps, he must go before autumn, before the first snows and the shortened days. Diana grieved in vain. He wrote to her:

'Since I cannot see you as I wish and as you wish, with bodily eyes, I have written to you several times... so that in spite of the inexact and diverse rumours which may have reached you, your soul shall not be in the least troubled... Know then that after having suffered with fever at Brescia, I am, by God's grace, now convalescent and have been able to come to Milan, whence I hope that I can happily continue my journey. Console yourself then in the Lord, so that I may myself be consoled thereby in the Lord, for your consolation is my joy and comfort before God. Greet all the Sisters for me and recommend me to them. To them also, good health.'

CHAPTER VII
EN ROUTE

THE Master General had an important reason for taking the road by the Alps and the Jura. The bishop of Besançon, that same Gerard de Rougemont who had recently entertained Everard and Jordan, had just established a Priory of Friars Preachers near his episcopal see. For ten years he had prepared for this foundation. It was now ready and Jordan was awaited at Besançon to settle the final details and to preside at its actual inauguration.

After leaving Milan, the most direct way to the Jura is the Simplon Pass, whose pathways were frequented by the muleteers who carried wine and salt from Ticine to Valais. Its hospice, recently constructed by the Knights of St John, assured a shelter for travellers. Perhaps after this, in order to make haste, Jordan decided against going around by Lausanne and this time took the Roman road which, going from Sion to Avenches, by the shores of Lake Neuchatel, leads into the valley of Doubs. At this time it was a common way for foot-passengers. He reached Besançon, but, worn out by this hurried journey, he suffered a serious relapse of his fever, and in spite of the scruples which the spirit of poverty inspired in him and to which the stories in the Lives of the Brethren and by Thomas de Cantimpré have given a legendary form, he had to submit to the affectionate hospitality of Bishop Gerard, who kept him a long while in his palace, in his own room and bed.[1]

---

[1] Thomas de Cantimpré speaks of an episcopal city 'not far from the Alps'—'per Alpium juga non longe a montis pede digressus acutam febrem gravissimam labore itineris fatigatus, incurrit', but allowing for the geographical notions of the times, this definition could apply to Besançon. According to Cantimpré, Jordan was accompanied and cared for by a Prior of his Order, a wise and prudent man, very learned, and practised in the art of medicine.

At last a letter to Diana announced his arrival at Paris. 'Here am I, dearest one, preceded by the grace of God, accompanied also and surrounded by your prayers and those of my daughters, happily arrived at Paris in good health... Brother Archangel and Brother John greet you.'

It must have been about All Saints' Day; Jordan, who liked to find inspiration for his exhortations in the liturgical season, briefly spoke to Diana of the City of the Saints, 'a region truly divine and worthy for a creature formed in the image of God to aspire to dwell in'.

This letter recommends Diana to keep herself and her sisters 'in the unity of religious practices, concord and peace' which would have had no meaning for the early group of four or five nuns. The little convent had certainly grown. 'My greetings also', Jordan wrote, 'to the lay-sisters of St Agnes, I mean the familiars, the ladies and friends of the house.' Clearly then a secular family had assembled round the cloistered sisters; Diana's mother, doubtless, and her younger sister, a choice few ladies and young girls of Bologna frequented the house, were present at its offices or associated themselves in its prayers, contributing by their offerings or their work to its support, receiving spiritual direction, hearing the letters of the Master General and having their share in his recommendations. This little society is a new thing; we did not see it appear at St Sixtus or Prouille. Maybe Diana was the promoter of it, or perhaps it was only that she was able to gather together what was already to hand and in some way to centre the group around herself and the Sisters of St Agnes.

Both suppositions are likely and are indeed complementary. Recalling the movement inspired by Reginald amongst the Bologna aristocracy and reading the chronicles of St Agnes, we can see that it is because of the example of Diana d'Andalo that 'many noble ladies and illustrious matrons of the city have come—and this since 1219—to converse with the Friars Preachers about the health of their souls'.[2] These became the auxiliaries and benefactresses of the convent.

This attraction of penitents from high society towards the Friars Preachers would later become general and not without attendant difficulties, particularly in Germany. At the start of the thirteenth century there was only a very small number of preachers who, exercising the double ministry of preaching and of penance, confessed and directed lay-people.[3]

At Bologna in particular—in this learned Bologna so much loved by Jordan—where even the women had an advanced intellectual culture, extending sometimes even to medicine[4] and to law, responding so well to sacred eloquence and outstripping the men in the zeal of their spiritual ambitions, there was already, if not in law at least in fact, a veritable Third Order which began to form around the Friars Preachers.

Some texts of the Dominican Constitutions make allusion to certain of these pious noble ladies of Bologna, calling them the 'Vestitae', the 'Clothed' of Bologna. Probably the most fervent and most free among them, young women who had renounced marriage, widows desirous of keeping themselves in retreat, made vows of a life of penance and continence and, while living outside the convent, were clothed in the habit of St Agnes. It appears even that later some of these 'lay-sisters' were provided with a lodging in the dependencies of the convent, nevertheless without becoming a part of the community and going inside only on

---

[2] 'Ceperunt preterea multe nobiles domine et illustres matronae de civitate Bononiae *ipsius exemplo* cum Fratribus Praedicatoribus familiaritatem et colloquium habere de salute animae. Exinde expergefacta est devotio militum nobilium et consanguinearum dominarum, qui ceperunt fratres adjuvare et vernerari.'—Melloni, Cormier.

[3] At this time, the Franciscans, who confessed one another, did not yet hear the confessions of lay-people with few exceptions.

[4] There is in the old cloister of San Francesco the tomb of a woman of Bologna who was a professor of medicine.

certain days. Jordan wrote in his last letter to Diana, 'Greet our special friends outside, and especially those who are with you in the house, when they come to see you.'[5]

Diana, then, had gradually grouped around her the nucleus of a budding Third Order. And Jordan never ceased to uphold and encourage her in this apostolate alongside the cloister. Probably he himself, while he was at Bologna, willingly gave the habit to these 'outside friends' whom he greeted so affectionately in his letters. All his colleagues were far from sharing his liberality on this point. There is reason to believe that an ordination of the Chapter of 1220 forbade non-cloistered women to wear in the world the habit of St Agnes. This habit was, at least, reduced to the leather belt, the belt which in those times was the characteristic sign of the Dominican habit.[6]

Thus light is cast on the singular story[7] of that exchange which Master Jordan, when he was already old, made one day: his belt for the belt with silver ends which had belonged to a devoted and noble lady. Could it not have been to console her for her distress at having to give up the habit of St Agnes that the Master had made her a gift of his own belt and accepted hers in return?

It can be seen by what followed how great a struggle Diana and he had to maintain on behalf of these secular associates, who were so devoted to the Order. We see them, under the patronage

---

[5] 'Saluta extrinsecus amicas nostras singulas, specialiter maxime illas quae in domo tua sunt tecum, si ad te forte venerint.'

[6] Dante by antonomasia called the Friar Preacher the 'Corrigier' (Paradisio, XI, 138.)

The satirical poet Rutebeuf, living in Paris about 1250, refers in his 'Diet des Béguines' to women 'who wish to be grafted on to these holy people'; this means the Preachers, whose belt they wore:

'Et riche femme est mal baillie
qui n'est de tel corroie sainte;
Qui plus bèle est, si est plus sainte.'

[7] told at the end of Chapter I.

of Sister Diana, as the authentic predecessors of the Third Order. Their small and persevering family gave it birth, more than these diverse 'militias of Christ', kinds of religious knighthood, in which some historians have believed they see the beginnings of the Third Order. Dominicans may have taken part in the direction and even in the foundation of these confraternities, but they were not the starting-point of the Dominican Third Order and never had anything specifically Dominican about them. Here, on the contrary, in the immediate neighbourhood of the house of St Agnes, and under the protection of Master Jordan, was sheltered a branch of the Order of Preachers—modest enough, but efficiently grafted on to the very trunk of the tree planted by St Dominic. This development of St Agnes made it more necessary than ever to have a regular constitution for the plan and interior administration of the convent. Pope Honorius III had not given in; the prior of the Roman province had not yet the authorization to send some of the nuns of St Sixtus to Bologna. It appeared as though they must give up that idea. Jordan had turned consequently to the Sisters of Prouille. In a letter difficult to date, but which seems to be more or less contemporary with the preceding one, he wrote to Diana, in a postscript to a beautiful exhortation on the three chief virtues of the religious life, poverty, chastity and humility, the following lines: 'The Sisters of Prouille will be coming soon. The Prior of Montpellier wrote me so... You will greet them affectionately and share with them the letter which I address to you... Pray fervently for me.'

What he begged from all his daughters at Bologna, repeatedly and always, was prayers, and always for the support of his preaching in the scholastic world. 'Ask the Sisters to pray for the students of Paris, so that God may open their hearts and dispose them to a prompt conversion, and that those who have already made good resolutions may put them into action.' After Padua, Paris; after Albert the Great, Humbert of Romans and Hugh of St Cher.

'Between the Advent of the Lord, and Easter', wrote Jordan to Diana in the following Spring, 1225, 'about forty novices have entered the Order. Several are masters, others are well-educated and we have good hopes for many others also... I have, thanks be to God, happily succeeded in my preaching among the students of the University.'

We know from Humbert of Romans that after he and Hugh of St Cher entered the Priory of St Jacques they were followed by forty other University students. It is probable, then, that it was in the course of this winter of 1224-1225 that the preaching of Master Jordan won for the Order these two illustrious recruits—Humbert and Hugh.

Hugh of St Cher, Master of Arts and Canon Law, was then a Bachelor in Theology, which means that he was already teaching it. He became one of the first Dominican masters of the University of Paris (1230-1235). He made a celebrated emendation of the Bible; made concordances of the Sacred Books and wrote the first complete commentary on Sacred Scripture. He administered the Province of France and was raised to the cardinalate in 1244. Made Papal legate to Germany 1251-1253 to promote the acceptance of the new king, William of Holland, he died in Orvieto in 1263.

Humbert of Romans was his disciple. A young Master of Arts, he was studying canon law and went often in the early morning to listen to lectures in theology. Son of a good family, de Romans, in the Dauphinate, the example of the monks from the Grand Chartreuse, who received hospitality in his father's house, had early turned his pure and charming soul to the religious life. Sent very young to the schools of Paris, he had also frequented the Friars Preachers and saw their house and their influence grow, and felt drawn to them.[8]

---

[8] According to the Vitae Fratrum, it would be the priest of his parish, St Pierre aux Boeufs, who decided him, on the Vigil of All Saints, by saying to him: 'See how many masters, and some of the greatest of them, have left the world to

He was to become Master General of the Order (1245-1263) and to die at Valencia in 1277, after having resigned his office. He exercised a profound influence over the Order during his government and was one of the thirteenth-century men who best understood the state of Christianity.

It was he who, at the General Chapter of 1256, at Paris, invited the Brethren who had known the holiest Friars Preachers at the beginnings of the Order to write down what they remembered. Gerard de Frachet, then Provincial of Provence, was charged with the duty of collecting and editing the work. Humbert furnished him with many notes himself, giving to these 'Lives of the Brethren' precision of facts, dates and names which added a historical character to their edifying legends. Spiritual son of Jordan, he particularly insisted on things which concerned Jordan. It was he also who codified the Dominican liturgy. He was one of the greatest servants of the Order during its first century.

Having triumphed over the last of his hesitations and paid his student debts, he said goodbye to the world and received the habit of a Friar Preacher at St Jacques on the feast of St Andrew, November 30, 1224. Hugh of St Cher came to join him on the feast of the Chair of St Peter, February 22. Such conquests were not made without deeply affecting the whole scholastic world. Even the students who did not decide to enter the 'Jacobins' went to Master Jordan to consult him on the salvation of their souls and about their vocation.

It was one day that same Spring[9] (or at least we can suppose so with all probability), that four Masters of the English nation came to Jordan.

The chief of these, Haymon of Faversham, already had a great

---

enter the Priory of St Jacques.' An interesting observation, as it underlines the striking progress of the Order among the students of Paris.

[9] To understand dates we must remember that the civil year, in the thirteenth century, began either at the Annunciation, March 25, or at Easter.

reputation. He was a priest and a preacher of talent. All the time he had studied and taught at Paris he had frequented the Friars Minor, and had deliberated about embracing their rule. His compatriot and companion, Master Simon of Sandwich, was similarly inclined; and two other 'famous masters'[10] were ready to follow the same impulse as Haymon of Faversham; so much so that, Master Haymon having celebrated Mass in their presence, all implored God to let them know his will; they were confirmed in their plan of not separating and of making profession together in the Franciscan Order. Nevertheless 'for more certainty', says the contemporary chronicler, 'they went together to find the Master of the Preachers, Brother Jordan, of holy memory and obliged him to give them his advice in conscience and in all sincerity.' The latter confirmed them in their original plan. Without any more wavering, they were then received by the Minister of the Friars Minor, Brother Gregory of Naples, and 'on Good Friday, in the church of St Denys de la Chartre, after Haymon of Faversham had preached on the verse "In convertendo Dominus captivitatem Sion, facti sumus consolati", all of them took the Franciscan habit.'

It does not seem, in this instance, that Master Jordan had felt the least hesitation, nor had he done anything whatsoever to draw this learned preacher Haymon of Faversham to the Order of Preachers. He knew the virtues of the Franciscans and readily used

---

[10] *Analecta Franciscana*, Tome I, 1885, p. 228-9: '...adventus fratris Haymonis de Faversham, qui cum tribus aliis magistris apud sanctum Dionysium in die Parasceves Ordinem sacerdos et famosus praedicator intravit... Cum vidisset fratres Minores Parisiis... socium suum magistrum Simonem de Sanwyz et duos alios famosos magistros sagiciter induxit, ut, ipso celebrante missam, ipsi a Domino Jesu Christo peterent quid sibi consultius foret ad salutem. Cumque simul omnibus Minorum professio complaceret, accesserunt, ad majorem securitatem, ad sanctae memoriae fratrem Jordanum magistrum Ordinis Praedicatorum et obligaverunt eum in animam suam, ut eis consilium suum fideliter daret. Qui, sicut erat veraciter inspiratus, consilio suo conceptum propositum confirmavit...'

them as an example.[11] He knew also their needs and their difficulties, and doubtless, in directing Haymon of Faversham to their Order, he foresaw the good influence he would there exert. Haymon of Faversham was to be named Provincial Minister of the Franciscans of England in 1238, then, the next year, elected Minister General of all the Order; he died at Anagni, where the Papal Curia resided, in 1244.

In 1225 he was already a mature man and of wide understanding. His deference to the advice of Master Jordan says more than many words could about the moral authority of the latter. As for the breadth of view Jordan showed in this matter, it proved him to be a man who was not 'of only one book' or rather of one religious rule, but one who served not only his own Order but the Universal Church.

Meanwhile the General Chapter of the Friars Preachers which was held in Paris on Pentecost 1224 brought him, through its definitors, news of all the Provinces. And soon after he embarked upon a long journey which, after detours to visit various newly-founded Priories,[12] was to end at Bologna. There he convened the General Chapter of May 1225, and in accordance with his custom he preached the Lent.

Probably the summer of 1224 found him again at Lille to open the new Priory which was so soon to spread its influence. From Lille the road was easy, by the plain of Flanders to the Rhine and to the Moselle. We do not know whether he pushed on as far as Cologne to see his dear friend Henry again and to visit Henry's

---

[11] *Analecta Francjscana*, T. I, p. 227: Primitiva pietas fratrum: 'Unde magister Praedicatorum bonae memoriae frater Jordanus dixit quod diabolus, cum aliquando ei apparuisset dixerat ei quod "mea culpa" abstulit sibi omne, quod lucrari credidit inter fratres Minores, quia scilicet dicebant culpas suas invicem, si quis alium offendisset.'

[12] In about 1224-1225 Houses of Friars Preachers were opened at Rouen, Angers, Lille, Strasbourg, Treves, Magdebourg, Cahors, Genoa, Treviso, Pavia; and in Ireland, at Dublin, Drogheda, and Kilkenny.

Priory. But he certainly stopped at Trier (Trèves). A little group of Friars had come there in 1222, under the guidance of a certain Brother Gautier or Walter (Gualterius). But they were not established in a priory until 1224. Trier, 'the Rome of the Gauls', flattered itself on being the most ancient See of all Germany and also of all Belgian Gaul; and since the Carolingian epoch, it had been a religious centre. For many reasons Jordan would have been drawn to it.

Three letters from him, addressed to a religious at Trier,[13] prove that he went there and stayed there, and this was before October 23, 1225, since two of the letters recount the death of Henry of Cologne.

He certainly must have gone from Lille to Brussels across Brabant, then from Brussels to Tongres and Liège, and from there followed the ancient Roman road to Trier. This country was covered with religious houses, regular chapters of canons and canonesses, Benedictines and Beguine monasteries. A great friend of Jordan's, future suffragan of the bishop of Liège, bishop of Lausanne from 1231 to 1239, master of theology of Paris and Cologne, a Cistercian, Boniface of Brussels, could have been in these parts then. But above all indication of Jordan's passage through Brabant is given by his correspondence, probably started at this time, with a saintly Flemish nun, the celebrated Lutgarde.

'Father Jordan knew her well', says the *Lives of the Brethren*, 'and she was greatly devoted to him.' She was a very original person. Born at Tongres, where her relics are honoured, she vowed herself to God at the age of twelve, in the Benedictine monastery of St Catherine. But a dozen years later she had transferred to the Cistercian Order, which was then flourishing vigorously; she lived at the convent of Aywières in Brabant, leading a life of

---

[13] These three letters, and a fourth addressed to an unknown young woman (*ad Virginem devotam*), were edited by Bayonne in 1865 and by Berthier in 1891.

extraordinary mortification and continual prayer, favoured with the gift of prophecy and enlightened by visions; besides Flemish and German which were the familiar tongues of her youth, she had learned, in a marvellous fashion, French and Latin which she read and even wrote; and having become learned, she was, even though a recluse, known and consulted by many great personages of her time, notably the future Cardinal Jacques de Vitry, who directed her in the spiritual way until his departure for the Holy Land and kept her acquainted with all that was going on in the Christian world. She fasted for seven years 'on bread and ale', to obtain the conversion of the Albigensians.

After Jacques de Vitry, Master Jordan became her spiritual director and was for her the very incarnation of the apostolic life. In the year of her death she was already very old and had become blind. 'On Christmas Eve', says the old chronicle, 'applying herself to prayer, she felt only disgust, and breathed this plea: "O good Lord! If I but had a friend in heaven or on earth, who would be praying now for me!" and at once before the eyes of her soul appeared a Friar Preacher, so shining and so glorious that the brilliance of the light did not allow her to recognize him. She asked, "Who are you, master?" He replied, "I am Master Jordan, formerly Master of the Order of Preachers. I was sent to you to bring you consolation on this beautiful feast-day. Be tranquil; you are on the eve of being crowned by God. Meanwhile recite faithfully the psalm 'Deus misereatur nostri', and the collect of the Holy Spirit, which when I was living I asked you and you promised to say until death for our Order."'

This revelation caused Lutgarde to be venerated in the Order of Preachers 'above all women', says her biographer, Thomas de Cantimpré, who called her 'matrem et nutricem', the mother and nurse of the entire Order. In default of letters, which undoubtedly they exchanged but are now lost, and of precise information about the visit which Jordan made her, this witness at least affirms their connection, and the spirit which the Master had imprinted on it.

At Trier he also found some Sisters who were friends of the Order. One especially, a certain Marie, seemed to have some relationship to Henry of Cologne, and perhaps was first drawn by him to the religious life.[14]

Perhaps when Jordan arrived she was already a nun of the convent of St Hermine.[15] Or maybe she was getting ready to enter and Jordan's ministry confirmed her resolution. In the letter, placed third in the manuscript, but which, from the sense, seems anterior to the two others, the Master writes to her: 'Since the day when you resolved to detach your heart perfectly, not only from your relatives and your property, but also from yourself, you have become the very dear friend of God.' In another letter he calls her 'my sister' and even more often 'my daughter' and speaks to her of the profound and reciprocal charity which unites them in Jesus Christ.

She was evidently a woman of noble family, learned, of a fine intelligence and delicate sensibilities.

These texts throw a brief but intense light on the ministry of Jordan; his travels did not consist only of visiting priories and of official preaching to students, but a more intimate apostolate of certain elect souls, in particular of religious women.

How long he stayed at Trier, and whether Henry of Cologne accompanied him or followed him, we do not know. They met, as we know by the sequel, at the Pentecost Chapter at Bologna. They may have passed by Strasbourg together, where the Friars this same year, 1224, started their convent and then, going back to Burgundy, made their way towards Provence.

---

[14] Jordan writes to her about Henry of Cologne, '...your friend... our friend in common... you have near to Christ a faithful friend...'

[15] This convent of St Hermine, or St Oehren (Horreum monasterium), was founded by Saint Modoald, archbishop of Trier, at the request of the princesses Modeste and Hermine, daughters of King Dagobert. Its nuns were recruited from the German aristocracy; they faithfully kept the rule of St Benedict and devoted themselves to the choral life, prayer and manual labour.

The only indication of Jordan's itinerary is provided by the text of a letter to Diana, the postscript of which, relative to the Sisters of Prouille and to the next arrival of the Master General at Bologna, dates it definitely before Pentecost 1225. Jordan sent to the nuns the greetings of the Prior of Provence, the venerable Bertrand of Garrigua.[16] He was then on his way to Bologna by way of Provence, doubtless through Avignon, Arles, perhaps Marseilles, and Genoa.[17] He saw Bertrand of Garrigua. Together they planned to select some nuns from the convent of Prouille whom Jordan would take to Bologna.

But while he was making the journey the Master must have received news from the Roman Curia, where Brother Guala of Bergamo was still in negotiation. To his entreaties and those of Cardinal Ugolino Honorius III had finally yielded; he consented to send some nuns from St Sixtus to Bologna. They would arrive after Lent.

'As to the Sisters of Prouille', wrote Jordan, 'it does not seem well to send you any of them at present. I will explain this when I see you. I hope to see you soon in person.'

Bologna received him with joy. It was this year that, according to a contemporary account, all the city, forewarned of his coming, wanted to go in procession before him. But having heard of it, he evaded this ovation and 'going around the city by unfrequented paths, he entered unobserved by an opposite gate and arrived at the Priory of the Friars'.

The nuns and laysisters of St Agnes gave him a great welcome. He settled among them the Sisters of St Sixtus finally sent by

---

[16] It is evidently by mistake that the two manuscript copies of Rome and of Wurtzbourg have 'Frater Bernadus' instead of 'Frater Bertrandus'; the Prior of Provence was then certainly Bertrand of Garrigua. *Vit. Fratr.* p. 338.

[17] Diana's older brother, Brancaleone d'Andalo, was at this time podesta of Genoa; he was able to facilitate the establishment of the Friars Preachers in that city.

Honorius III who, it was said, had wished to choose them from among the first nuns taken by St Dominic and himself to bring them out of the cloister. There were four or, perhaps, five; Agnes, who must have been the oldest, was immediately named Prioress of the convent of Bologna. A legal document dated June 12, 1225, effecting the acquisition of a piece of land situated at Bagno Marino and Valsampero and destined for the enlargement of their church, attests, together with the presence of sisters Diana and Julita, the lady Jacobina and her daughter, the presence of 'Lady Agnes, of the city of Rome, now Prioress of St Agnes', and it is to her that the sale was made. The other Roman sisters sent to Bologna were Cecilia and Amata, Constance and Theodora.[18]

From that time the regular observance of the convent was assured. As for its recruiting, it seems to have been fruitful from then on; it even extended, thanks to the Master, beyond Lombardy, since two Sisters of German origin, certainly brought to Bologna by the influence of Jordan and of Brother Henry, made profession at the same time, probably into the hands of the Master General himself; one took the name Maria, the other, Jordana.[19] Henry of

---

[18] This was the Blessed Cecilia who in her old age—she lived to be extremely old— dictated her memoirs to a certain Sister Angelica, who is probably the author of the primitive chronicles of St Agnes dated about 1254.

[19] Letters XI and XII Aron, XXIV and XXX Berth. In letter XII Henry of Cologne, greeting the two novices in his own name and in Jordan's, wrote, 'Mariam nostram', *our* Maria. I have wondered in reading Jordan's letter to a pious unknown virgin ('ad virginem devotam') if she could be identified with this Marie. Jordan wrote to her, 'You loved me because you believed you had received by my ministry the word of salvation and *the grace of conversion*; and I believe that the Holy Ghost had prepared your soul before we met. You have such confidence in me that you do not want to do anything without my advice... *I know that you wish to leave your country and your family...* I do not dare to urge you to do so at present... Wait a little while.' Either these things were done in haste, or the family gave up, and it was perhaps this noble and well-educated girl, of Cologne, Trier or Strasbourg, who entered the cloister of St Agnes then. And we understand that the Preachers called her 'Miriam nostram'.

Cologne, Conrad of Hoxter and Bernard the Teuton had come to assist at the General Chapter of May 18, 1225, at Bologna.

Soon after they left again for Germany with Master Jordan. The route which the travellers followed is neatly punctuated for us by the letters of Jordan to Diana. They climbed toward Brenner Pass by the Trentine Alps and their first important stop was Verona.

At Verona there was one of the first Priories of Lombardy, established by St Dominic himself between 1218 and 1221. In the immediate neighbourhood of Verona, and on its territory, the village of Cologna was known for its rustic weaving of cloths which were neither milled nor dyed, which the peasants wore, and which were used for religious habits.[20] So, in the letter which Jordan sent to Diana d'Andalo, Henry of Cologne who doubtless took the pen and added a word, announced the sending of a piece of cloth destined to make a tunic and hood for Sister Jordana.[21]

Brother Bernard is charged with the message. Master Jordan sent back in haste to Bologna this faithful friend, one of the first witnesses of Diana's vocation, so that he could console her in the blow which had just struck her. For doubtless at the same time as she, he had learned of the death of her elder brother, the nearest to her and the most dear, Brancaleone.

The circumstances of this death, and its date, June 7 (on the kalends of May), are recorded in the annals of Genoa. Brancaleone, who had qualified as a great captain, wise and brave, a prudent and noble man,[22] had been that year called to Genoa as podesta.

---

[20] Certain commentators of Dante, Zombani in particular, think that it is this Veronese village and not Cologne on the Rhine, which is referred to in Canto XXIII of the Inferno (61-64): Egli avelui cappe con cappucci bassi—Dinanzi agli occhi, fatti della tagliache per li monaci in *Cologna fassi*.'

[21] Novices paid the cost of the habit. Maria, who was noble and rich, had had hers made. Jordana, who probably followed her, perhaps was poor.

[22] 'Miles formosus, sapiens, largus, animosus... vir prudens et nobilis...'

The ambitious republic wished to have at its head a man capable of bringing to a victorious conclusion the war which it was waging against Alessandria. It was one of those wars of artful skirmishing, sudden attacks interrupted by subtle arbitrations and rather equivocal discussions, which the Lombard cities were constantly waging among themselves. This one had already lasted some time, and might be prolonged seven or eight years more. It concerned the territory of Gari and Vultrabio, and the fortress of Capriata, a strategic point which commanded the road to Genoa. It was waged between the Alessandrians and the people of Tortoni on the one side, and the people of Genoa on the other.

In April, things had flared up again. Brancaleone, leaving his wife and daughter at Bologna, probably with the lay-sisters of St Agnes—since Lady Jacobina and her daughter are witnesses of the deed of purchase of the Bagnio-Marino land on June 12—had actively fortified Gavi and raised fresh troops. But he fell gravely ill and was carried out of the tumult of men-at-arms into a purer air, to the monastery of St John at Paravano. Meanwhile the Alessandrians and their allies, taking the offensive, invaded the territory of Asti and threatened Genoa. In spite of his illness, the impetuous Brancaleone arose, went back to Genoa, set the army on the march, conducted the operations, and died at Gavi in the joy of triumph which his death overshadowed.

By the emotion of the scribe who wrote the Genoese account, we can judge the bravery of his death and the violent grief which must have seized his kindred.

Jordan's fatherly heart shared their grief. He knew the sensitivity of his daughter; he sympathized with the sadness of the wife and mother of Brancaleone.

'I know that you are surely weighed down by sadness. But your sorrow shall be changed into joy, for the more abundant are the sufferings of your heart, the more abundant will be the consolations of the Lord and the more the Paraclete, whom the Father shall send to you, will console you in truth.

'For my part I send you Brother Bernard to bring to you, as well as to Lady Jacobina, some comfort, and I continue to pray and beg him to soothe the anguish of your hearts, since it is he himself who consoles his own in all their tribulations. We must in this present life be saddened, but not beyond measure, and only, as says the Apostle Peter, to resemble in some way him who said, "My soul is sorrowful even unto death." ... Your brother is taken out of this world that malice might not corrupt his spirit nor worldly vanity deceive his soul. That is why, my dears, you should not sorrow too much, as those grieve who have no hope. Let your hope be full of immortality, and ask God to give joy to your hearts again. Greet the two ladies, Otha and Lady Jacobina, and all the convent of St Agnes.' Henry of Cologne adds: 'Brother Henry greets you very affectionately and sympathizes deeply in your grief. But the Lord, who makes the calm after the tempest, will re-establish serenity in your souls, change the hurricane to a favourable breeze, and pilot you into the port of his very tranquil will. I greet you. Greet Jordana and our Maria. With the permission of Master Jordan, I send to Jordana some cloth for a tunic and a hood, and I pray you to have them made for her. Goodbye.'

Brother Bernard must have made good speed and soon returned to Verona. The letter which follows, still offering consolation, indicates that Jordan had had news of St Agnes: 'I am happy that you are not too much disturbed and desolated by the death of your Brother...' The danger for Diana was not that she would despair, but that she might pursue God too ardently by excessive austerity. 'Your Spouse, Jesus Christ, will never abandon you', Jordan wrote to her. ... 'He seems at times to withdraw so far from you that you cry out, "Why, O Lord, have you gone so far away and left me in my need?"... It is certain that the Lord does not go away, but that he comes nearer, since he is near to those who are afflicted in heart... If you suffer too much, think how he said: "Look and see if there is any sorrow like unto my sorrow." He alone knows the pain and the grief... Do not abstain too much from food, drink, sleep; act in all things with moderation and patience. Take care that the Sisters do not mortify themselves too much... I write this letter with my own hand.'

Greetings are addressed to the two ladies Otha, mother and sister of Diana, to Lady Jacobina, and to Agnes, the Prioress of the convent. He thinks of everyone. He is worried about the sorrowful isolation of the young widow of Brancaleone. He is not sure that Diana, in her own prostration, and her wholly contemplative piety, takes enough care of the soul of her sister-in-law, and helps her effectively to turn herself gradually towards the religious life. In a note which seems, soon after, to complete the preceding letter, he says to Diana, 'Since the greatest duty of piety is to offer spiritual help to the sorrowful, I beg of you in your charity to do all that is in your power to console the widow, Lady Jacobina, and take care to do so generously; thus you will render yourself agreeable to God and you may be able to gain her soul.'

This short note is also a farewell. Jordan asks prayers for himself, for Brother Henry, Brother Bernard and his other travelling and preaching companions. He was making ready to leave Verona in a few days, it is evident. But he fell ill, seriously enough to worry his companions, and he was kept at Verona until August 10. At last, on August 15, he is in Trent, and there he preaches. 'Your prayer and that of your sisters', he wrote to Diana, 'has come into the presence of God, and in his mercy he has again extended the time I am to live, or rather, to do penance. On St Lawrence's Day I was able, with the permission of the doctor, to leave Verona, though still weak; I have gained strength on the road, so much so that, on the feast of the Assumption, I preached to the people, and the next day to the clergy... I am worried on your account and that of the Sisters, and wish to know all about the things that threaten you. As for you yourself, however, my very dear daughter, be steadfastly confident in the Lord. Whatever cares you have, whatever your burdens, God is with you. Do not

En Route

let yourself be in the least uneasy... I am writing you from Trent, the day after the Assumption.'

It is to be noticed that Jordan preached, not only to the clergy, but to the people. Is this because he was in Trent, a country probably then using the German language? For he does not seem to have managed Italian or French with the same eloquent ease as he did clerical Latin.[23] The anecdotes gathered from the sermons of Master Jordan in the Lives of the Brethren, in the Life of the Bees of Thomas de Cantimpré, in the collection of Stephen of Bourbon, have sometimes a savour and an easy humour which seem to reveal the familiar and direct eloquence of a man who is delighted to speak to people more often than we should perhaps think, and who succeeded brilliantly at it.

As for the uneasiness which the Master showed about the convent of St Agnes and his wish to hear exact news about it, these are both explained by the reconstruction of the Lombard League in the summer of 1225. Bologna, rather than Milan, was the centre of it this time, and we can be certain that Bologna was surrounded by the troops of Emperor Frederick II. St Agnes was, as we know, outside the walls; therefore it was particularly exposed, and perhaps there was some question of evacuating the religious. It was to keep them from becoming too agitated that Jordan reminded Diana to have unshakable confidence in the Lord. As for himself, he continued his travels. It was one of the traits of

---

[23] *Vit. Fratr.* Cap. 42, no. 16. In his travels beyond the sea, visiting a Commandery of French Templars, he was asked, the story goes, to give a sermon or, rather, a collation, as they then called the evening conference. The Master was ready to do it, but before starting, as if they were on a terrace and had before them a wall the height of a man: 'If there was a donkey behind the wall and it raised its head so as to let us see only its ears, we should understand nevertheless that a whole donkey was there; for by a little part of the whole, we have knowledge of the whole; that is what is going to happen to you, if I succeed in telling you great truths in a few French words, mingling with them, if you will allow me, some German words.'

his character never to go back or to dissipate his activity in useless or uncertain things, but to perform, day by day, the work in hand, without letting it trouble him.

Towards the end of August the Brenner Pass was crossed without incident and in about five weeks the travellers reached Magdeburg. 'I reached Magdeburg', writes Jordan to Diana, 'the third day after the feast of St Matthew.[24] There the friars of the Priory, who had been for a long while uneasy about me, and numerous other friars, surrounded by many people, all glad to see me in good health, gave me a joyful reception. I was happy to find the Priory well arranged, and the recent entry of several novices into the Order increased my happiness still more.'

The convent of Magdeburg had scarcely been one year in existence; it had been founded the previous year on the feast of St Lawrence; but it was in full and vigorous growth. Its situation and its recruiting made it become one of the hearthstones of the German province. A large gathering of friars had assembled there. We can infer from this that it was for the first Provincial Chapter and that they were waiting for Jordan to solemnize it. Nothing is more probable. The year which had just ended marked a notable increase of the Order in Germany; since the opening of the first house of the German language at Friesach in Carinthia, in 1220, Cologne had been the first to have a Priory in 1221, but in 1224 there were founded, all at the same time, Trier, Strasbourg, and Magdeburg.

This feast had a morrow of grief. In the night of the following October 23-24, Brother Henry died at Cologne in Jordan's arms. The rapidity with which these events followed one another makes some doubt the reality of their connection.[25] There is really no proof that Henry of Cologne died in 1225, and the name of his successor as Prior of Cologne, Brother Leo, does not appear until

---

[24] Then September 24.
[25] Dr B. Altaner.

a document of 1229. Still it is certain that Henry, Prior of Cologne from 1221, was there only a few years and that he died young and in a manner, if not sudden, at least unforeseen, since Jordan wrote to the Benedictine nun of Trier, 'See, most dear, how God has afflicted me in a sudden and unforeseen way.'[26] And then: 'This excellent workman in the vineyard of the Lord was called not at the end of the day, but toward the sixth hour, to claim his wages.' After 1225, there is never any mention of him in Jordan's correspondence and no trace of his presence at any Chapter. As for the little time spent between the stop of the travellers at Magdeburg and their arrival at Cologne, pilgrims who, without hurrying, had come from Trent to Magdeburg in five weeks, would not need more than fifteen or twenty days to go from Magdeburg to Cologne. The Provincial Chapter must have been celebrated as soon as the Master General arrived, between the 24th and the 30th of September at the latest; by October 15, Henry and Jordan could have been at Cologne. It was on the direct way to Paris where Jordan was to preach Advent.[27]

Finally, a less psychological argument but convincing enough to settle the question, the letter in which Jordan announced to Diana the death of his friend is undoubtedly written only a few months after the death of Brancaleone. In the interval Diana had also lost her young sister Otha. Jordan says to her: 'And you, my daughter, most dear Diana, do not grieve too much about your brother or your beloved sister Otha... It is good for us to be saddened now at the same time, to go sowing our seed in tears; at the harvest we shall come carrying our sheaves in joy.' And also in the postscript. 'Diana, greet Lady Otha, your mother, and tell

---

[26] 'Vide, carissima, quam inopinate et insperate hoc mihi Deus fecerit.'

[27] It seems improbable to place the death of Henry of Cologne, as Dr Altaner suggests, on October 23, 1227. There are too many chances that Jordan had stayed in Rome and in Italy during the summer of 1227; it would have then been impossible for him to have been in Cologne in October.

her that I should like to be with her dear Otha and my dear Henry.'

Grief drew from Jordan expressions of a pathetic tenderness in which nevertheless there is a note of invincible hope: 'I weep for my very dear friends, I weep for the brother who loved me so much, my very dear son Henry.[28] All Cologne wept over him; what lamentations amongst the Brethren, the holy widows and virgins[29] ... When I resolved to enter the Order, I asked my Queen, the glorious Virgin Mary, to grant him the will to enter with me; he begged this grace and obtained it... He was entirely devoted to the Order... I confess, I do not believe I have ever wept so much... In this very night of the kalends of November (October 23-24) after the Matins bell had sounded, I went to see him before going to choir. Having found him breathless and already on the point of entering his last agony, I asked him if he wished to receive Extreme Unction. He replied that he ardently desired it. We wished to satisfy his desire before starting the Office; and he seemed to give the Unction more than to receive it, so fervently did he recite the prayers... We then went down to choir and in honour of St Severin, patron of Cologne, we celebrated the Office with its nine lessons. I was struck with their significance and in my heart I applied them to him who was already on the road to Heaven... I was bathed in tears, but the more they flowed the more this time did they seem sweet to me... Returned to him, I found him talking in transports of God and to God, singing, exciting in himself and in others a desire for our heavenly home... repeating often with joy the invocation "Pray, Virgin Mary, that we may be made worthy of the Bread of Heaven". He spoke again a little and said:

---

[28] Fragments from a letter to Diana and letters to Maria, at the convent of St Hermine at Trier.

[29] The nuns and doubtless the beguines of Cologne who were under the spiritual direction of the Friars Preachers and, as we see, were very much devoted to the ministry of Brother Henry. This confirms the supposition that the sisters who were taken to Bologna could have been his penitents.

"Here comes the prince of the world, but he can have nothing in me." After this, he began his agony. Let us follow him, let us make haste to enter into this eternal peace... Nevertheless, do not be too precipitate;[30] there is still a long way to go. If you are tired, your Jesus was so also; and in his fatigue he sat on the edge of the well. (John IV, 6.) In all humility, in all patience he knew how to wait. As does the labourer who patiently waits for the fruits of the earth, cultivate your souls without weakening your bodies, and wait for the precious fruit, the blessed fruit of the womb of the glorious Virgin Mary... I am well enough as far as my body is concerned, and I hope that Christ will sustain my spirit.'

---

[30] Jordan was writing to the Sisters of St Agnes as well as to Diana, and even in this moment of tragic emotion, he remained their prudent spiritual director.

Chapter VIII
'I AM GOING TO ROME'

HEN he was leaving Cologne, Jordan ended his letter with these words: 'Brother Conrad, who was with us at Bologna, greets you and asks you to pray for him.'

This was Conrad of Hoxter, Prior Provincial of Germany. A famous lawyer, author of a *Summa Confessorum* from which Raymond of Pennafort borrowed, he was one of the lights of the Order. He was at the Chapter of Bologna in 1225; he was at the one in Paris in 1226; his name is found at the end of a letter written from Paris after the Purification, February 2, 1226. Very probably he was now the travelling companion of the Master on his return to France.

And now soon once more the saddened eyes of Jordan fall upon the familiar outline of the Priory of St Jacques. It continued to grow. It was in full prosperity. An interesting conquest was made there; on November 11, the feast of St Martin, a student of noble birth and brilliant prospects received the habit from the hands of Matthew of France. He would make profession in the hands of Jordan on the feast of the Annunciation, March 25, 1226. He was the future biographer of the Master, the historian of the Lives of the Brethren,[1] Gerard de Frachet. Elected prior of Limoges in 1233, he moved the city so greatly by his preaching that the women of the place, giving up their extravagant, stylish headdresses, covered their heads with 'capitèges', linen bonnets such as were still found a few years ago in country places of Limousin. He was to become Prior of Provence, and then of

---

[1] Undertaken on the orders of the General Chapter of Paris, 1256, approved by the Chapter of Montpellier in 1260, Humbert de Romans being Master General of the Order.

Montpellier. He was to die at Limoges in 1271. Bernard Guidonis, his contemporary and colleague, said of him: 'He was a preacher liked equally by the clergy and the people, fully instructed in doctrine, who, from his earliest years, had built up his knowledge by continual study... knowing the history of the saints and of famous men, acquainted with the memorable historical events, and speaking of them when occasion offered.'

It is through him we know that, in the same year as he himself was received into the Order, during Lent, Jordan gave the habit to twenty-one students of the schools of Paris on the feast of the Purification. 'Several of them taught theology later in divers places. Among them was a young German whom the Master had several times refused because of his extreme youth. He slipped in among the twenty others, and the Master, finding it too hard to refuse him again, especially in the presence of a thousand students, contented himself with saying with a smile: "One of you is stealing the Order from us." ... The Brother in charge of the wardrobe had made ready only twenty habits, and as he could not reach the door to the chapter room because of the crowd of students pressing round it, the Friars had to divest themselves, one of his cappa, another of his tunic, another of his scapular, to clothe the young German... Often on such occasions Master Jordan would pawn his Bible in order to pay the debts of the students entering the Order.'

This vivid picture corresponds perfectly with a letter which, doubtless about the same time, Jordan addressed to Diana d'Andalo. 'I do not wish, most dear, for you to be ignorant of the grace which God has given to our Order, nor of how our Brothers increase in number and merit. Since my arrival in Paris, twenty-one novices have entered—in only four weeks! Six of them were Masters of Arts, the others Bachelors of Arts, well-instructed and entirely suited to the duties of the Friars Preachers. Also, the Bishop of Paris has developed such an affection for the friars that he assisted in person at our sermon and ate with the friars in the refectory. Likewise the legate of France came to dine with the friars on the feast of the Annunciation of the Blessed Virgin. Finally, the Queen loves the Friars Preachers so tenderly that she talks with me familiarly about her affairs.'

The harmony is complete. Jordan had doubtless reached Paris only a little before Christmas, and his presence and his preaching had borne rapid fruit. The Priory was growing marvellously. The immense refectory had just been finished; the chapter room scarcely could contain the crowd of clerics. The newly consecrated bishop, Bartholomew of Chartres, successor of William of Siegnelay, was a man of study, ex-chancellor of the schools of Chartres. The papal legate was Cardinal Romanus de Sant'Angelo, a learned man, favourably disposed toward the Friars Preachers. The Queen was Blanche of Castile. She was then the reigning queen, the wife of Louis VIII whom she had just urged to take up the crusade against the Albigensians again. On November 8 of the same year, 1226, by the King's death, she was to become Regent of the Kingdom. Already, at this time, without having the title, she exercised the duties of that office, and 'her affairs' of which she spoke familiarly with Jordan, undoubtedly to obtain his advice, were those of France.

St Jacques had become an incomparable home of the spiritual life and, by the same token, a home of social action. The General Chapter of Pentecost, 1226 (June 7), was celebrated there with a great many Friars Preachers.

Jordan left soon after, as was his custom. Diana d'Andalo had hoped that he would direct his steps toward Bologna. This city was in a state of unrest. The tension created between Ghibellines and Guelfs by the tightening of the Lombard League and the stormy quarrels between the Pope and the Emperor Frederick II kept all Italy in suspense. The civic squabbles of city against city, family against family, had become more heated, especially in Lombardy.

The least friction could set everything aflame, and doubtless the Sisters of St Agnes were troubled by a certain diversity of view. 'In this affair', writes Jordan, evidently answering Diana's pressing questions, 'I can offer you no advice or remedy, except what can be obtained by my prayers—those of a poor sinner—and the prayers of our Brethren... Cast all your cares with confidence upon him whose power is invincible, whose wisdom is infallible, whose goodness unceasing... Remember that he, being what he was, delivered himself up and did not deliver up his own... In your soul then you will not be troubled.'

With a powerful movement of faith, Jordan deliberately raised all the sentiments of his spiritual daughter to the supernatural plane. Not because he was at all unaware of what was happening. Friar Guala of Bergamo, formerly Prior of Brescia, was now attached to the Roman Curia. He had been one of the papal delegates to the Diet which was held on March 6 at Mercaria, near Mantua, with the object of effecting an accord between the Pope and the Emperor. Jordan had most certainly been given information by him. He knew Frederick; he had no illusions about this strange personality, faithless and superstitious, a dilettante, fierce, delighting in Arabian science and Oriental art, a complex figure of the Renaissance strayed into the thirteenth century.

'The Emperor', Jordan wrote to Diana, 'is a man who can neither respect nor listen to religious; but rather, as he says himself, it is painful to him to see them.'

She had certainly hoped and wished for Jordan's intervention, but that was, in his view, completely useless. 'I am certain of it', he says, 'so I shall not come at present... I shall come, if it please God, a little later, in the course of this year, and we shall see one another then and our hearts will rejoice. Thus joy and sorrow follow one another.' This was a virile understanding of life, the philosophy of a traveller who goes straightway where present duty calls.

He was, in fact, on the road again and again this time towards

Germany, for Brother Conrad was his new travelling companion.[2] They were probably going to establish a Priory of Friars Preachers at Worms; then, crossing the Rhine, going up the valley of the Main, they reached Wurtzburg, where in 1226 a house of the Order was opened—Wurtzburg, whose library has gathered together such valuable documents of Dominican history; Ratisbonne then drew them to its recent foundation; finally, perhaps, they pushed on as far as Vienna where a Priory was organized that same year. Jordan had not been able to visit the first Priory of the Order in German territory until then; this time, with Carinthia linking Austria to Carniola and Istria by much-travelled roads, Friesach was on his way. He surely made a stop there, and it was probably the Roman road, so much used then, of the Seuil de Tarvis that took him to Venice by way of Udine and Aquilea, at the end of the summer.

He could not have stayed very long at Bologna. Three letters to Diana[3] show him to us preaching to the students outside Bologna and gathering for St Agnes a young German orphan who was at the home of a certain Lord Gerard 'where she heard nothing spoken but Lombard'. A story told by Thomas de Cantimpré shows Jordan visiting the Priory of the friars at Santa Sabina, and preaching at Rome in the presence of Pope Honorius before the death of the latter on March 18, 1227.[4]

As difficult as it is to establish absolutely precise times, we shall not be wrong in supposing that between Advent 1226 and Pentecost 1227, when the General Chapter was celebrated at Bologna, Master Jordan was sometimes at Padua, Vercelli, Reggio, Treviso or Cremona, with students scattered by the war, and

---

[2] Letter XX A, XXVIII B. 'I ought to see you soon, I hope... Brother Conrad who was with us at Bologna greets you and asks your prayers.'

[3] The allusion to the Bull of December 17, 1226, dates these letters at the very end of the year 1226 and the spring or summer of 1227.

[4] ... Nec mora, felix Papa Honorius, audito adventu ejus, mandat eum dormitatione facta post prandium intrare curiam facturum in clero sermonem...

sometimes at Rome. The untiring recruiter of the Order was at work. 'Let me tell you of the mercies which our Saviour has showered upon me since I left you', he writes to Diana, ... 'for Christ has drawn to the Order eighteen men famous for their learning... I recommend them to you, both these and others too who have holy intentions' ... and later: 'The Lord has drawn to our Order, by the power of the Holy Ghost, thirty students who are very learned and entirely suited to the needs of the Order.'

The more the Priories multiplied, the more lectors and masters were needed to instruct the novices in them. So Jordan is on the look-out for the best students in all the Italian Universities. But, as well as his keen judgment as a man of knowledge, his goodness was increasingly alert. 'I send to you the young girl on whose behalf I have appealed to your charity', he writes to Diana. 'You will treat her as I confidently expect you to do. I am afraid though that she will be a burden to you, but there is no one to care for her and I had compassion on her for the love of him who suffered for our salvation. I should like some German brother to come and talk with her once or twice a week so that she will not forget German, which she knows as well as Lombard. Tell the conventual Prior to send you a Brother, and oblige the child to talk with him in that language; she has lost the habit of speaking German because since Easter she has been in the house of Lord Gerard where she heard nothing spoken but Lombard. He says she is a good child and he lets her go with regret.'

Nothing was neglected by the Master, not even precise directions as to teaching. This child was assuredly not the only one of her age that the nuns of Bologna took to care for. The radiation of the religious life and its virtues, the personality of Diana d'Andalo and its influence, continued to enlarge the activities of the convent, where pious works were multiplied. This letter is probably after Pentecost ('from Easter until now', he says). But, several months before, the rapidly-growing activity of St Agnes and the complex duties which resulted for the Friars Preachers called to confess and direct lay-sisters and boarders must have created serious difficulties for Diana. Her recent cares were not all caused by political events. The departure of Brother Ventura, who in 1225 became Prior of Viterbo, had taken away her principal support. Already, in a letter which was a homily to the whole convent, Jordan insists especially on the Dominican character of the vocations of the St Agnes novices, and on the certainty of conscience they must have in responding to God's call into the Order of Preachers. But they were far from being officially recognized and to this trend of opinion the Master General could not oppose the absolute authority which would be that of a sovereign abbot, but which did not belong to the liberal Constitutions of the Friars Preachers. To secure the intervention of the Pope would be the most efficacious procedure; but his fraternal spirit and delicacy as a superior prevented Jordan from calling down upon his brothers a papal reprimand. So it was to himself that he had it addressed! Since we know all that Jordan had done for Diana and her sisters, all his paternal care for the convent of St Agnes, the tone of the Bull of Honorius III cannot deceive anyone; this Bull was drawn up in agreement with Jordan, acting on his information, and perhaps even written in his presence.[5]

---

[5] *Bull. Ord.* T. VI, p. 7, December 17, 1226. 'Honorius, bishop, servant of the servants of God, to Our dear son the Master of the Order of Preachers... It has come to Our notice that, although our dear daughter Diana the foundress and certain other Sisters of the convent of St Agnes at Bologna, have made profession according to the Order of Friars Preachers into the hands of Brother Dominic... your predecessor, with the firm hope and confidence of remaining perpetually under the government of the same Order' (this evidently could come only from Jordan himself) 'you, nevertheless, have abandoned the convent, the prioress and the other sisters, without fulfilling the duties of your office toward them. So that these sisters shall not be grievously frustrated, by your failure, in the hope they have held, of belonging to the aforesaid Order, We enjoin to your discretion, by these present apostolic Letters, to take under your care and correction both these sisters and their convent, the same as the

Honorius III would never admonish Jordan like that except at Jordan's own request. And it is without doubt at this time—October or November 1226—that we must place the strange incident recorded by Thomas de Cantimpré.

When he reached Rome, the Master stayed at the House of the Preachers, Santa Sabina. After he had said Mass, his first visits were to the sick. He found in the infirmary 'a lay-brother who had but little sanity and whom they had prudently tied up'. He seemed peaceful. Jordan ordered them to untie him. Pope Honorius learnt of Jordan's arrival and he ordered him to come and give a sermon to the Curia, after the siesta which followed 'prandium' (lunch). Jordan had his meal, said grace, and lay down to rest. He had with him the lay-brother, who seemed quite restored to his senses. But when the Master had fallen asleep, the lay-brother, taking a razor, slashed at his throat, and although he did not cut him deeply, he made a large wound. Waking up, Jordan seized the razor, cutting two or three fingers. There was an uproar. The Prior commanded silence and ordered all to conceal what had happened, to avoid scandal. The time came for the sermon and the Prior went to preach in place of the Master; he was in tears, so that one of the Cardinals took him aside and made him tell the cause of his trouble. Both went to find the Pope, who exclaimed weeping: 'Alas, a great pillar of the Church has fallen today!' He sent his own surgeon to the Priory. On the third day the Master called a very young novice and prepared to say Mass. The novice told the Prior, who was amazed and frightened, thinking Jordan was delirious. Jordan calmed him, celebrated Mass and, having washed his wounds with the water of the ablutions, declared himself cured; and that same day before the Pope, the Cardinals and the clerics of the Curia he preached 'gloriosissime'.

---

other houses of the Order entrusted to your direction. Given at the Lateran Palace, the XVI of the kalends of January, in the eleventh year of Our Pontificate.'

Either from Rome or from a Lombard city he sent to Diana the letter of the Sovereign Pontiff, or perhaps a second Bull, destined for the archives of St Agnes, which confirmed it. 'I congratulate all the sisters, whose joy is my joy', he writes. 'As for you, my dear daughter, while you are not ignorant how much always and everywhere I have desired your well-being and that of your sisters, be sure that in the future, if it please God, I shall take even more care of you. I give into your keeping the letter that the Sovereign Pontiff has addressed to me on the subject; be its faithful guardian.' This letter gives the convent its titles, and definitely stabilizes its Rule. Diana's happiness was great. She saw her mission blessed and accomplished. She could die now for she would die a Dominican, leaving behind her the monastery of St Agnes belonging to the Order of Preachers; and with the passionate ardour of love which characterized her, she was eager to leave the world and to be with Christ. 'You have written to me', Jordan answered her from a city of northern Italy, Vercelli or Padua, 'that you did not wish to die and enter the home of your Father... so long as the house of St Agnes was not established and confirmed in the jurisdiction of the Order; and now that it is an assured thing, you desire to be dissolved and to be with Christ.' (*Phil.* I, 23.) And prudently he rebuked her: 'I wish you to preserve this desire in the deepest places of your heart, but I do not wish you, by an excessive compunction or immoderate mortifications, to hasten towards your end... That is why I exhort you not to run so fast, for fear that you may fall on the way. If we run, let it be as the Apostle says, in such a way as to receive the prize; and let our blessed God deign to draw us after him.' (*I Cor.* X, 24.)

The General Chapter of May 30, 1227, had called Jordan back to Bologna; but the roads of Lombardy and Tuscany soon saw him again. Rome drew him. 'Vado Romam', he wrote to the sisters of St Agnes. 'I am going to Rome; pray for me.'

Meanwhile an event had taken place which was of great importance to the whole of Christianity, and particularly for the

Order of Preachers which had been, since its beginning, so closely united to and so obedient to the Chair of Peter. Honorius III died on March 18, 1227, and the next day the conclave raised Cardinal Ugolino to the Papal See.

This great figure had already, for six years, dominated the background of Dominican history. Protector, confidant and friend of St Dominic, he was one of the first to recognize his genius, one of the first to proclaim his sanctity; he presided at Dominic's funeral and was to proclaim his canonization; Cardinal Ugolino was the patron of the mendicant Orders. Even the name of Gregory—Gregory IX—which he chose when he ascended the Roman throne was a promise for them; 'As Gregory VII pressed his reform with the aid of the monks of Cluny, so Gregory IX entrusted the triumph of his plans to the support of the mendicant Orders whose patron he had been before he became Pope.' (Héfélé.) Through them he intended to stamp out heresy, put an end to war, instruct the clergy, and establish true doctrine and peace everywhere.

But if he loved tenderly and tenderly admired the holy charity of the Poor Man of God, St Francis, he did not find in his Order, then almost entirely recruited from among illiterates, the same assurance as in the Order of Preachers, all students and scholars and with few exceptions all priests, all prepared to teach or to learn how to teach.

As he had been the legate to Lombardy when Jordan was there, he knew him; perhaps he had known him before that in the University world. The accord between St Dominic and himself had been so deep, and in some ways the resemblance between them was so close, that it was possible to say that 'St Dominic is almost Ugolino become a saint'. (Brem.) Perhaps, at any rate in the human domain of realities, he was still closer to Jordan, because he also had been and basically remained a University product.

Born about 1170 at Anagni, in the palace where Alexander III had hurled the anathema against Frederick Barbarossa, nephew of

Pope Innocent III, Ugo de Segni probably studied canon law at Bologna, and certainly studied theology at Paris. He remained all his long life a theologian and a canonist; in 1234 he dedicated to the University of Bologna the first edition of his Decretals; in 1231 he reconciled the University of Paris and the King of France; in 1229, he founded the University of Toulouse. At Paris and at Bologna he had known and been friendly with the most famous clerics and the most learned masters of his time. It is in that milieu that he is best seen. He knew its worth and its failings; but he remained attached to it. He remained faithful to the friendships born during his youth in the schools. His palace at Rome was a hospice for his former classmates, and his benevolence extended to all within the Church who wished to devote themselves to study, to learn and to teach how to worship in spirit and in truth.

He had been chaplain and confessor to the Pope since the accession of Innocent III in 1198, then bishop of Ostia and cardinal-deacon; nevertheless diplomatic and administrative affairs would turn his thoughts towards immediate action. He brought to them a breadth of view rare in that period. Twice legate to Germany, then to France and then to England where he settled the conflicts raised by John Lackland; preacher of the Crusade in 1217; finally in 1218, when he was legate to Lombardy, he sought rest in the ascetic solitude of the religious houses of the Apennines, in the silence of the Camaldulese cloister in Florence, or with contemplative religious—St Clare of Assisi, Diana d'Andalo, the sisters of St Mary of Sienna whose house he loved. He seems to have known St Dominic first in 1215, at the Lateran Council. On his last trip to Rome, the founder of the Friars Preachers was his guest. It was at his house and through him that Dominic met the bishop of Cracow and his nephews Hyacinth and Ceslaus, that he had won over Reginald, and that he had decided, with his approval, to gather the Roman nuns together at St Sixtus.

But it was in Lombardy above all that Ugolino had favoured the growth of the Friars Preachers. His influence guarded their establishment in Bologna, for he knew that 'the Universities were the true doors through which the Preachers gained entrance to the world'. (Brem.) One senses it in connection with Reginald and Diana d'Andalo, at St Nicholas of the Vineyards, and at St Agnes. He had helped install the friars at Florence in 1229, in Sienna in 1220, in Trani, at Pisa, and in 1221 at Viterbo, so often visited by the Curia. He was in Venice with St Dominic a few weeks before the latter's death. The following year he consolidated the foundation which had been started there. Thanks to him, Jordan had already been able to open houses at Padua, Asti, Trier, Genoa, Cremona and Pavia. Cardinal Ugolino had brought to bear all the financial resources of the Roman Curia for the fight against heresy and for the progress of the Friars Preachers in Lombardy. This generosity was the only point on which Pope Honorius, successor of Innocent III from 1216, sometimes opposed him; for in all else he made no decision without consulting him. Now in his turn Ugolino was called to succeed him, at the moment when the conflict with Frederick II, the insolvency of the Crusade, the war with the Albigensians, were all threats against western Europe. But this vigorous sexagenarian had a firm energy in action, a far-seeing penetration in counsel. He knew how to surround himself with competence. One of the first collaborators whom he called to him was Master Jordan.

The Bulls granted on March 29, 1227, by the new Pope to the Master of the Preachers[6] bear witness to an understanding which

---

[6] We find them in the *Bull. Ord. Praed.* and in Potthast, but more completely in V. Ligier—P. Mothon, *Epitome Bullarii Ordinis Praedicatorum, Romae*, 1898, which alone contains the letter of March 29 addressed to Jordan and to the Preachers who were in France, to ask the help of their prayers. The Pope recalled to them on this occasion how old their friendship was: 'Vos... quibus ab olim nos iunximus bitumine caritatis, sollicitandos duximus et prece affectuosa rogandos, pro grandi munere postulantes, quatenus in ora cordis vestri ei pro nobis orationum vestrarum sacrificium crebrius offeratis.' p. 31, no. 143.

could result only from previous relationships.[7] In giving to Jordan the right to preach everywhere, and to release the novices himself from any canonical penalties they might have incurred as clerics before entering the Order, these Bulls made him independent of the bishops and removed from the latter all rights of jurisdiction henceforth over the Order of Preachers. It was their obvious purpose to remove all obstacles that might stand in the way of Jordan's particular function, namely recruiting for the Order. They gave to Master Jordan a new and hitherto unprecedented power over the academic world. It was the joyful accession gift which Cardinal Ugolino made to him on becoming Gregory IX. He must receive it at Rome itself.

It was very probably at Rome also, and under papal direction, that Jordan decided upon and prepared the gathering of a Most General Chapter of Friars Preachers for the following Pentecost at Paris, May 14, 1228.

The agenda of this Chapter is the widest to be proposed to the Order since the first Chapter held by St Dominic in Bologna in 1220. It was wholly inspired by the great needs of Christendom, which only the vision of the Sovereign Pontiff could encompass.

It provided for the extension of the Order by four new provinces — the Holy Land, Greece, Dacia and Poland.

The Holy Land! It was in that direction that Gregory IX turned first, only four days after his election, when by his Encyclical of March 23, 1227, he called all the princes of Christian Europe to the Crusades. He summoned the Emperor, Frederick II, calling a truce to all the Lombard and Sicilian dissensions, to take the cross and set out. And when the Emperor was slow to respond, when the

---

[7] That Jordan had presented himself to the Roman Curia after the papal election is proved by the letters of Gregory IX, June 20,1227, which entrust to Jordan of Saxony and to two Florentine ecclesiastics the duty of pursuing Philip, bishop of Cathares, arrested at Florence and imprudently set free, as were his supporters, in accordance with the constitution of the General Council, 1215.—Ligier-Monthon, *Epitome*, p. 34, No. 157.

Landgrave of Thurigen, husband of St Elizabeth of Hungary—one whom Jordan knew well—the true head of the Crusades and most faithful crusader, died mysteriously at Brindisi, the Pope hurled at Frederick in September the decree of excommunication.

To establish in the Holy Land not a few isolated houses but organized groups of Friars, who would settle themselves there and develop steadily, would be to assure to the Crusaders solid bases of support, and would perpetuate, in the midst of the disorder and the insecurity of expeditions which were too often adventurous, the teaching of apostolic and roman doctrine and would establish a permanent mission. To create a Dominican province in the Holy Land was probably one of the desires of St Dominic; it was an idea in the mind of Jordan of Saxony; it was also, certainly, the wish of Gregory IX.

As for Greece, it was the road to the Orient, one of the most important frontiers of the southern Occident.[8] Poland and Dacia then represented the plains of central and northern Europe, that is to say, besides Poland itself and the confines of the Ukraine, also Brandenburg, Denmark, Sweden and Norway. These countries, where the remnant of the barbarian world had taken refuge, retained something of their fabulous mystery. Towards them, as we know, the ambitions of St Dominic, a missionary at heart, had reached out. He had to limit his first extension of the Order to closer boundaries. Only a few of his sons had ventured so far. For them to secure a foothold there by lasting foundations was to

---

[8] Dr B. Altaner discovers that in 1227 there seemed to be already seven priories of Friars Preachers in Greece and Crete. In the Holy Land, in 1222—after the Chapter which elected Jordan as Master General—the first Friars Preachers had set foot in Palestine; then in 1225, after the Chapter of Bologna, '*ex decreto Jordanis*', several friars were sent out to the Holy Land, but being stopped on their journey, settled at Ragusa and there began to establish a house which was definitely founded in 1228. Nicosia or Nemosia in the Limassol language, in Cyprus, had a priory in 1226. It was attached to the Province of the Holy Land.

extend and fortify the frontiers of Christendom. But these things could not have been accomplished without the help of the Papacy. Jordan could not hope to throw the nets of the Fisher of Men so far if Peter himself, in the person of Gregory IX, had not directed and supported the effort.

Now that he had received full assurances, he would call all the Priors Provincial and two definitors for each Province to the priory of St Jacques, for Pentecost, 1228. Leaving Rome himself, he set out for Paris.

He certainly did not reach there before the following December 10.[9] What was his route? Did he stay longer in Italy? He does not seem to have gone by way of Bologna. Perhaps the interview with Frederick II should be put at this time rather than in 1229, between the return of the Crusades and the peace of San Germano.[10]

Frederick, according to the Lives of the Brethren, had scorned the canonical decisions; which fits in with the imperial attitude during the events of 1227. On the other hand, if Master Jordan, in spite of his repugnance, resolved to go and find the Emperor, it is evidently upon orders from the Pope and to fulfil a duty. No indication of time or place allows us to be precise about this interview.

'They sat down together', says the account, 'and there was a

---

[9] Letter XXIV A, XXXIX B: 'Know then at present... that I reached the priory in Paris in good health fifteen days before Christmas. I stayed there and am still staying there, preaching and awaiting the mercy of God. You and all the Sisters, then, pray assiduously and constantly that the Lord will increase our numbers and will touch the hearts of the Parisian students in His sweetness.' Dr B. Altaner assigns to this letter the date December 10, 1223, because it contains ascetical advice belonging, he says, to young nuns still without a Prioress. It is rather a vague hypothesis. Jordan often returned to the same spiritual counsels. He says here 'videlicet saepe'—'As I have often done'.

[10] It is there, between June 1229 and July 23, 1230, that Bayonne, Fleury (Church Flistory) and E. Bernard place it.

long silence. Finally the Master spoke: 'Sire, I go through many provinces to fulfil my duties, and I am surprised that you do not ask me to give you the rumours which are going around." The Emperor replied: "I have faithful messengers in all the courts and in all the provinces, and I know everything that everyone in the world is doing." The Master retorted: "The Lord Jesus knew everything, since he was God; nevertheless he asked his disciples to tell him what was being said about the Son of Man. As for you, you are certainly only a man and you are unaware of much that is said about you which it is important for you to know. They say that you oppress the churches, that you despise canonical decisions, that you consult soothsayers, that you favour Jews and Saracens too much, that you do not listen to truthful counsellors, that you do not honour the Vicar of Christ, the successor of Peter, the father of Christians and our spiritual head." '

These courageous criticisms seem to have been fruitless. Be that as it may, Jordan reached France again in the course of the autumn. He left the Curia, having received great honours there. According to Thomas de Cantimpré, Pope Gregory had even forced him, on the day of his departure, to break the Rule of his Order and sit at the Pope's own table. The meal finished, he left for France.[11] Finding himself at nightfall at the entrance to a village, he asked hospitality of the priest of the place, and it was refused him; it was in the home of a poor man that he was received, and seeing the poverty of the supper table he said joyfully to the friars who were with him: 'Blessed be the priest who closed his door to us, so as to take away from me the false glory of having been seated today at the table of the Sovereign Pontiff.'

We cannot be at all sure that, so late in the season, he took the Brenner Pass and crossed Germany again.[12] Seeing that the house of the Friars Preachers at Clermont-Ferrand was opened between

---

[11] 'Fine egressurus erat phrasi Gallica.'—Vit. Fr.

[12] Hypothesis of Dr Altaner.

1227 and 1228, we are tempted to think with some probability that, using the ancient way of the 'Codex Calixtenus', through Provence, Arles, Nimes, Le Puy, Brioude, Clermont-Ferrand, Jordan travelled through the Auvergne, where memory of him was preserved for a long time after.[13]

Preaching to the students of Paris and the preparations for the Most General Chapter must have provided the Master with a full winter's work at the priory of St Jacques. His letters were few. He had no time to write, not even time to pray: 'I shall speak to you at greater length some other time (of the fruits of his preaching to the students of the University of Paris)', he wrote to his spiritual daughter. 'For the present, I must make haste.' And elsewhere: 'I must finish this letter briefly... Pray for me... I have great need of it... and I do not pray often; that is why I need you to exhort your sisters to supply for me during their prayers.'

We have every reason to believe that the nuns of Bologna fervently did what he had asked them. Moreover the time was a vital one for the Order of Preachers. By reason of the Most General Chapter, and due to divers circumstances, the Master was about to enlarge the scope of the Order singularly and to tie it up definitely on the one hand with full missionary activity, on the other with the pursuit of study and teaching to which it was essentially destined.

---

[13] *Vit. Frat.* 3a p., c XXXIV and XXXV—'in Alvernia'. It concerns a miracle obtained by Jordan in the house of a great lady who had generously received the Preachers in Auvergne.

Chapter IX
CREATIONS AND CONQUESTS

HE work of the Most General Chapter, the organization of far-off Provinces, and even his incessant preaching to the students of the University, were not in fact the only preoccupations of Master Jordan. What probably absorbed him still more, for he put it before everything else, was the question of the studies. What good would it be to send out preachers if they were not well taught and able to teach in their turn? And, at a period when study was not possible without a master, there could be good preachers only to the extent that there were good professors. That is why the Friars Preachers had organized their Order from the time of its origin as a vast scholastic system; and this is why it has been said that St Dominic was the first Minister of Public Instruction known to Europe. The Friars Preachers could have established schools for their own use alone; but that would have been to forget that they were especially created for the service of the Christian society and that the lack of schools of theology for clerics was then one of the most serious difficulties engaging the attention of the Church. Thus, teaching of the sacred sciences was demanded of the Friars Preachers as a sine qua non for the foundation of every priory, and this teaching was public. To establish a house of Friars Preachers in a diocese was to create a school of theology; a great number of bishops were decided in favour of the new Order by this consideration; as the bishop of Metz, Chancellor of the Holy Empire, wrote on April 1221 in recommendation of the Friars in his episcopal city: 'Having the Preachers living here will be of great profit not only to the layfolk, because of the preaching of these religious, but also to the clerics because of their lectures in the sacred sciences. Moreover, this is to follow the example given by the Pope who has given them a house in Rome.'

The Dominican priories had their scholastic hierarchy. Each house had its own conventual school, attended by all the religious present and by clerics from outside; the teaching in it was given by a master who was called sometimes Doctor and sometimes Lector. The course consisted of the reading of Holy Writ, the Sentences of Peter Lombard, scholastic history, and the *Summa* of cases of conscience. This was the first degree. The larger priories had, besides the principal master, a sub-lector, sometimes one or two bachelors, and also the master of Students (*Magister Studentium*) who watched over the students as regards discipline and work, and a tutor. The principal Master held public disputations twice a month. That was the second degree: *studia solemnia*. Finally, besides the priory schools or the *studia solemnia*, there were also established general schools: *studia generalia*. Here the students could acquire a still higher culture, in imitation of the University of Paris, and after having received and themselves given a more or less prolonged teaching course, they could go into other centres and preside in their turn over other schools.

It was on the University of Paris that the scholastic life of the thirteenth century was modelled, and it is there that the Order of Preachers, precisely as a teaching Order, was to make its official entry; a Chair of Theology was conceded to it when the lectures were resumed in September, 1228.

The moment was opportune; the students loved the house of St Jacques and came to it in their crowds; the new bishop of Paris, William of Auvergne, consecrated in Rome in April 1228 by Gregory IX, was a former Master of the Faculty of Theology and a friend of the Friars Preachers; the Sovereign Pontiff, we cannot doubt, desired to see the religious in whom he had so much confidence teaching theology with all the authority which Paris alone at that time could give; finally, the occasion was propitious because the man who was needed was there.

For several years the Friars Preachers at St Jacques had had in their midst a personality already famous in the University world:

Brother Roland of Cremona.

Entering the Order in Bologna under the priorship of Reginald, when he was a Master of Arts of great repute and probably also a Master of Medicine, Roland of Cremona had come to Paris to follow and complete his academic career. There is reason to think that he had even accompanied Reginald when the latter left St Nicholas of the Vineyards for St Jacques. There is in fact no mention after that time of Roland having had any office in Lombardy or elsewhere. He must have been given freedom to devote himself entirely to theological studies. He did so brilliantly, at first no doubt under the direction of the first Master of the Friars Preachers at Paris, Jean de Barastre; afterwards perhaps under the direction of John of St Giles. He ended his course finally and could receive the doctor's hood.

At this point, at the end of the scholastic year 1228, Jean de Barastre left Paris, his University, and the Friars Preachers of St Jacques. Some letters of June 1228 allow us to establish his presence again at Paris; but in August other letters indicate his presence at Rheims, at the bishop's palace. Then, at the same time as a Chair in Theology was in the appointment of the Faculty at Paris, the Friars Preachers of St Jacques were looking for a professor. It was probably the Most General Chapter of Pentecost, with Master Jordan presiding, which then proposed Roland of Cremona to succeed Jean de Barastre. The candidacy of the new doctor was agreeable to the bishop, William of Auvergne, and to the chancellor of Notre Dame. When the students returned in September 1228, Roland of Cremona took possession of the master's chair in the theological school of St Jacques.

This is an important event in the history of the Order, and an important event for the University of Paris. The teaching of the new master was to mark an epoch there. The substance of his lectures has been preserved for us in a single manuscript, preserved in the Mazarine Library,[1] of the *Summa Theologica* of Roland of Cremona. This *Summa* has, says Cardinal Ehrle, 'a Parisian flavour', but it is also the most important Summa of the times; it shows a very new scientific tendency, and provides a remarkable prelude to similar works which were subsequently produced by other theologians of St Jacques, Hugh of St Cher, Peter of Tarentaise and their successors.

A little further on we shall again come across the learned and forceful figure of Master Roland of Cremona. Leaving him in his Chair of Theology, we must now set out again towards Lombardy with the tireless Jordan.

He seldom remained, as we know, after the celebration of the annual Chapter, and regularly alternated between Paris and Bologna in preaching the Lent. It is to Lombardy, therefore, that he is now called. Perhaps he prolonged his stay at Paris to be present at the inauguration of the chair given to Roland of Cremona in the middle of September, 1228. Meanwhile he could, during the course of the summer, have gone to visit the new priories of the Province of France—La Rochelle, Sens, Gand. These are vague suppositions, for nothing definite appears in the contemporary texts as to this itinerary. But what is fairly certain is that, whatever way he had come there, Master Jordan was at Milan before the beginning of Lent. A letter to Diana is dated from there, a letter of consolation on the death of d'Andalo, Diana's father, who died, it is thought, in the first months of the year 1229.

'You have preceded your father in death, since for a long time you have been dead,[2] your life hidden in Christ, while your father, as I have learned at Milan, has just died; it is not fitting, then, for

---

[1] MS. No. 795—143 pages from the books of Si Martini a campis ordinis Cluniacensis (Moliner, catalogue of the MSS. of the Mazarine Library, 1888). This *Summa* is divided into four parts: 'De Deo Uno et Trino'; 'De Creaturis'; 'De Incarnatione'; 'De Sacramentis'.

[2] i.e., to the world.

you to grieve. I do not wish to say that his death does not move me; on the contrary it does move me, especially on your account. You can admire, nevertheless, the mercy of God, for he has taken away your parents according to the flesh, your parents in this transitory life, to grant you a spiritual and permanent friend—to give you the Eternal One. I am writing to you briefly from Milan. I shall see you soon, if it pleases God.'

Lent and the Paschal season must have kept Jordan at Bologna until the General Chapter of June 3, 1229. According to custom he visited Diana and her sisters, exercised his spiritual ministry among them and was pleased with the increase in number and with the spiritual progress of his daughters, for a little later he wrote to them: 'Joy is in my heart, my dear daughters, when I remember you, for I saw you so united and so bright, walking in spirit with the Lord.' Yet, if we are to credit certain texts whose positive sources are difficult to estimate, the Chapter of June 3 had shown itself to be without indulgence towards the convent of St Agnes and above all towards the growing apostolate which it exercised with regard to the pious women, lay-sisters or clothed, who wore the habit. It is beyond doubt that in many places, particularly in Germany, the Friars Preachers had begun to be overwhelmed by the influx of penitents, whether nuns or beguines. The General Chapter of 1228, having considered the question, forbade the Friars of the Order to accept the direction of convents of women, or to receive them to the vows of religion. But this admonition did not concern the religious nor even the Tertiaries or the lay-sisters of the Order of Preachers. The Chapter of 1229 returned to the same subject, and did all it possibly could to take away the habit of St Agnes from widowed ladies and young girls of the world who had previously been clothed with it. The regulation enacted against them is singularly harsh.[3] If they did not leave off the habit, they could not be visited by the Friars, neither for preaching nor for confession. It seems that this regulation was not applied—or for only a very short time—for Jordan addressed his greetings to 'sisters and outside friends' in a letter of 1235 or 1236, which proves that the group of lay-sisters or those ladies clothed in the habit still existed around St Agnes. In leaving Bologna, after the Chapter of June 3, 1229, the Master did not even seem to suppose that, from the exchange of ideas in which these questions were discussed among the friars, there could result an ordination of such a kind as to disturb his daughters. The first letters to Diana and her sisters after he left make no allusion to it.

Nevertheless, a short time afterwards, Diana was troubled over it, and the same day that he writes to reassure her, Jordan sends to the Provincial of Lombardy, Brother Stephen of Spain, a letter which puts him right in no uncertain manner.

What had happened? There was evidently indiscreet talk, and indiscreet talk that was without good will towards the Sisters; 'Rustling of leaves', as Jordan says. 'I see', he wrote to Stephen of Spain, 'that your conscience is alarmed by a rustling of leaves', and at the same time to Diana: 'I understand that you are troubled because of a constitution about which they have spoken to you... but it is only a question of an indiscreet interpretation.'

What incident gave rise to this little storm? According to what we can gather from reading the text of Jordan's two letters to Diana and to Friar Stephen, it was set off suddenly, following we do not know what conversations. Friar Stephen was seized with scruples and, justifying himself by the resolutions of the last two

---

[3] 'Admonemus quod nullae mulieres induantur per fratres nostros ad suscipiendum habitum S. Agnetis, et si quae habuerint, nullo modo visitentur per fratres nec causa predicationis vel confessionis... quamdiu habuerint hunc...'

Chapters, made difficulties about admitting to profession certain sisters, probably lay-sisters (*conversae*), friends of St Agnes; and, besides that, sharp tongues were not lacking to raise doubts about the validity of the reception into the Order of 'sisters of outside' and perhaps even of sisters from within.

Thus fear and feeling had been at work round the enclosure of St Agnes and doubtless also in the convent itself; fear, feeling, perhaps a little feminine, perhaps a little Italian in vivacity, but profoundly touching and worthy of respect, for what aroused them was attachment to the Order of Preachers, voluntary fidelity to its direction and love of its rule. That is how Master Jordan judges it. Briefly, without going into embarrassing details, he brings the thing to a head. Haven't they accused him themselves, in regard to this very matter, of an extreme breadth of mind? He is the one who opens wide the doors to recruits of good will; he is the Master who liberally gives out dispensations, especially those which facilitate study. Timorous spirits thought him imprudent. He was not unaware of that. It was to them that he gave a lesson in his answer to the Prior of Lombardy, because their rigorism had found some echo in the too-scrupulous Brother Stephen.

Jordan explained to him that it was not in accordance with the spirit of true children of God to create useless difficulties. He recalled to his mind the papal Bull which had placed St Agnes under the jurisdiction of the Order, without differentiating between the Sisters and the Friars. He charged him to re-establish confidence where there had been anxiety. Let no doubt remain.

'I know very well the acts and decrees of all the Chapters as well as the secret reasons which inspired them, and I can affirm that although one of them carries this prohibition[4] it is not a question of the Sisters of our Order at all; that would have been to

---

[4] forbidding the Preachers to administer convents of women and to admit to religious vows penitents and 'continentes'. (Chapter of Paris, 1228).

separate them entirely from us[5]; and supposing that such had been the intention, should we have had the right to do it? Not at all, for we should have been acting against the directions of the Sovereign Pontiff who has charged us to watch over them as over the friars... Be then entirely re-assured in this regard... Reassure also the Sisters of St Agnes and tell them that they have nothing to fear and that they may continue in peace in the name of the Lord... This point must be regarded as certainly and clearly defined... It is useless to raise the question again... As for the other points of the rule, to think that I have not the right to dispense from them is to believe that the Order has not given to me the office of Master General.[6] There is not one of them, however grave, from which I cannot dispense according to my judgment as to the divers needs of people, places and times. I except always the three articles which, after the last Chapter celebrated at Paris, are irrevocable, which must be inviolably observed, and which we have even thought to have confirmed by the Roman Curia. This exception taken, I have the general power of giving dispensations, to permit, for example, someone to travel on horseback, or to carry money on his journeys or to grant other permissions for large things or small. If it were otherwise, would I have dared to arrogate to myself a right which I had never received? Thank God, I have nothing to reproach myself with on this point... So, my dear friend, banish from your conscience these too meticulous scruples and, on the contrary, recognize... that it is not wise to change your mind every time you hear a new opinion expressed.'

To stifle gossiping, keep silent. 'Do not talk about it any more', Jordan advises him, and to Diana, he says more gently; 'Do not

---

[5] It is clear that this applies more probably to Tertiaries than to nuns.

[6] It is the well-balanced tendency of the mind of Master Jordan to delimit at the same time that he is re-enforcing the authority of the Priors and of the General. The democratic Constitutions of the Preachers must not turn into anarchy; the Chapter of 1236 will return to these questions and will regulate them by legislation.

speak of it to anyone, do not be upset, keep calm... If we have some statute of the sort,[7] it is not concerned with our sisters, but because of certain foreigners, for, in various provinces,[8] the better to assure the conversion of women,[9] our Brothers have been accustomed to admit them too easily to the vow of chastity and to the habit... These sisters who are due to make profession can do so in all security into the hands of the Prioress, or the Prior, or the Provincial who will receive them in my name. I shall be as happy about their profession as if I had received them myself and, for their part, they can never have any doubts [as to the validity of their reception]... Be in everything confident and joyful. As for that which you lack by my absence, find it in a better Friend, in your Spouse, Jesus Christ, whose presence you have more often than mine, in spirit and in truth; and he will speak to you more sweetly and more helpfully than Brother Jordan.'

Brother Jordan has resumed his itinerant apostolate and he did not return to Bologna for two years. He went to Padua first and then to Vercelli to meet again with certain groups of Ultramontan students whom these cities, the rivals of Bologna, had attracted by offering rich salaries to the masters and generous privileges to the students.

He preached and he recruited Friars Preachers.

'You have been heard', he writes, 'in your prayers for the students of Padua, for shortly after I had begged your prayers for this intention twenty of them, and twenty of the best, entered the Order.'

At Vercelli his conquests were still more striking. Thirteen students entered the Order; they were notably learned, and in particular the regent, who seems to have brought in the rest, was one of the most important recruits the Friars Preachers could have

---

[7] In the same Constitution of 1228, doubtless confirmed in 1229.
[8] particularly in Germany.
[9] i.e. repentant prostitutes.

gained. This was 'Master Walter of Germany, regent of logic and perfect in his art, who was considered at the University of Paris to be one of the leading masters', writes Jordan himself to Brother Stephen of Spain. Better known in the Order afterwards under the name of Walter of Strasbourg, he was already about forty-five years old and enjoyed great prestige in the scholastic world. Almost immediately after his entry he was to be named Prior at Strasbourg; but since he was a logician and theologian of all-round ability, the Order was in too great need of his teaching to confine him long to administrative work. Made Lector at Strasbourg and later at Basle, he shone especially by reason of his scientific knowledge and his spiritual direction during the short number of years that he was to live in the Order, for he died at Basle soon after, in 1234.

He founded and directed—clearly on the advice of and supported by Jordan—the famous monastery of the 'Unterlinden' of Colmar; 'In the year of our Lord 1232, two pious widows, Agnes of Mittelheim and Agnes of Herkenheim, were inspired to found a convent. They opened their minds first to Brother Walter, Lector and Prior of the house of Friars Preachers at Strasbourg, a holy man right venerated, and he approved their plan.'[10] He gave them the habit and the enclosure at St Andrew's, 1232, and Beguines and Augustinians joined them and adopted the rule of the Dominicans. This convent became a centre of contemplative life.

Walter was so much attached to it that it was probably in order to keep the government of Unterlinden that he went from Strasbourg to Basle when they were changed from the jurisdiction of the Preachers of Strasbourg to that of the Priory of Basle. He was less fearful than Stephen of Spain and, like Jordan, considered the prayers and penances of nuns to have great value before God.

---

[10] Cl. Champion. See also J. Ancelet-Hustache, Critical Edition of MS. 508 of the Library of Colmar (*Vitae Sororum d'Unterlinden*) in the T.U. of the historical and literary Archives of the M.A.

Besides being a master, learned and sure, we also see in this Walter of Germany glimpses of a profound and attractive mystic.[11]

Jordan already knew him and perhaps had seen the depth of his soul. But he, still a prey to his period, attached to the world by his great appointments in the University of Vercelli, resisted this interior vocation which would make him leave it all and shrank from Jordan's winning words. When he knew that the Master was coming to preach at Vercelli, 'he said to his colleagues and students: "Take care; do not go to his sermons; do not listen to even one of his words; like a courtesan who takes men captive, he captures them by his discourses."[12] But here is the miraculous thing, the work of God; he who kept others away was the first to be captured; and when his miserable worldliness would have kept him from entering the Order, closing his fists he struck himself as if to urge himself on, saying to himself: "You will go!" He came therefore, was received, and became an example to all.'

'He was, in fact, followed', writes Jordan, 'by two of the most outstanding bachelors, both ready to teach logic; the one is from Provence, the other from Lombardy. There also came an excellent German student in canon law, canon of Spire, and rector at Vercelli of the students of his nation:[13] another German who was

---

[11] According to tradition, he received the stigmata while in prayer at the Church of the Franciscans at Colmar, which he often visited. Vit. Frat., p. 222-223, -300. Pez. p. 65, 66. Perdrizet, Speculum Salvationis humanae.

[12] 'The Siren of the Schools' was Jordan's nickname among his contemporaries.

[13] He also put up a good fight; but having learned that one after the other of his friends had been won over, he forgot his books, open before him, which he left without closing them... and began to run like a madman toward the Friars... arrived at the place where they met, for the Preachers still had no house at Vercelli, and finding them all assembled around Master Jordan, he threw off his silk mantle and lay down on the ground like a drunken man, without saying anything but, 'I am God's'... Master Jordan said to him, 'Since you are God's, we consign you to him' and, raising him up, gave him the habit.—Vit. Frat. 4a, X, 4, p. 173.

very learned and well esteemed, Master Godescalc, canon of Maestricht; two Provençals full of talent, both associated with the principal Master, the one teaching canon law, the other civil law. It might have been said that we had chosen all these recruits from among all the students of Vercelli... I have taken almost all of them with me to Genoa; and two left immediately for Montpellier. The others will wait here a while.'

There was not yet a priory at Vercelli. Jordan took care to conduct his new recruits to Genoa himself; it is at this time, in an inn on the way, that the incident took place—so illustrative of the way in which Jordan behaved toward his novices—of the foolish laughter of the new Friars Preachers at the Office of Compline.[14]

Not only was the Master not scandalized, but he shared in the lightheartedness of these young men, became young again with them; nevertheless he observed them, scrutinized them, 'filtered' them if one may say so, and finally oriented them to the best advantage of the Order according to their degree of culture and their special aptitudes, urging those who were gifted toward study, using talents already developed. He recommended the Provincial of Lombardy not to lose sight of a man from Cremona left at Genoa, saying that he was 'learned in logic, of noble birth, and very much gifted; his name is Peregrine; he must be sent to the best studium of the Province'.

As for the two students whom he had already sent to Montpellier, they were evidently destined to strengthen the Provençal nucleus amongst the Friars Preachers, which was to be called upon, in fact, to furnish Masters for the new University of Toulouse. And it is to Toulouse also that Jordan went, by sea; he embarked at Genoa[15] and set sail for Montpellier.

---

[14] This anecdote is told later, in Chapter XII.

[15] 'I am writing from Genoa, where I intend to set sail for Montpellier.' (Letter to Stephen of Spain.) 'This very day when I am writing, I am going to leave Genoa.' (Letter to Diana, A, XIX B.)

The creation of the University of Toulouse is one of the great events of the year 1229. It is one of the results of the Peace of Languedoc finally settled by the Treaty of Meaux. The court of France and the Roman Curia agreed to endow Toulouse with new schools whose teaching, given by approved Masters, carefully watched by the Apostolic See, might preserve the youth of the land from a possible return to the Albigensian heresy and would propagate the true doctrine in this section so profoundly shaken by the Cathari and the Vaudois. It was, moreover, the spiritual policy of Gregory IX to teach and to reform, by means of the best brains, the mass of the Christian people. In the discussions which doubtless dated from the first months of his accession, he had opened his mind to Jordan of Saxony; and at the Chapter of 1229 at Bologna the Friars Preachers were officially charged by him to take care of the theological teaching at Toulouse. Already, in spite of earlier difficulties, this teaching had been maintained at St Romain by the Friars Preachers of the first Priory of the Order. It was the only Chair of Theology which the bishop had at his command; and it was to be incorporated into the new University.

But that was not enough; in the programme as planned—and as desired by the Roman Curia—the schools of Toulouse, hereafter arranged in four Faculties, would have to include, besides the masters in the liberal arts, in law and in medicine, four professors of theology. The first chair continued to be at St Romain. The second was entrusted to Roland of Cremona.

From the first Master of Grammar, the poet Jean de Garlande, we learn that in the summer of 1229 Roland of Cremona arrived at Toulouse to occupy a Chair in Theology. Evidently he had been appointed by the General Chapter of Bologna. It is very probable that he was there himself and accompanied Jordan in his journey from Padua to Vercelli, Genoa and Montpellier. He may have been sent for from Paris and met the Master General at Toulouse again by arrangement.

But it cannot be doubted that his nomination to Toulouse was

Jordan's work. It was, in fact, part of a whole University 'movement'. Roland of Cremona had made a magnificent beginning in the first Chair of the Friars Preachers at the University of Paris; for his successor they would have to find a Friar Preacher as well qualified and agreed to by the Chancellor of Notre Dame. In this year, 1228-1229, Roland of Cremona had as assistant Lector at the studium of St Jacques, Brother Hugh of Cher, who entered the Order with Humbert of Romans in 1225 and had already a reputation as an established theologian. Before the end of the school year he received the doctor's hood. Roland of Cremona could leave Paris; he would be adequately replaced by a Parisian master. Himself a Lombard, accustomed to the *langue d'oc* (the language used south of the Loire), he would be still better in his new post in Toulouse. His colleague, Jean de Garlande, greeted his installation with enthusiasm[16] and, like the good rhetorician he was, exalted his oratorical combats against the heretics above the exploits of the legendary Roland at Roncevaux.

Roland of Cremona had in fact to prove his courage. He stayed at Toulouse until 1233 and was remembered in his day for not having fallen, as he might, to the threatening dagger of the heretics. The Pope had then given him an inquisitorial mission, which was also dangerous enough, first at Plaisance and afterwards at Florence. He then came back to Bologna as Lector. There his reputation as an incomparable debater caused him to be designated in 1238 to oppose the astrologer-philosopher and magician of Frederick II, the famous Theodore. Frederick was then besieging Brescia. Roland, who was suffering from gout in his knee, was taken on a donkey to the imperial camp. He held his own in the dispute and reduced Theodore to silence. His was evidently an energetic and belligerent personality, especially as he

---

[16] Annum millenum Domini centum bis et annos—vigintque novem semita solis agit—sanguine... Italus huc veniens ad robora nostra magister—Rolandus, verbi claruit ense sacri—Forti Rolando major quia corpora stravit—Ille, sed hereticum contudit, ille nefas—Gaudia... etc. (*op. cit.*; p. 101.)

was both a subtle scholar and a religious of outspoken enthusiasm. Jordan knew what he was doing when he called him to Toulouse. He had the joy of installing him himself in his chair. It is probable that he had time to be present at the solemn inauguration of the course, since he did not return to Paris until after October 9. 'Know that, aided by your prayers', he writes to the Sisters of St Agnes, 'I have crossed safe and sound, having left Lombardy, Provence, Auvergne[17], Burgundy and France, and have reached Paris, where I am writing to you, after the feast of St Denis.' He had visited important Priories on his way; doubtless Limoges, Orléans, and Sens. 'I found the friars increasing in number, in knowledge and in virtue. But', he added, 'I exhort you, my very dear daughter, in your devoted prayers to call upon the God of peace, Author of all peace, to maintain this peace in his holy Church; for in many places they rebel against the Friars, and these attacks give rise to strife which imperils many souls.' This vague allusion could have reference to the difficulties which Roland of Cremona would have with the heretics of Toulouse; perhaps Roland had foreseen the insidious intrigues of the secular masters against the University Friars Preachers, which reached their apex twenty-five years later in the debate between William of St Amour and Thomas Aquinas. The maintenance of the chair conceded to the Friars Preachers of St Jacques, and now occupied by Hugh of St Cher, probably raised some jealousy.

And finally—another cause of trouble—in October, 1229, Jordan found the University of Paris in a turmoil.

It was not the first time that violent friction had been produced between the students and the townsmen of Paris. Many

---

[17] A reading adopted by Berthier and Bayonne gives 'Alemaniam', but evidently it should read 'Alverniam' (see Altaner, commentary on Letter X) which must be read. The itinerary of Jordan must have been: Toulouse, Brive, Limoges, Bourges—perhaps Orléans—Auxerre, Sens, Paris, Auvergne, Burgundy, France.

times, since the number of students of diverse nations was on the increase in the city, quarrels had broken out among the turbulent youth and the city's population. These affairs were generally not important. If there was too much uproar, a real brawl, the students were hauled before the tribunal of the Bishop, who, though he had a prison and considerable power at his disposal, generally showed himself fatherly in dealing with them.

In 1219 a conflict had arisen between the University and the Chancellor of Notre Dame, and the latter had been called to Rome and reprimanded by Honorius III. About the same time a provost of the police had taken it upon himself to arrest and molest some rioting students, and the hue and cry in the ecclesiastical world was such that the King, Philip Augustus, put the provost in prison, and some say that he was hanged.

The affair of Mardi Gras 1229 had other consequences.

It is all obscure enough. It began in a skirmish at Faubourg St Marcel. The students were at liberty, the two days before Ash Wednesday and the start of Lent, to engage in feasting and games. A group of students of arts had gone out to amuse themselves, not far from the banks of the Bievre, at the Faubourg St Marcel. The quarrel started in a tavern between the inn-keeper and the students. The people of the quarter took part in it, and there were blows and wounds. According to Matthew Paris, the English contemporary chronicler, the students, angry with the townsmen who had at first put them to flight, went so far that the dean of St Marcel, aghast, appealed to the bishop, and the latter to the legate; all three went to find the Queen Regent, who summoned her provost-at-arms; and the students were attacked indiscriminately on a field outside the ramparts, where they were peacefully amusing themselves; two were killed, a Flemish and a Norman of great promise, both of them innocent of any part in the St Marcel brawl. According to the inquiry ordered two years later by the Pope, and the Bull of April 19, 1231, which concluded the inquiry, it was the dean of St Marcel and the townsfolk, not the provost, who had shed blood; this was confirmed by the great Chronicle of Limoges of the year 1229. Was this a police action thoughtlessly consented to by Blanche of Castile to give satisfaction to the Parisian commune? Or was it a popular uprising against foreign students? Perhaps both; the townsfolk would not have taken the risk if they had not had the provost on their side.

In any case emotion ran high. Murder had been committed. University privileges had been violated. The masters made a pact with their students. The schools suspended their lectures; at least those of the Trivium and the Quadrivium, for it does not seem that the rioting extended to the medical and law students, and it is certain that the Faculty of Theology, at any rate at the start, remained aloof from the arts students' strike. Paris was, however, emptied of a large number of its students. When the schools opened in September, 1229, the masters had moved their chairs to Orléans, Chartres, Rheims, or Poitiers. Many found it easier and more practical to return to their home countries. Those from Angers went back to Angers and called to this friendly capital with its pleasant climate other companions in study. The English took the road to England. The King, Henry III Plantagenet, who was always alert to what was going on on the Continent, seized the opportunity thus offered to lower the University prestige of France to the profit of England and hastened to offer to the masters and students of Paris 'if it pleased them to enter his kingdom and to live there, towns and villages of their choice and all the immunities due them'.[18] The proposal was alluring and was accepted by a chosen group, and the University of Oxford received a considerable influx.

These divers exoduses had destroyed the unity of discipline which gave the University of Paris its superiority; the masters, become independent, did not scruple to grant degrees without the

---

[18] Letters patent of July 16,1229, delivered and sealed at Reading. Text quoted by Bernard.

control of the episcopal chancellery. They had had recourse to the Pope with their grievances against the bishop, William of Auvergne; and in a letter to the latter of November 23, 1229, the Pope had replied blaming the bishop severely.[19] The disgrace of the legate, Romain de St Ange, who was recalled and replaced by the bishop of Tournai, Gauthier de Marvis, doctor of the University of Paris; the nomination of three arbitrators[20] to restore peace between the parties; and finally the letter of November 26 to King Louis and Queen Blanche, all bear witness to the activity of the Roman Curia on this occasion and the concern with which it viewed the dispersal of the students of the University of Paris. 'See', said Gregory IX to William of Auvergne, 'how you have diverted and divided the course of the river—that is to say, the studium—which watered and fertilized the city of Paris'; and to the King, 'If this river (of knowledge—and knowledge nourishes wisdom)—turned from its course, loses itself in streams, and dries up, the science of Holy Letters will be obscured. This would be a misfortune, not only for the kingdom of France, but for the garden of the Universal Church.' He named the chosen arbitrators to the King and Queen. But the discussions lasted a long time. Probably there was a trip to Rome by Philip the chancellor; then a delegation of three masters in 1231. In the interval, the Pope did not neglect to get more detailed information[21] and to seek out people who knew what had happened. Among these 'discreet personages', as Matthew Paris calls them,[22] the best informed

---

[19] De Perouse. Text Coll., Moreau MS. 1184, folio 321 B.N., quoted by Noel Valois.

[20] Maurice, bishop of Mans; Guerin, bishop of Senlis; John, archbishop of Chalons. November 24, 1229.

[21] Letter of May 10, 1230, to the doctors of Angers and of Paris to obtain from them an exact copy of their privileges.

[22] 'Tandem procurantibus discretis personis elaboratum est, ut factis quibusdam pro tempore exigentibus utrobique culpis, pax est clero et civibus reformata.'—M. Paris, 1229.

about University matters and the most experienced also, was the former student and Master of Arts of the Parisian schools, the faithful friend of the students of arts, the man from whom Blanche of Castile took advice, to whom an audience with the Sovereign Pontiff was always available, Master Jordan. If his name is not recorded in the archives of the affair, if he is not one of those appointed to undertake the arbitration, we have a right to suppose that it was so as not to excite unfavourably the distrustful susceptibilities of the secular masters in regard to the Friars Preachers newly come to the University. Prudence of this sort fitted both Gregory IX and Jordan. The spring months of 1231 would see Jordan in Italy, moreover, and at the Roman Curia, at the very time when the conflict between the students and the townsfolk of Paris was to be finally resolved. For the time being, since he was deprived of the largest and most fruitful part of his audience in Paris, and everything was otherwise calm at the priory of St Jacques, which was now under the priorship of Philip of Vercelli and the scholastic regency of Hugh of St Cher, the studies serious and hard, the preaching assured and conventual peace established, Master Jordan left France; he went to preach Lent at Oxford.

CHAPTER X
FROM OXFORD TO MILAN

HE way frequented by pilgrims from Great Britain going to Puy, to Rome or to Compostello, was that of the daily merchant traffic between Paris and London; it went through St Denis, Beauvais, St Riquier on the Somme, and reached the coast at Boulogne or at Wissant. The crossing was made to Dover or to the mouth of the Thames; and if the wind was favourable, the voyage was relatively rapid.

Jordan set foot on English soil in January, 1230. He was not unknown when he disembarked. He was awaited both by the Friars Preachers, who would take advantage of his visit to celebrate the first Provincial Chapter in England, and by the Friars Minor, amongst whom he would find Haymon of Faversham and his companions, and among the higher clergy and in the schools where his reputation had preceded him.

His first stop was London. His visit there is marked by an anecdote of the Franciscan Annals, which show him visiting the Guardian of the Friary of the Minors in London, Brother Solomon. This gentle friar, model of poverty and of neighbourly love, had been received into the Order of St Francis by the Bishop of Canterbury and had come from there to London barefoot in the snow. As a result he had so bad a foot that he languished for two years in the London house, incapable of moving and threatened with an amputation. In his infirmity he merited to receive the visit of Brother Jordan, Master of the Friars Preachers, who comforted him and said to him; 'Why are you ashamed, brother, if the Father of our Lord Jesus Christ wished to draw you to him by the foot?'[1]

---

[1] *Analecta Francis.* T. I, p. 222: 'In hac infirmitate visitari meruit a sanctae memoriae fratre Jordano magistro totius Ordinis Praedicatorum qui dixit ei: "Frater, non verecunderis si Pater Domini nostri Jesu Christi traxerit te ad ipsum per pedem".'

If Jordan visited this sick man, who was soon to be cured, he also visited other Friars Minor and their houses. He doubtless had a mission from the Pope to the English Franciscan houses.

But his object was Oxford.

This beautiful English university was beginning to extend, under the shadows of its great parks, the noble colleges whose traditional architecture has preserved a cloistral aspect. It was said to owe its still recent origin to a first migration of students from Paris in 1167. The influx of 'strikers' from the Continent infused into it a wholly new life. Jordan was received in the house which the Friars Preachers had received from the Countess of Oxford when, after they had landed in the county of Kent in 1221, they had hastened to Oxford. It was modest; but there was adjoined to it a prosperous school, St Edward's, which from its origin had kept a Chair in Theology.[2] The comings and goings of the Friars Preachers and the students who frequented their school took them through the Jewish quarter of Oxford which surrounded the Church of St Edward; and so great a number of Jews were baptized by the friars that the king granted them a dwelling for the new converts.

But it was the University world which was the aim of Master Jordan's preaching. As soon as he arrived, he set to work: 'I write to you in good health, from England, before the Purification of the Blessed Virgin (February 2, 1230)', he writes to the Sisters of St Agnes. 'Pray for me unceasingly to the Lord that he may put his word into our mouths, for his own honour, the extension of the Church, and the increase of the Order. I have the hope that God will give us a good catch at the University of Oxford where I am now staying.'

---

[2] Its Lector in 1230 must have been Richard Fishacre, former student of the Faculty of Theology of Paris, who perhaps entered the Order at St Jacques. He died in 1248. Robert Killwardby succeeded him. The first Lector was Robert Bacon, who was probably still at Oxford in 1230.

What this preaching was and what its results, we do not know exactly. But the visit of Master Jordan left a lasting impression. We have proof of this in a letter to him later by Robert of Lincoln. This person with the singular surname, Master Robert Grosseteste (Greathead), called also Master Capito, was then teaching theology at Oxford.[3] He was a vigorous person, of a combative disposition, quick to act, the victim of frequent whims. At Paris he had studied and taught arts, medicine and theology; his Sentences, which are probably a resume of his lectures at Oxford, his commentaries on the pseudo-Dionysius, his translation from the Greek of Aristotle's *Ethics*, bear witness to the wealth and variety of his talent. He had experience as a physician and passed for a magician in the eyes of the common people. He must have known at Paris, among the physicians, his compatriot, the celebrated physician of Philip Augustus, John of St Giles, who later became a great theologian. It was in regard to the latter, then become a Dominican, that Robert Grosseteste, recently appointed Bishop of London, addresses this curious letter to Jordan in about 1235.

He first refers to their conversations at Oxford: 'We believe that your charity has not lost the memory of the frequent conversations which, with sweet affability, you accorded to us when you were at Oxford, nor with what an affectionate familiarity you were ready to welcome us.' Then he made his request. It was twofold; that Master Jordan should write to the Friars Preachers living at the Curia (Raymond of Pennafort was advocate of the Rota in 1235) for them to hurry the business of the diocese of Lincoln.[4]

---

[3] He had opened a school at Oxford; he was also the first professor of Sacred Sciences amongst the Franciscans of the Oxford Friary.—*Monumenta Francis.*, I, 37.

[4] These business matters were perhaps not without interest to the Friars Preachers themselves, and also to the Friars Minors. Robert of Lincoln had made himself the patron and propagator of the mendicant Orders in his diocese.

This diocese was the largest in the kingdom of Great Britain and had the largest population also, and this led to his second request: 'We have great need of an auxiliary to preach the word of God, to hear confessions, to impose penances, and with a sound knowledge of the Scriptures and a right judgment to advise us prudently in the cases which every day come up before our jurisdiction; and we could not wish to have for coadjutor a more efficient man than Brother John of St Giles, whose generosity, in consideration of our extreme necessity, would consent with good grace to our desire if your charity would give him liberty to do so.'[5]

Subsequent events showed that Jordan agreed to Robert's request, for John of St Giles left France for England in 1235 and looked after the bishop of Lincoln in his last illness. He died in 1253.

Meanwhile Lent came to a close and the General Chapter of Pentecost would soon require the presence of the Master of the Friars Preachers in Paris. But when in the very year of his visit to England and in the time immediately following, we see Priories multiplying one after the other in Great Britain, at Arundel, in Sussex, at Chichester and at Salisbury, and in Scotland, at Berwick, Edinburgh, Perth and Ayr, we are tempted to believe that before the Lent in Oxford Master Jordan had visited the bishops, and that the most-travelled roads of England and Scotland had seen him pass along them. The kind of people he could have seen at the principal stopping-places reinforces this hypothesis. Not far from Oxford, on the road to Lincoln, Coventry had for its bishop Alexander of Stavensby, the same who, when he was a professor of Holy Writ at Toulouse, had seen St Dominic attending his lectures with the first friars; afterwards, as a master at Bologna,

---

[5] A similar letter, probably written at about the same time, was addressed by R. Grosseteste to the Minister General of the Franciscans to ask them also for two friars who could preach and hear confessions.

probably from 1218 to 1224, he had known Jordan and liked him so well that he had encouraged several of his scholars to enter the Order of Preachers; later, consecrated bishop of Coventry and Lichfield, he could not have failed to want Jordan to visit him; and Jordan would have wanted to see him. At Lincoln, the see having jurisdiction over the clerics of Oxford, lived a learned prelate, Hugh Wells, the greatest friend of Robert Grosseteste who succeeded him and who said that there had never been but one heart and soul between them. He was then building the lordly nave of the cathedral. From Lincoln to Hull the distance was short; and the boats which sailed along the coast easily reached the mouth of the Tweed. The Friars Preachers crossed the latter, we know, in 1230 and established their first Priory on Scots soil at Berwick.[6] The foundation at Edinburgh followed almost immediately.

If Jordan did not go as far as Scotland, it is inconceivable that he did not at least make a stop in the south of Great Britain—at Reading where the court resided; at Salisbury whose treasurer, former master at Oxford—where he had had the Friars Preachers Bacon and Fishacre as disciples—was no other than St Edmund; at Chichester where, a few years later, the bishop would be Richard of Wych, that Saint Richard, sprung from the common people, learned in theology and ordained priest by the Friars Preachers at Orléans, meanwhile studying at Bologna and at Paris, a figure of edification whose biographer was an English Dominican.[7]

Perhaps it was during the course of these visits that it was decided to create an official house of Friars Preachers at Bordeaux, where the Plantagenet influence was then dominant.[8] It was a

---

[6] The first Prior was Brother Clement, a Scot, received into the Order in Paris in 1219, and in 1233 made bishop of Dunblane.

[7] Ralph Booking, *op. cit.*

[8] The act conceding to the Friars Preachers an establishment at Bordeaux is dated 1230.

quick journey from Salisbury or from Chichester to Southampton or Newhaven. Jordan returned to Paris on May 26, 1230.

He came back rich with information about the generous welcome given in England to the students from Paris. No doubt the Regent, the bishop and the new legate all consulted the traveller on his return. The situation had become serious. The strike was being prolonged. Nobody knew whether the deserters would return in September. The Paris of the University, like a desert now, was lugubrious. The townsfolk themselves bitterly regretted the exodus of these young men on whose spending they depended for their livelihood.

While the students and masters sent a representative to the Pope, the pride of Blanche of Castile and the rigidity of William of Auvergne and the stand taken by public opinion began to relent.

Jordan would leave soon for Italy and his influence would make itself felt both in Paris and in Rome in the outcome of this conflict. But he stayed a little while longer at St Jacques. He was there, we are certain, at a noteworthy ceremony on September 22, 1230.

On this day Master John of St Giles took the habit from Jordan's hands; and his entrance into the Order would give the Friars Preachers of St Jacques their second Chair of Theology at the University of Paris.

The entrance of John of St Giles amongst the Friars Preachers of St Jacques raised again and finally resolved the question of the incorporation of the Dominicans into the University of Paris and the conferring of the second Chair of Theology which had been conceded to them.

Too much credence has been given to the letter written on the subject on February 4, 1254, by the secular Masters of the schools of Paris. Formulated to meet the needs of the cause, at the height of the quarrel between the seculars and the religious, this document, as Humbert of Romans declared only a few years later, is 'a tissue of lies'. It was meant to rouse opinion against the Friars

Preachers, who were supposed to have profited by the circumstances of the strike of 1229-1231 to infiltrate in some degree into the University.

First of all, it sought to establish that with a master created by the doctors pertaining to their first chair the Friars Preachers had themselves established a second, and that after the return of the secession of 1229.[9] But, if Roland of Cremona, occupant of the first chair, left that chair to his confrere Hugh of St Cher when he departed for Toulouse in the summer of 1229, we have a simple succession in the same chair, not a multiplication.

The holder of the second chair was a Master in Theology well before he put on the habit of the Friars Preachers; he was John of St Giles. And—this is an important point which is established by the manuscript text of the sermon he gave on the day he was clothed—it was not after the return of the seculars, but in 1230, when, passing from the secular clergy into the Dominican rule, John of St Giles gave the Priory of St Jacques the chair which he already occupied.

John of St Giles, an Englishman by birth, was first famous in the arts and in medicine, which he studied and taught at Montpellier (where he probably got his surname of St Giles) and then at Paris. He never ceased to practise medicine; he effected numerous cures in England and took care of Robert of Lincoln until his last illness; Oxford still preserves manuscript treatises on medicine attributed to him. According to tradition, which is somewhat mixed up with a legend about a certain Giles of Corbeil, who was also a physician at the same time, he had given medical attention to Philip Augustus. But later he entered upon the study of theology. A doctor of good repute, he wrote his lectures in theology, after he entered the Order, at the urgent request of his

---

[9] Deinde studio nostro apostolica provisione Parisiis reformato, per eandem cathedram multiplicatis sibi doctoribus... per se ipsos secundam cathedram erexerunt. Chart. Un. Par. p. 253 I.

hearers. The annotated manuscripts of his books, which certain contemporaries of Nicholas Trivet seem to have seen, bear witness to his profound knowledge of the Scriptures.

The letter of Robert Grosseteste which asks for him to be sent back to the diocese of Lincoln, describes him as a reliable jurist and a fine case-lawyer. After teaching at St Jacques from 1233, he was to occupy the chair of Toulouse for two years as the successor of Roland of Cremona, and then he was to return to England where Robert of Lincoln would make him his coadjutor. He was an excellent preacher and very much appreciated by his students.

His entry into the Order of Preachers must be counted as one of Jordan's most decisive victories. John of St Giles had passed through and obtained all the University degrees; he enjoyed fame and wealth; and, already mature, ripe with experience of things and of men, he came to put all his knowledge at the service of the Friars Preachers and to embrace their life of poverty. Doubtless he did not enter without a struggle. He also, like Walter of Strasbourg and many others, had resisted this late vocation. But it won this time and he desired to make his taking of the habit an example for others.

It was on a Sunday, the feast of St Maurus and companions, martyrs. John of St Giles must have preached the sermon at the High Mass to the friars of St Jacques and the students who filled the nave of the church. He preached, according to the account given by Nicholas Trivet, on voluntary poverty; and striving to persuade the students to follow a life of poverty, and the better to enforce his words by a public act, he went down from the pulpit, received the habit of the Friars Preachers, and then went up again and finished his sermon.[10]

He had himself gone through 'the narrow gate, the gate of

---

[10] '... quorum Joannes de sancto Ægidio... in domo fratrum Praedicatorum sermonem faciens ad clerum, cum suasisset paupertatem voluntariam, ut verba sua exemplo confirmaret, descendens de ambone, habitum fratrum recepit, et oedem regressus ad pulpitam sermonem explevit.'—Nich. Trivet.

death-to-self which leads to life'—'the clerics know it is so, but they abound in reasonings against reason. The latter tells them that it is good to enter religion and to bear the yoke of obedience; the former says, on the contrary, that it is freedom which is good, and they play the devil's game. So, the world is a house in ruins; is it not senseless to take a ladder to climb up it (in coveting titles, houses, riches, horses) at the very moment when it is going to crumble?'[11] In this way, more or less, John of St Giles tries to induce his listeners to imitate him. Noted down, doubtless, by a listener, the transcription of this sermon which has come down to us is only approximate, but it is a prize; Master Jordan heard these words and approved of them; they show the kind of eloquence which he loved to hear spoken to students, of which he himself must have given example with even more force and charm.

There he was, on this September 22, 1230; and if we could reconstruct the living sermon of John of St Giles on this slope of Mount St Geneviève, which today is levelled, something of Jordan himself would live again.

While he listened to him, however, the Master General was far from in a dream. This reception of one of the principal theologians of the University of Paris into the Priory of St Jacques was the fulfilment of his dearest wish.

Of one mind with the Roman Curia, the bishop, and the legate, he had been able two years before to give the studium of the Friars Preachers an official chair. Roland of Cremona and then Hugh of St Cher, had founded and maintained it. Now it was John of St Giles who, having become a Dominican, doctor that he was, brought his own professorship into the studium of St Jacques and, at the opening of the scholastic year of 1230, brought his students with him. By force of circumstances, or even more by the

---

[11] The text of this sermon is found in MS. 338BN Nelles acq. lat. fo 9. It was edited by M. M. Davy. Supplement to the Spiritual Life, September 1928, p. 80 et seq.

irresistible attraction of an apostolate which drew the best of the Parisian masters towards St Jacques, a second professorship was added to the first in the cloister of the Friars for the triumphant teaching of truth, for the salvation of souls and for the service of the Church. The Order went straight ahead in a way truly its own; and at the end of the liturgical year Jordan could write to his dear daughters, the nuns of St Agnes, who, near or far, he knew were always praying for the intentions of the Order: 'Give thanks to the generous Lord for the great number of famous and learned men, already having their master's degree, whom he has given this year to our Order.'

He added at the end of the same letter: 'Pray for me that I may be brought soon and happily to you.'

He was already in Italy, but doubtless he had come by the Corniche and Genoa, the most convenient way in winter to cross the Alps, and he had not yet touched Bologna. Where was he? The forceful Bull—sent from Anagni by Gregory IX to the canons of Chartres on November 9—which would decide finally the establishment of the schools of the Friars Preachers at Chartres, where many Parisian students were still to be found, shows such precision and reflects so accurately Jordan's activities in that same place in the Province of France, that we are inclined to think that his steps were first turned toward the Roman Curia. In that same month of November 1231, another document witnesses his passage through Anagni; it is an official document[12] drawn up in the church of the Friars Preachers at Bologna in execution of a letter of the Pope addressed to three apostolic visitors: 'In consideration of the decline of the monastery of St Adalbert at Padua and the necessities of the poor Sisters of St Agnes at Bologna, whose pure

---

[12] Text in Melloni. *Appendice degli atti della B. Diana d'Andalo.* A document of March 14, 1331, completes the concession of a group of neighbouring lands to the Sisters of St Agnes by the Fathers of St Jacques of Cella, Volana, 'adtendentes quod de voluntate Domini Pape proceditur, sicut ex relatione Fr Rodulfi Ord. Praed. intelleximus'. This must have been Bro. Rudolph of Faenza.

life and fervent devotion should receive a recompense, there is assigned to the aforesaid Sisters the properties of St Adalbert and the revenues of all its possessions, lands, woods, fields, and fishponds.' Jordan surely must have had something to do with such a donation!

At the same time there was effected, as Gregory IX and certainly Master Jordan also greatly desired, one of the most wished-for and one of the most important foundations of the Order of Preachers. In spite of the opposition of Frederick II, the friars had secured a footing in Naples, near that would-be University, rival of Bologna, the most modern and the most daring of the centres of medieval studies. Their Priory, and soon their studium of theology, would become singularly attractive to the best of the students of Naples. If Lombardy had canonists and lawyers, the kingdom of Naples, a land alight with mirthful knowledge, subtle versifiers, erudite inquirers, curious doctors of medicine, gathered the flower of brilliant youth into its schools, those interested in science and art. That Master Jordan went to Naples, preached there, and prepared, if he did not gather in, future harvests, cannot be doubted; and it is probable that he was influential in turning the attention of the Sovereign Pontiff in this direction.

But where his presence shows most plainly is in the work of providing information and of diplomacy which, by a series of acts emanating from the Apostolic See, finally terminated the strike of the Parisian clerics. Who then, if not he, could have informed Gregory IX in such detail about the facts, places and persons, could have had such a knowledge of complex causes of strife, such moderation in the appreciation of responsibilities, such a care for the proper pursuit of studies, and all the while such a paternal indulgence for the youth of the schools?

All these traits characterize the Bull addressed from the Lateran Palace on April 13, 1231, to the masters and students of the University of Paris. It guaranteed, first, the level of studies and independence and peace in the schools; in all the Faculties only those would be admitted to the mastership who were worthy of it in the opinion of their masters, and the bishop himself must bow to the sole authority of the masters.[13] The books of physics of Aristotle were forbidden. The students must not bear arms. But all the scholastic privileges were restored to them, very much reinforced.

Neither the bishop, nor the abbots who had schools under their jurisdiction, would be concerned with the hours of lectures, the expulsion of students, the fixing of agreed rents by the townsfolk, matters all to be left to the care of the masters. The students could not be put into protective custody, they could not be imprisoned for debt; those who were excommunicated could receive absolution without paying fines. The chancellor took an oath to respect the rights of the University. The latter retained the right of suspending its courses if its privileges were violated. They made the University a sort of inviolable person. It was the opposite of what Frederick II was attempting at Naples, and of what Roland of Cremona had to fight at Toulouse; Jordan of Saxony and Gregory IX were the first to understand all the worth of intellectual and spiritual power that the University of Paris then represented.

The Bull of April 13, 1231, was also followed up by three individual letters addressed respectively to the bishop of Paris, the dean of St Marcel, and the Abbot of St Germain des Prés, inviting them to have the townsfolk under their jurisdiction take an oath to keep peace with the students; by a letter to the chapter of Notre Dame—written, doubtless, not to stir up discord again, but to frighten agitators—directing a judicial inquiry into the violences

---

[13] In a Bull of September 7,1237, annulling the degrees of canon law granted by the bishop of Paris without the permission of the Masters, Gregory IX wrote to the Professors of the University: 'We do not intend to let your rights be violated, even by a Bishop of Paris.' Jordan was then dead; but his spirit still lived.

of the Faubourg St Marcel; by a letter to the King of France asking him to ensure the carrying out of the apostolic commands.[14] The honour of his kingdom, the generous traditions of his ancestors, who were protectors of sciences and arts, and the renown of his capital were all involved.

Such preciseness, calculated to touch so many people at the same time and at the very points where they must be touched to be convinced, all this shows the experience and almost the hand of Master Jordan. The Curia could certainly not have had any collaborator more devoted and better informed about the delicately balanced government of the schools.

If he went to Rome, he left nevertheless afterwards to preach the Lent at Padua.[15] He did not go back through Bologna, and he writes to Diana: 'Soon, God willing, we shall be able to console one another. Meanwhile Brother Henry, Provincial of the overseas Province, will console you and until my arrival will take my place near you.'

This was Henry of Germany, appointed by the Most General Chapter of 1228 as Prior of the Holy Land. He had come to get himself absolved from his office at the Chapter of Bologna (May 11, 1231). Landing at Brindisi or Naples, he went first to Rome, no doubt accompanied the Master General part of the way, then left him and went on ahead to Bologna, instructed by Jordan to visit the Sisters of St Agnes.

Master Jordan was reaping a full and laborious harvest among the students of Padua.

Two letters, one addressed to Diana, the other to the Prior and Brethren of St Jacques in Paris, were written by him from Padua

---

[14] The Bull specified one of the sharpest grievances of the students against the townsfolk: the excessive price of lodgings! The king was to watch that the prices of lodgings were established by a committee of arbitrators in which, against two townsfolk, there should be two doctors of the University.

[15] 'Jordanus Paduae praedicabat annis 1229 et 1231.'—Berthier.

during the octave of Easter[16] and most probably on the same day.

The letter to Diana was a short one, urging her to have patience.

The letter to the Brethren at St Jacques was an instruction on the occasion of Paschaltide.

This letter seems to coincide with the end of the students' strike and the return of concord to the University world. Its wording seems to indicate also, very probably, the completion of the work of enlarging the Priory of St Jacques, which finally allowed the Friars Preachers who had been lodged in nearby houses to be united and to begin to practise regular observance in a large house suitable for study and recollection.

'I have learned, most dear ones, and this news fills me with joy, that, all reunited under the same roof and in the most perfect accord, you persevere in prayer, applying yourselves to study and growing in peace and in mutual charity.'

A holy tenderness, a gentle confidence, reflect in these fatherly pages the joy of the apostle who sees his work blessed. 'I write to you from Padua. The Lord has just given us thirty novices, learned and entirely suited to the Order; several are of noble birth and were masters in the University. On Holy Wednesday I received Master James, archdeacon of Ravenna, provost of Bobbio, the best professor of law in all Lombardy, a man of good counsel, of a great reputation, excellent habits, rare amiability, who has refused a bishopric to enter the Order.[17] I have received with him a young man of great talent, very well versed in arts, son of one of the most noble families of Hungary.'

He adds with a touching modesty about himself and a careful solicitude for the Order, '—thanks be to Heaven, our friars work in

---

[16] Between March 14 and 21, 1231

[17] This man may be James Buoncambio, already a witness in Bologna in 1213-1214; later charged with important duties in the Roman Curia and bishop of Bologna.

the Church with great success and abundant fruits.'

The same news, in the same terms, was given to Diana.

A few weeks later, Diana saw her Father at last. The General Chapter was held at Bologna on Whit Sunday (May 11, 1231), with Master Jordan presiding.

Shortly after that, he had departed and was preaching to the students at Modena, then at Reggio, at Milan, and finally at Vercelli.

'I stayed a week at Modena; there I sowed much seed, but because of my sins had little harvest. Then leaving Modena, I came to Reggio.'

He had renewed contact with his daughters at St Agnes, both those inside and those outside, the old and the new; for he greets the Prioress, who must then have been Cecilia Caesarini, the successor of Lady Agnes; he greets Sister Jordana, and Galiana, and Julietta, and Cardiana, and 'all the others' he says to Diana 'whom you know to be my friends'. But the visit was short, the leaving abrupt; Jordan had not taken leave of his nuns by a formal farewell and they complained about it, and Jordan himself felt it too; but he reproached Diana for her excessive sensitiveness: 'When I have to leave you, I do not do so without anguish of heart; nevertheless you add to my pain... Why do you torment yourself like this? ... What would you do if I should die? ... Even at my death you ought not to mourn in such an unconsolable way... I should be more useful to you living with the Lord than kept in this world and dying here each day... Be braver.'

In a subsequent letter he says to her again: 'Do not be at all anxious about me.'

Evidently Diana was uneasy. She was worried, it seems, about Jordan's health. He must have seemed tired; and in spite of her prayers, perhaps against the advice of the doctors, the untiring preacher had taken to the road again.

Let him at least come back to have a rest at Bologna; the air of the Emelia is more healthy in the summer and autumn than the climate of the swampy Lombard plain. But no; he will arrange for stopping places, that is all. 'I have made plans to go by short stages, from priory to priory, until I have crossed the mountains; I would like to do so before winter. It has become too difficult for me to return to Bologna.'

This crossing of the mountains is the passage of the Alps, toward Germany, doubtless by way of the Gotthard Pass.[18] Henry of Germany went with Jordan, and it was he who first fell dangerously ill at Vercelli. 'Brother Henry is dangerously ill; I recommend him to you urgently and to your Sisters to pray fervently for him, for we fear that we may lose him.' He got better, however, but Jordan in his turn was laid low with fever. His preaching at Reggio had been very fruitful. 'I believe that you know enough'—intermediary letters evidently have been lost—'on the subject of those who entered the Order at Reggio. I ask you only to give thanks to God.' At Vercelli an important group of students had been won over; as there was still no house of Friars Preachers at Vercelli, the Master had taken them to Milan; from there he was preparing to continue the crossing of the Alps. Sickness prevented him.

'You know, my dear, what has happened to me and how, when I came back from Vercelli with eight novices—eight good novices, learned and well made for your Order—and was planning to go next into Germany, I was taken with a tertian fever. I had three attacks of it, as I said in my previous letter, and I am awaiting the fourth... I write to you myself, because perhaps you would be worried otherwise', he adds with affectionate concern, 'if you heard this news from someone else... Brother Henry has been

---

[18] Leaving Milan, this is the shortest route; it had not long been open. It was the development of the Hapsburg power which had, between 1218 and 1226, or about that, given it importance, and, abandoning the slopes of the Grisons, the people of Uri had widened and graded the muleteer road of the Gotthard. The Benedictines of Disentis soon established a hospice there. (Geographical Dictionary of Switzerland.)

cured, I hope, by your prayers; he will go ahead of me into Germany. Take care not to be frightened by my illness, for I hope that it will improve me in soul and in body. The Lord has given us his gifts at Reggio and Vercelli; doubtless it has pleased him—as is right—that I should not receive them entirely gratuitously. Blessed be his name forever... Tell the Brothers how I am.' This illness must have lasted some months. The letters to Diana permit us to follow its principal phases in the medical language of the times; after the tertian fever there followed, with several disorders, the quartian fever or fevers, doubtless of different kinds, for Jordan says he had endured three. 'After having been severely tried, not only with quartian fever, but with other disorders too, I am now free of them. They even think that I am completely free of one of the three quartian fevers which I have had.'

Convalescence was long: 'I am exhausted with suffering and worn out by the illness I have undergone.'

He had to give up his visit to Germany. The winter was over and spring was at hand; Master Jordan was still at Milan. That he was still there at the end of February, 1232, is proved by a parchment from the archives of Genoa, copied from a document drawn up at Milan in the house of the Friars Preachers, in his presence, and doubtless upon his orders.

This curious document relates to an obscure affair between Alessandrians and Genoese, in which a Friar Preacher of great renown, Brother Bartholomew of Vicenza, was strangely mixed up. The war between Alessandria and Genoa about the possession of the fortress of Capriata had not even yet, since the death of Brancaleone in 1225, come to a lasting truce. Constant skirmishes took place which kindled the conflict again. Sometimes it was the Alessandrians invading the territory of Asti, sometimes it was the Genoese who, in spite of the watchfulness of the Alessandrians, favoured the immigration into Capriata of mercenaries in search of adventure and thus, little by little, would succeed in introducing a menacing garrison into that place; then the Alessandrians would attack, pillaging everything, and afterwards would reconstruct the ruins they had caused and fortify them in their turn, and it would start all over again.

Milan was interested in these turbulent intrigues. Capriata commanded the road which, coming from the coast, penetrated into the interior. The commune of Milan had tried to mediate, but without success.

Finally, towards the end of the year 1230, the arrival of a new *podesta* allowed the party in favour of peace to triumph at Alessandria. A compromise with Genoa was envisaged and arbitrators appointed to effect it: for Alessandria a certain Sardus, archpriest of Alba: for Genoa, the Prior of the Hospitallers of St John, William of Vultabio. But, as they could not come to an agreement, they made Genoa and Alessandria agree upon a third arbitrator chosen by them as a mediator: Brother Bartholomew of Vicenza. He was a distinguished lawyer, who had been born at Vicenza of the patrician family of the Broganza; he had been received into the Order at Padua probably about 1219 or 1220 by St Dominic himself. Having studied theology, from 1224 he was lector and then Master of Sacred Science at the Priory of Bologna. The chronicle of Salimbene shows him arriving at Padua in 1233, where he preached marvellously, worked miracles, and founded an association of lay-men consecrated to the service of the Church, the militia of Jesus Christ. He taught later, in 1235, at the Roman Curia and became chaplain and confessor to Gregory IX. He assisted at the Council of Lyons in 1245 and was appointed bishop of Cyprus, where he received and confessed St Louis; he was bishop of Vicenza from 1255 to 1270. He was an eminent preacher, a great lawyer and diplomat.

His dealings with the Genoese were astonishing.

They took place just between the years 1230 and 1233, which his biographers have left empty, whether because they were ignorant of the facts or because they did not wish to relate such a painful incident.

But this story shows too well how Jordan of Saxony handled these diplomatic affairs to be left in obscurity. Moreover, it does not diminish in any way the holiness or the delicacy of Brother Bartholomew. It seems rather that he was a victim of his own confidence. He was, at this time, a very much esteemed and very popular peacemaker in Lombardy. He had left Bologna and was attached in 1231—with what duties we do not know—either to the Priory at Milan or to that at Genoa. It was he then who brought Sardus and William of Vultabio into agreement, and made them accept one of those provisional arrangements which, by gaining time, calm anger and check violence. After a year of truce, dating from the feast of the Purification of the Blessed Virgin, February 2, 1231, a final peace could be concluded between the Genoese and the Alessandrians. What were to be the conditions of it? Exactly what was contained in these documents, sealed with the seals of the three arbitrators and secretly deposited, according to the usage of the times? The complete silence of the Genoese annalist—one of the three who drew up the documents—and the absence of the signature of the Alessandrian legal representative at the bottom of the documents, gives one to suppose that there was interpolation or fraud. In truth, even after the scrupulous and scholarly publication of the documents in the Genoese archives by Dr G. Caro, this whole affair remains insoluble. A letter written by Brother Bartholomew to William of Vultabio, at a time when the Friar Preacher, discouraged by the difficulties of these long debates, had doubtless returned to Milan, bears witness only to the tension between the arbitrators and the uneasiness of the mediator. Faithful to his obligations, he did not wish to break off negotiations. He could not nor did he wish to change the tenor of the judgment which he had dictated, he said; he knew, moreover, what dangers he ran, especially on the part of the Alessandrians, and he could not look forward without anguish to the end of the year and the opening of the treaty which would deceive their hopes. He suffered bitterly from the slanders spread against him, and threw himself on the mercy of God.

This letter seemed to have been solicited, or at least provoked, by the *podesta* of Genoa, who put it on record to calm the rumours which were current in the councils of the commune.

But what happened in the interval? The year passed by and the seals of the secret treaty were broken; it was at Genoa that public anger flared out. The Genoese would not accept the sharing of Capiatra with the Alessandrians. The Alessandrians, exasperated, laid waste the surroundings of Capiatra. Then finally peace was restored and eventually Capiatra was taken over by the Genoese.

We get the impression of a certain confusion, perhaps voluntary, in the whole conduct of this affair; it even seems that Brother Bartholomew had not only been deceived, but that someone had tried to pin on to him, one way or another, all the suspicions.

The thing could have grave consequences for the Friars Preachers. They had not acquired in Lombardy the privileged position which would permit them to preach everywhere and increase the number of their houses there except by the favour of the Communes. If the latter became hostile to them, it would mean stopping the Friars' apostolate in a very short time, a disaster both temporal and spiritual.

This was in February, 1232. Master Jordan was at Milan. With him was the Provincial of Lombardy, Stephen of Spain. At their request, doubtless, an inquiry was held, led by the archbishop of Genoa. A document in the Genoese archives shows that a number of notables were gathered in the presence of the archbishop in his own palace. The Prior of the Friars Preachers of Genoa read the judgment delivered by Brother Bartholomew, which the latter had believed was really placed under seal; he affirmed that no other Preachers had ever been a witness in this affair; if a signature, and moreover one that had been altered, was followed by the title of the Prior of the Friars Preachers of Genoa, it was a forgery. The responsibility of the Order was cleared. All the blame fell back on Bartholomew alone.

That was not all.

A few days later, at Milan, another scene took place, more solemn, more dramatic, and in the presence of Jordan.

The Master General had exacted from Brother Bartholomew of Vicenza a sort of public confession, the terms of which seem to have been carefully chosen and dictated in advance. Humbly prostrate, poor Bartholomew vowed that he had let himself be deceived by weakness, to the prejudice of the Genoese, that he had failed in firmness and in clarity during the debates with the arbitrators, and—the essential thing—'having come to himself, whole in body and mind', he accused himself in vehement terms 'of having sinned against the Order, of having broken the Constitution (issued doubtless in a preceding provincial chapter held at Milan) which forbade Friars ever to intervene in civil litigation, or ever to be arbitrators or mediators except in cases where faith or doctrine were in question.'[19]

The act which recorded this curious declaration was drawn up forthwith 'in the house of the Friars Preachers, near the church of St Eustorgius' at Milan, and a certified copy was also made by a Genoese notary and taken back to Genoa.

This rapidity, this precision, the decisive authority; at a comprehensive glance, there can be no doubt but that this was all

---

[19] G. Caro: legalized copy by a Genoese notary of the document drawn up at Milan in the house of the Friars: 'Actu Mediolani iuxta S. Eustorgi in domo fratrum predicatorum.' Here is the beginning of the document: 'Ego frater Bartholomeus Vicentinus nunc ad eos et ad meam sanam conscientiam reversus, spontaneus et voluntarius, coram vobis magistro, Jordano ordinis fratrum predicatorum magistro et coram frate Stephano priore provinciali in Lombardia et coram fratre Olrico prior fratrum predicatorum de Januis, protestore confiteor, et dico me... Deum... et totum nostrum ordinem graviter offendisse... fera me eligi in arbitrum... inter duos arbitros... de discordis et litibus seu controversiis quod vertebantur inter commune... contra mandatum speciale factum in capitulo provinciali quod fuit Mediolani...'

Master Jordan's doing.

We know how numerous Dominican peacemakers were at this time in Italy. Brother John of Vicenza would soon play, at Bologna itself, a striking public role. It is to be remarked that Jordan is never mentioned where John of Vicenza's activities are concerned and that he seems never to have been present at his preaching. He let him go on at his own risk and peril; that was all. He himself—as we have seen in relation to the Emperor Frederick II—never engaged in negotiations of a political character. He knew too well the danger of this slippery and so unstable ground.

At Milan, he did not hesitate to oblige a Brother whom he esteemed and he loved, and whom he certainly knew was destined for a high career in the Roman Curia, to proclaim himself 'a poor imbecile', deprived of good sense, astray even in the judgment of his conscience, rather than compromise the security of the Priory of Genoa and risk the good name of the Friars Preachers in Lombardy.

It is possible that some time after that Jordan went to Genoa to put the last finishing touch to this thorny story. His itinerary is not known to us. He left Milan with the intention of being present at the General Chapter in Paris (Pentecost 1232).

Diana had doubtless hoped that the Chapter of the Lombard Province would bring Jordan back to Bologna before he left for Paris. But no. He writes to her: 'Feeble as I am, to come to Bologna and go back would be too long a journey for me; already my time draws near to take the road to Paris so as to be there for the General Chapter (Pentecost 1232), if thanks to your prayers the Lord condescends to permit me to do so. As for the state in which I find myself at present, Prior Nicholas and his companions will be able to give you details about it.'

This Prior Nicholas must be the Prior of the Roman Province, Brother Nicholas Palea, of Giovinazzo. It is known of him that he was received into the Order by St Dominic and was an excellent physician; Thomas de Cantimpré has an account of Jordan being sick and being cared for by a Prior of the Order, learned in medicine, who asked of him to forget the fact that he was Master General and to submit to his prescriptions in all obedience. Perhaps the good chronicler, to be more edifying, had mixed up times and places a little; a part of his account, which took place in the palace of a bishop, belongs to Besançon; another is better fitted to some town 'at the foot of the Alps' also possessed of a bishopric. This could be Milan. As for Prior Nicholas, if he was not sent to Jordan in his capacity of physician, which is quite possible, he had come to discuss various pieces of business with him; a later letter lends credence to this: 'I have written to the Provincial (of Lombardy) telling him that I shall be glad to grant the request of Brother Nicholas concerning this young girl. Let this not trouble you', writes Jordan to Diana. (Perhaps it was a question of taking some young novice away from St Agnes to transfer her to St Sixtus?) 'Brother Nicholas worries very much over it and has been very insistent, and I should find it difficult not to give ear to a man like him, who is so dear to us, and who is so necessary to our Order.'

Leaving Jordan convalescent at Milan, Brother Nicholas took the road to Rome again; he would go by way of Bologna and he was charged with messages from the Master; he carried letters.

As always, Jordan mingled attention to practical details with the highest spirituality in his advice to Diana: 'I warn you, in case you meet some contrariness to your will in regard to this little Lambertina girl, that you do not allow yourself to be in the least troubled about it; but bear it with patience'; and later: 'If you judge that you ought to receive the Lambertina girl, you have leave to do so, and whatever you may do, I approve of in advance.' It was probably a question of a little 'conversa' whose profession was meeting with some obstacle. In the same letter Jordan greets, besides his daughters in Christ the nuns of the convent, 'the other persons living outside the convent, to whom you know that I love to send a spiritual greeting' and 'all those whom I love and who love me, more especially those whom you know to be particularly my friends'. His meaning is transparent; it is a question of the Tertiaries. The General Chapter of Paris would try again to make some anti-feminist ruling which could affect them; and Jordan, 'judging that this decision was worth nothing', would have it entirely withdrawn.

Meanwhile he lifts the discussion to the spiritual plane: 'Only over the loss of the grace of God, must the souls of holy people sigh and be troubled. And should God even permit (that you have such a loss) I should hope in his mercy and I expect of his grace that he would give you more abundant consolations... The words of the Apostle (Rom. VIII, 28) are true; all things work together for good for those who love God and are called by him unto sanctification.'

This meditation, Jordan could apply to himself.

He had tried to take the road to France. He did leave Milan; but he fell ill before having reached the end of the journey and could not be present at the General Chapter in Paris.

'After I left Lombardy and was making my way towards the Chapter; I reached Turegum and again fell gravely ill, so much so that I was prevented from going to the General Chapter. It is because I was not there that the definitors, who knew little about the situation at St Agnes, made a certain decision which was not good for you. But as soon as I was informed of it, I had it entirely withdrawn.' Where was this letter written? Had Jordan arrived at Paris after the General Chapter, and did he spend the summer there? Had he changed his itinerary?

There is a complete gap here, without any pointers to help us. In spirit, however, the Master was present both in Bologna and Paris, and at Colmar where this year (1232) Walter of Strasbourg established the Unterlinden, and at Chartres where the new Priory expanded in study and teaching. Everywhere obstacles had been overcome and dangers removed; the pilot was at the helm.

CHAPTER XI
THE LAST YEARS

HE years passed; soon St Dominic had been dead twelve years, and the full life of Dominican work grew stronger from day to day; its characteristics more sharply defined, its place in the world more certain. The year 1233 was to be a sort of triumphal year for the Order. The making of peace in Lombardy, largely due to the Friars Preachers, made the people of Lombardy call it the year of Alleluia or of 'devotion'; it was also the year of the first solemn translation of St Dominic and the opening of the process of his canonization.

Master Jordan did not take any primary part, at any rate by direct action, either in the Alleluia or the process of canonization. Not that there could have been any voluntary withdrawal on his part; no one was more convinced of the sanctity of St Dominic than he. But he left it to those to speak who were best qualified to bear witness to St Dominic's life and acts, to those who had been the companions of his studies and his journeys, to those first associated with his earliest endeavours, to those already favoured with miracles in his name—Stephen of Spain, John of Navarre, Guala of Bergamo.

As for public enthusiasm, he admired the way it clung to the Friars Preachers, but he did not trust its capricious waves. Seeing John of Vicenza threatened at Bologna with a quasi-dictatorship, he did not hesitate to remove him, in spite of the request of the commune. Himself a man of learning as well as a magnificent orator, he was not a man for public affairs. On the contrary, he fashioned for himself more and more, it seems, a perfectly-defined conception of his proper role as Master General and as a preacher, and he adhered to it with a firm moderation.

While Guala of Bergamo, bishop and legate, exercised his influence over the Diet of Ravenna, while John of Vicenza, by his speech to the assembly of Paquara, effected the reconciliation of

400,000 men, as contemporaries tell us, and afterwards entered Brescia in the municipal state coach, while Bartholomew of Vicenza was acclaimed at Parma, while Jacobin of Reggio and Peter of Verona brought peace in the market-towns between families which had been divided by heresy and politics, Master Jordan went back to the students of Padua.

He was already there during Advent of the year 1232. He may have come there before the snows, in the golden autumn, by the familiar roads of the Jura and the Vaudois country.

Something new drew him to Lausanne. His old friend Boniface of Brussels had been installed in the episcopal see there on March 11, 1232, and one of the first things he did, in the year 1232, was to give a house and a church to the Friars Preachers there.

The poetical anecdote of the *Vitae Fratrum* which describes Master Jordan walking outside Lausanne and interrupting his talk about things of God to admire and bless an ermine, took place very probably at this time.

He had gone out of the city, the account tells us, to go and see the bishop who was at his country house, for they had long had a great friendship for one another. Several friars walked ahead of him and he followed behind, speaking of Jesus with the treasurer of the church in Lausanne. The light was shining on the summits, as in the approach of winter, the lake showed below, between the bare red wild-grape vines which lined the pathway. And here a little animal shot across the road like an arrow and disappeared into a hole. The friars stopped; it was a weasel, they thought, but it was all white![1] They had never seen anything so pretty. The Master joined them, asking: 'What is the matter?' They told him; and leaning over the hole he said: 'Come out, beautiful little animal, and let us see you.' And the little animal showed itself at

---

[1] The ermine is a member of the weasel family. The weasel is the most common of the Martens and it is reddish. The ermine is white, especially in winter. This is why the anecdote probably took place between November and April, most likely in November.

the opening of its burrow and stayed there without moving, fixing the master with its piercing little eyes. And he, placing a hand under its front paws, with the other stroked its head and its back; it allowed him to do this and did not disappear until he said to it: 'Now go back to your home, and bless the Lord who created you.' The friars of Lausanne re-told this story one to another, and it was written down by Gerard de Frachet.

We are not told whether it was by the St Bernard or the Simplon pass that Jordan went from Lausanne to Lombardy, then to Padua and then to Reggio where he opened a Priory.

But a letter to Diana, written certainly a little before Christmas,[2] tells us about his preaching to the students and about the recruits whom he had drawn to the Order: 'Already our Lord Jesus has given us several students of Padua, learned, suited to the office of preachers, and he has touched the hearts of many others living in the world but who in the present and in the future will be aided by the power of your prayers; one of the others is in great peril, to such an extent that he fears he is in mortal sin; so I recommend him to you earnestly that you breathe for him such warm prayers that God will not abandon him but will come to his help and deliver him from all harmful assaults.'

He came to the Order, in fact, if this is the young German of whom the *Vitae Fratrum* speaks, and he drew his Master to it.[3] Advent at Padua, Lent at Reggio, Jordan then journeyed toward Bologna where the General Chapter of Pentecost (May 24, 1233)

---

[2] Letter XLIV A, L B: 'Fortify yourself and console yourself in the Little Child who will soon be born for you...'

[3] Vit. Fratr. 3a Chap. 14, p. 110, Bertheir: 'Cum idem magister (Jordanus) Padua ubi tunc erat studium magnum instantissime predicaret, recipit quendam scolarem Theutonicum genere nobilem... cujus magister et socii prescientes ingressum tanquam ministri dyaboli quandem mulierem secundum carnem formosam cum eo in camera clauserunt ut per voluptatem camis ejus meritum averterent a proposito suo sacrato. Sed Christus eo vincit et ad ordinem eum forcius traxit... qui etiam post modum magistrum suum ad ordinem induxit.'

was to be celebrated, and where would take place with great ceremony, in the presence of the Pope and a great concourse of cardinals, bishops and notabilities, the translation of the body of St Dominic to the first tomb which replaced the poor slab of his first burial-place. It was the prelude to his canonization, which was to be proclaimed by Gregory IX on July 9, 1234. Jordan then drafted a long circular letter to send to all the Priories of the Friars Preachers, relating the circumstances of this translation and the miracles which accompanied it. We again find the precision which was habitual to him and which he knew how to combine with the most moving piety. It is the only one of his circular letters—although assuredly they must have been numerous during his mastership—which has come down to modern times.

Other cares soon made him take the road of the Alps again, doubtless in August, 1233.

It was most probably during this summer of 1233 that the journey by the St Gotthard took place which is told of in the miracle stories of the *Vitae Fratrum*. The text says positively that Jordan was on his way from Lombardy to Germany. On the other hand, the crowd of travellers in the inn indicates a traffic which could not take place in these regions except at the height of summer. Jordan did not cross the Alps in the Lombardy-Germany direction until after the chapter of Bologna in 1225; he was then with Henry of Cologne; they had taken the most direct way for them, the Brenner; the Gotthard was not then frequented; in 1231, Jordan was to have followed this route with Henry the German, but sickness prevented it. In the intermediate years (1222-24-26-28-30-32-34), it was in the other direction, from France, Alsace or Provence to Lombardy that the Master came; in 1235, the chance is that he was again held back by poor health; in 1236 the Most General Chapter was at Paris.

Only the summer of 1233 fits in with this itinerary. From another angle, seeing the way the people crowded round, at every halting-place, to see the Friars Preachers and seek their prayers, it would seem that something of the 'great devotion' of the Alleluia and some echo of the ceremonies of the translation of St Dominic and of the edifying stories to which it gave rise, had accompanied Jordan to the pass of St Gotthard and the Uri country.

Coming from Rome or from Bologna, he must have gone by way of Milan. He was in the company of two Brothers and a secular cleric, rich and noble, whose name we do not know, who later on was to become a Dominican. Behind other pilgrims, they climbed the wild, rocky road, crossed the pass and, tired and hungry, descended to Andermatt at the end of the day. It was late; the innkeeper had only two loaves of bread, which he was keeping for his family; and here already at the sight of the Friars Preachers the poor came running. Then Master Jordan blessed the loaves, broke them, and distributed large pieces to thirty poor people, then they themselves, the four travellers, ate their fill, and the innkeeper and his family still had some left over for their supper. The innkeeper refused the payment which the secular cleric offered for the meal, and filled his gourd with wine, so that on the road he could give a drink to the Friars. From Andermatt, the travellers went down across the Uri country; a priest who had been sick for a long while with quartian fever and whose doctors had expended all their resources in vain, was dying. He asked Jordan to hear his confession, and he was cured. The next halt was at Zug where a blacksmith was delivered from an infirmity by the prayers and the touch of Jordan.

If we reflect that in this romantic framework of mountains and lakes in the heart of what was to become Switzerland, popular piety, from Stans to Zurich, from Andermatt to Basle, was already directed toward the Friars Preachers and that soon all through this region the houses of the Friars and the cloisters of the Sisters were to abound, raising most sweet mystical prayers towards heaven, this miraculous journey of Master Jordan stands out in singular relief and is clothed with a poetical charm.

His journey ended at Zurich. The Friars Preachers had had an important Priory there for four years.

The Priory of Basle, founded this very year, 1233, and that of Frankfort, probably indicate then a journey of which the final stopping-place for the winter and the spring could not be anywhere but Paris, where the General Chapter of 1234 would meet.

After the Pentecost of 1234 Jordan undertook the visitation of the Rhenish Priories. Probably he first saw Flanders again and opened Priories of the Friars Preachers at Brussels and at Antwerp. But one thing is certain: on August 5, 1234, he was at Strasburg. There he received news of the canonization of St Dominic.

'I have learned by your letter, most dear one', he writes to Diana d'Andalo, 'good and pleasant news; the announcement of the canonization of our blessed Father and the joy that you receive therefrom in the Lord... I have not yet been able to reach the end of my journey (was it Basle, was it Freiburg-in-Bresgau or further into Germany, or in Austria where the Friars Preachers were established not far from Vienna, at Freyberg?) for the messenger of the Prior Provincial (of the Roman province) has caught up with me at Strasbourg, on the vigil of St Sixtus.[4] But as we had already learned of the canonization of our holy Father, from the letters of Brother Raymond who is attached to the Roman Curia[5] and the Friars of Strasbourg from Brother Godfrey, ... we celebrated its solemnity with joy on that same vigil of St Sixtus.'

The office celebrated at Strasbourg must have been, as in the other convents of the Order informed of the canonization, the common Office of a Confessor. But it is probable that the thought of introducing parts proper to St Dominic was already in the mind

---

[4] In those times the feast of St Sixtus was celebrated on August 6; it was the anniversary of the death of St Dominic. Fixing the feast of the Transfiguration of our Lord on August 6 caused St Dominic's feast to be transferred back to the 4th.

[5] Raymond of Pennafort. Bro. Godfrey of Strasbourg was then the papal confessor. He announced the death of Jordan to the friars of Paris in 1237.

of his sons.

Maybe Jordan drafted something. His prayer to St Dominic *'Sacerdos Dei sanctissime'* long figured in the primitive office of St Dominic. A breviary of Venice from the end of the fifteenth century, which Père Mortier saw, gives the text of it in the first six lessons of Matins. It must have been communicated to the entire Order in this year 1234 at the same time as the circular relative to the translation. 'Now', adds Jordan in his letter to Diana, 'I am ready to leave for Lombardy and I hope that in a little time, thank God, I shall see you. I knew that you had hurt your foot; I have pain in your foot.' A word of daring tenderness, which anticipates by more than four centuries the famous 'I suffer in your breast' of Madame de Sévigné to her daughter.

A departure for Lombardy in September, where the General Chapter of 1235 was to be celebrated, might seem to indicate that he preached the Advent in Italy. But no trace of it can be found for this year.

On the contrary, the comparison of a letter to Diana with texts of the *Vitae Fratrum* and of Thomas de Cantimpré leads us to suppose that Jordan spent the winter in Paris and received at St Jacques more than seventy-two novices. It would be at this time that the entry into the Order of a young German student of great family, Albert de Falkenburg, whom his family wished to take back by force of arms, occasioned an uproar at the door of St Jacques; at this time, too, Peter of Tarentaise, then fifteen years old and still almost illiterate, received the habit. He was to become a doctor of theology, Prior Provincial, Archbishop of Lyons, Cardinal of Ostia, and finally Pope under the name of Innocent V.

Many friars were opposed to his entering. They held that these recruits whom Jordan accepted so freely were too young: 'for among these sixty and more whom the Master received into the Order then, there were some so little advanced in their studies that they could scarcely read a lesson'. But Jordan, an old apostolic labourer, matured in the work of the harvest, replied: 'Let these young plants grow and do not despise any of these little ones whom God has sent us. I promise you that all, or nearly all, will preach fruitfully one day and will work for the salvation of souls more usefully than others whose talents we esteem more today.'

It was a remarkable thing that, the older he grew, the more indulgence and tenderness the Master had for these young men of the schools who, more and more, gathered round him and loved him; more than ever the students of arts were his preference. Neither their youthfulness, nor their inexperience, nor their gaiety were obstacles in his sight to their vocation as Friars Preachers. They, at least, could be entirely formed by the intellectual and theological discipline in the houses of study of the Order; nobody would cram their brains with more or less authentic Aristotelian formulas. Averroism was beginning to penetrate into the Universities. The old Master of Arts had a presentiment of the perils of extreme intellectualism, pseudo-scientific and not truly scientific at all. He who had received Walter of Strasbourg, John of St Giles, and so many other great masters, leaned now voluntarily towards these very young students who were still at their grammar and saw in them, in their candid enthusiasm and their freshness of mind, the best promise of the future.

The years were accumulating for him, and also grievous infirmities. To the attacks of marsh-fever from which he suffered periodically since the summer of 1223 when the first fevers took hold of him, were added still more serious trials of health. Certain people, who did not like him, vulgarly called him 'One-eye'; and in fact, after long sufferings, he was to lose an eye.

He was thus detained a long time at Paris and perhaps, although present, was unable to preside at the General Chapter of 1234. 'You see that the Lord has so ordered it', he wrote to the nuns at St Agnes, 'that I am not able to leave, nor, once again, to assist at the General Chapter.' In the *Vitae Fratrum*[6] there are indications of a General Chapter at a time when Jordan was gravely ill and could not preach to the Brethren. He came and gave them only a few words of consolation, inspired by the liturgy of Pentecost. Then probably about the same time, he writes to Diana: 'I believe it is the will of God that I have been hitherto prevented from coming; if such is the will of God, it is proper that we should mortify our own will until it is like to his; I have stayed at Paris all winter, since the Advent of our Lord; and by the grace of God many excellently endowed students and masters of the University have come into the Order. The last time I wrote you, the Brethren were saying that already seventy-two had been received. As for my health, the fevers left me a long while ago, but one of my eyes is giving me great pain and I am in danger of losing it.' We know from the *Vitae Fratrum* that he did lose it, and when the Brethren expressed their sympathy he replied: 'Let us give thanks to God. He has delivered me from an enemy.'

'One-eye' (*ceco*) is what certain naïve laybrothers would afterwards call him in the familiar tales of the *Vitae Fratrum*. But he was restored to health, a little less lively in his gait when on the road, but always inspired, always eloquent, always an apostle. Following once more the ebb and flow which year after year took him from Italy to France and from France to Italy, he must have taken the road again in the autumn of 1234. It is not known where he preached the Advent. He must at any rate have preached the Lent of 1235 at Naples. We know from a letter of Pope Gregory IX

---

[6] *Vit. Frat.* 3a, chapter 42, 12: Cum in quodam capitulo generali propter gravem infirmitatem non posset conventui predicare, tandem rogatus ut aliquod consolatorium eis diceret, ingressus capitulum, ait: Fratres, in hac septimana (Pentecost) frequenter dicimus: Repleti sunt omnes spiritu Sancto. Scitis autem quod plenum non impletur ab alio sed pocius effunditur quod infunditur. Sancti igitur apostoli repleti sunt a Spiritu sancto quia evacuati erant a spiritu suo... etc... Quo verbo fratres multum edificati sunt.

to the Archbishop of Naples, May 15, 1235[7] that after the entrance into the Order of a novice of some rank, his family had armed a band which attacked the Priory, sacked the house and maltreated the religious, so much so that a man's death resulted. But knowing the facts—probably from Master Jordan—the Pope energetically demanded that the Archbishop should excommunicate the guilty ones.

The memory of this event still survived at Naples when seven or eight years later the Friars Preachers hesitated somewhat before accepting a young student of high lineage who was to become St Thomas Aquinas.[8] The turn of events, its resemblance to the less offensive squabble which took place at the Faubourg St Jacques in the winter of the preceding year when young Albert of Falkenburgh entered the novitiate of the Friars Preachers, is enough to persuade us that Jordan of Saxony was present in Naples in the spring of 1235. His irresistible eloquence awakened, as we know, ardent vocations among the best students and, on the other hand, provoked violent reactions from their noble parents. This scandal marked his preaching at Naples and the memory which he retained of it, for it was to Naples that he wanted to return again when death surprised him on his return from the Holy Land. It is also to this year 1235—we know because of the epithet 'One-eye'—that a rather curious anecdote in the *Vitae*

---

[7] Mandonnet, *Th. d'Aquin, Friar Preacher novice*, p. 42, note 2: Non absque mentis amaritudine Nobis dilecti filii Fratres Praedicatores, commorantes Neapolim, nunciarunt, necnon sine turbatione didicimus nuntiatum, quod quidam filii Belial, cives Neapolitani, fautores haereticorum, ut creditur, occasione cujusdam no vitii, qui ordinem ipsorum intraverat, cum consanguineis ejusdem novitii in domum eorum nequiter irruentes, fractis ecclesiae januis, quosdam de fratribus lethaliter vulnerarunt, et nisi conversi domus ejusdem, et quidam alii eis praesidio adfuissent, occidissent plures de fratribus, devastassent domum incendio, et asportassent inventa ibidem omnia, prout prius fuerant terribiliter communati etc... (Bull Ord. Praed. I, p. 74.)

[8] The similarity of this case with that of St Thomas is so great that some later chroniclers have believed, though wrongly, that St Thomas is meant here.

The Last Years

Fratrum belongs,[9] telling of a friar of Bologna who, possessed by a devil and endowed at this moment with second sight, recommended to the Friars Preachers to pray 'for One-Eye who is preaching at Naples'. The Brethren noted the day and the hour and ascertained later that Jordan was really preaching at Naples at the very moment announced by the possessed friar.

From Naples the Master definitely went back to Bologna where the General Chapter was held at Pentecost.

It was decided there that the following chapter, to be held at Paris on May 18, 1236, would be a Most General Chapter. The needs of the expanding Order and the extension of its Provinces made desirable this Chapter armed with powers as wide as that of 1228.

Nothing or almost nothing of its proceedings was recorded or at any rate preserved in the archives of the Order. We know that one of its decisions increased from six months to one year the minimum time obligatory for the novitiate. On many points, doubtless, it confirmed and perhaps developed with greater precision the Constitutions of 1228.

In any case it reinforced the administrative scope of the first Most General Chapter and continued its work along the same lines. In eight years the prodigious growth of Provinces and Priories had showed that the early legislation was good.

No doubt it was at this Most General Chapter that the journey of Master Jordan to Palestine was decided upon.

This Province of the Holy Land, which was his own creation,

---

[9] *V. Fratr.*, part 3a, c. XXXI, p. 125, Reichert. In Italian, then added by Humbert de Romans. Quidam alius frater fuit Bononiae demoniacus qui dixit Fratribus: 'Fratres rogate dominum pro illo ceco qui modo Neapoli predicat. Gaudet enim multum et vana gloriatur diabolus quando potest futura predicare.' Qui statim penitens de verbo quod dixit: 'Non credatis michi, ait, quoniam ego mentitus sum.' Fratres autem notaverunt diem et horam et invenerunt postea, quod ipse eadem hora et die tunc magister Iordanis predicaverat Neapoli quando demon Bononiae ista predicaverat.

and numbered already, it is said, eighteen Priories, besought a visit from him. Very probably also Pope Gregory IX wished to send the legate in whom he had the greatest confidence on a mission to the Templars and the Hospitallers, military and monastic Orders which were more military than monastic.

Where did Jordan set sail from? Perhaps at Aigues-mortes or Fréjus if he came the shortest way from Paris; at Brindisi or Naples if he had the time to go by way of Italy once more. In the latter case he would have made his promise by word of mouth to the students of the University of Naples to preach the following Lent for them because the account of his shipwreck and death mentions that he was 'making sail in haste for Naples in order to preach again to the students'.

How long he spent in the Holy Land and what was the itinerary of his visits we do not positively know.

The fact that he was hurrying back to preach at Naples, after the beginning of February, leads us to think that he wished to reach Italy before the end of Lent. Also his voyage could not have lasted long. Doubtless he touched at Cyprus, where the Priory of Nicosia, in the vulgar tongue Limassol, opened in 1226, was the oldest in the Province and one of the most important. He must have disembarked at St Jean d'Acre—Acco or Accon, in the geography of those times—perhaps he touched at Tripoli, where the Friars Preachers were established. He certainly went to Jerusalem and preached to the French Templars. A trace of his sermon is found in an anecdote of the *Vitae Fratrum* where Jordan excuses himself for his mediocre French. This may have been at Jerusalem itself. Or it could have been in the formidable Krak des Chevaliers, of which a most imposing remnant of the fortified castle still stands at the entrance of modern Lebanon. He may have gone as far as Damascus.

The same mystery which envelops his last moments veils the itinerary of this distant journey.

His last letter (which seems really like the last because it has the tone of a sad and tender farewell, like an *au revoir* in eternal life above the tempests and the ills of life here below) carries no indication of time or place. It seems only to come from far off and to challenge the power of his correspondent to answer him. He writes to Diana d'Andalo:

'I would like to know how you are, for your progress and joys in God are the sweet food of my spirit. But you are not sure enough of the places I have gone to[10] to reach me by letters, and even if you knew you would find no messenger to bring them to me... It is of small importance, dear one, that we write to one another; in the depths of our hearts is the fervour and delight with which we love one another in the Lord; and it is there—in this intimate affection of charity—that you say to me and I say to you endlessly what no language can express and no letter can contain. O Diana, how miserable is the present state which we must endure since we cannot love one another without sorrow or think of one another without anxiety!... Who shall lead us into the fortified city, into the City of the Lord of Hosts, where we shall sigh no more nor yearn for him or for each other? Here each day we are lacerated and the depths of our hearts are torn, and each day our miseries force us to cry out: "Who shall deliver us from this body of death?"[11] ... Yet we must patiently endure this life and as far as possible in our daily wretchedness we must recollect our souls in him who alone can take away our poverty and in whom alone we can find rest... While waiting let us receive with joy whatever sadness comes to us; according to the same measure by which our tribulations have

---

[10] 'Ad quos fines orbis' in Biblical style, 'to what ends of the earth'. The expression gives the impression of great distance and allows us to think that this letter was sent from Palestine.

[11] Rom. vii, 24.

been measured out, joy shall be measured out to us; we shall be turned towards the Son of God, Jesus Christ, to whom be honour, glory, power and empire, for ever and ever. Amen.'

After the nostalgic appeal of heaven, the Master made his daughter listen, one last time, to the harmonious words of patience and serenity. But he added a few lines more; they were addressed to his 'dear friends outside the convent', to those lay women living in the surround of St Agnes, to the Sisters of the Third Order also, whom Jordan had defended against so many attacks and to whom went his last recommendations: 'Greet for me the Prioress and Galiana, greet our special friends outside the convent, above all and especially those who are in your house when they come to see you, and recommend me to their prayers... Goodbye, dear daughter, in the Son of God, Jesus Christ.'

Perhaps these are the last words ever written by Master Jordan. Did Diana know of them? Did this letter reach Bologna before her death? According to the old chronicle of St Agnes, still available in the eighteenth century to Melloni, Diana would have been about thirty-three years old at the time of her death, and she was fifteen when Reginald came to Bologna in 1218; the date of her death would thus have been in 1236.

The daughter and the Father followed one another closely, whichever way it was, in their passage into eternity. Doubtless Jordan had not time to learn of the death of Diana, and Diana left the world before Jordan came to his end in Syrian sea.

He boarded the ship at St Jean d'Acre, along with the two Brothers who accompanied him, Brother Gerard and Brother Albisus, on a galley whose destination was Naples. A violent tempest caused the ship to founder and probably no one among the passengers or the crew could save themselves, since ninety-nine people were drowned. This took place on February 13, 1237.

The bodies were soon washed up on the shore. A supernatural light, in the form of a cross, was seen by many over the body of

Jordan. The Friars Preachers of the Priory of St Jean d'Acre came by ship, to take possession of it, and also of the bodies of the two Brethren who were with him, and buried them in their church.

This was the news which was given to the Friars Preachers of St Jacques, in Paris, in a letter sent to them from Rome by Brother Godfrey and Brother Reginald, confessors to the Pope. It was inserted in the *Vitae Fratrum* by Gerard de Frachet and in the Chronicles of the Order by Humbert of Romans.[12]

A short while after, the Turks devastated St Jean d'Acre and the Priory of Preachers was destroyed; of the tomb of the Master and of his relics nothing was ever found.[13]

Proclaimed a saint by the voice of the public, invoked after his death by many of those whom he had directed during his life, a

---

[12] *Cronica Ordinis*—prior (Reichert-529)—et Vitae Fratrum (with some slight variations) Part 3a, chapter 37, p. 129 (Reichert).

[13] Letter of Brothers Godfrey and Reginald announcing the death of Jordan. Venerabilibus et dilectis priori et conventui fratrum predicatorum Pariensi frater Gotfridus et Reginaldus, domini pape penitenciarii, salutem et Spiritus sancti consolacionem.

Noveritis quod innundante maris sevicia et suo impetu propellente ad litus galeam in qua dulcis pater noster magister Jordanis cum duobus fratribus erat (Fratres Gerardus et Albisius) ipse et nonaginta novem personae aliae mortis vinculis liberati sunt ab hoc seculo nequam. Super hoc tamen, carissimi, non paveat cor vestrum quia nobis orphanis pius Pater et Deus consolacionis remedium et post tempestatem providit tranquillum. Nam dum iacerent corpora inhumata, ut testantur qui de illo naufragio evaserunt et qui eos tradiderunt propriis manibus sepulture, luminaria de caelo super eos singulis noctibus effulserunt, sed et cruces super eos multe visae sunt a multis.

Ad quod miraculum loci incole confluentes tanti odoris fragranciam hauserunt, ut iuxta testimonium eorum, qui post visa miracula eos tres sepelierunt, usque post X dies odor nimius ab eorum manibus non recessit; sed et per circuitum sepulture eiusdem odoris suavitas lacius emanabat, usquequo fratres de Acon venerunt cum barcha et eos in suam ecclesiam transtulerent, ubi dictus pater corruscat miraculis et multa multis beneficia prestat. Per omnia benedictus Deus. Amen.

(Hanc epistolam Gerardus inseruit libro Vitae Fratrum et consequenter IIa redactione Cronica omisit, cf. Vit. Fratr. p. 129.)—Reichert's note.

cult was formed about him and he was commonly called the Blessed Father. But no official ratification has consecrated this beatification which was conceded to common usage and that only in 1827.

Concerning his sanctity as concerning his person, some uncertainty had to remain, and this great figure fades into the background of the intellectual and religious history of the thirteenth century, and even into the background of the history of the Friars Preachers.

Chapter XII
THE WORK AND THE MAN

O Master Jordan of Saxony, first after St Dominic, the Order of Preachers owes the essential elements of its vitality, its decisive orientation and its particular characteristics. This is not saying too much. The best Dominican historians, Father Denifle and Père Mortier, show clearly that the Constitutions, drafted and codified later by Raymond of Pennafort and Humbert of Romans, had already been established by Jordan. It is around the General Chapter of 1228, so carefully planned by Jordan at Rome under the eye of Gregory IX himself, and the papal Bulls which preceded or immediately followed it that Dominican legislation crystallized and remained.

According to Père Mortier, it was at the Chapter of 1228 that the first book of the customs of the Order was published; and if we follow the progressive unification which took place in the observances of the customs of the Friars Preachers, as for example the regular establishment of the singing of the Salve Regina after Compline, the organization of studies, the duration of the novitiate, it can be established that it is from 1228 and the years immediately following that the fundamental usages of Dominican life became uniform in the entire Order.

This centralization, which reversed all the monastic customs of the Middle Ages, St Dominic had foreseen and certainly desired; it was Jordan who brought it to pass, a thing of unusual daring for those times.

A 'diplomatic code'—the expression is Père Mortier's—guaranteed it from without. The collection of papal Bulls concerning the Order allows us to estimate it—notably the two Bulls '*Quoniam abundavit*' of May 10, 1227, and '*Cum fratres*' of September 5 of the same year; the first enjoins all bishops to allow those Friars Preachers furnished with apostolic letters every right to preach and to hear confessions, under the sole control of the Master General of the Order; the second enjoins the Bishop of Bologna to refrain from intervening in the election of Dominican Priors in his diocese.

But these privileges, which make us think of the great freedoms which the communes were wresting from the feudal hierarchy at this same period, were balanced by firm internal discipline. And if the definitive action of Master Jordan in respect of the Roman Curia is revealed in the Bulls coming from the Holy See, his spirit can be seen in the provisions of the early customs of the Friars Preachers.

It was important that friars should be formed and governed to become preachers; canons, by the obligation of the choral office; monks, by obedience and community life; but still more, and above all else, preachers.

Accordingly, in the first section of the Rule which concerns the conventual observances, already some important modifications of the Rule of St Augustine and the customs of the Premonstratensians, which first served them as models, appeared. The recitation of the Office should be short. Individual dispensations should be accorded to the Brethren, lectors and preachers, to safeguard their studies, for it must never be forgotten that the supreme aim of the Order is the salvation of souls by means of preaching and teaching, and that the special vocation of the Friar Preacher is to study and to teach.[1] The period of novitiate was not to be less than six months. In 1236 it was increased to a year. This shows already a definite significance.

---

[1] '...haec tamen in conventu suo prefatus dispensandi cum fratribus habeat potestatem, cum sibi aliquando videbitur expedire, in hiis precipue, quae studium, vel predicationem, vel animarum fructum videbuntur impedire, cum ordo noster specialiter ab predicationem et animarum salutem ab initio noscatur fuisse institutus, et studium nostram ad hoc principaliter ardenterque summo opere debeat intendere, ut proximorum animabus possimus utiles esse.'

But in the second section, concerning the legislative power and administrative organization, the strong impulse which gave a practical start to an entirely new form of religious life is still better seen.

The Order is directed by the Capitular Fathers. They have the right of correction even over the Master General whom they have elected. But to maintain continuity in this republican government a very important arrangement was made: if any reform is necessary it must be submitted to a Most General Chapter or to three successive General Chapters. The authority of the Priors is also reinforced; Brother Visitors are named to substitute for the Master General in canonical visitations. All this tends to maintain the Order in its own special path, to ensure its asceticism by poverty, its activity by study and the apostolate.

The General has power to release the Friar Preacher from observances which would be an obstacle to his missionary activity. In fact, as seen in this early legislation, the Friar Preacher appears to be very much like a missioner; at twenty-five years, with his studies finished, under the control of his superiors and provided that he is furnished with apostolic letters, he is sent to preach everywhere; he is never attached to a cure of souls, to a parish; he goes without purse, satchel or money, through the whole world. The Benedictines called him a 'vagabond' and found it hard to understand how, in that monastic century, one could be so easily dispensed from residence in a religious house and be at the same time both a religious and a traveller.

Nevertheless, these same Constitutions which put a staff into the Friar Preacher's hand put a book in it also.

By 1228 each novice was already required on his entry in the Order, to buy, along with his habit, a Bible and a breviary. There was no Priory 'sine priore et doctore', without a prior and also a professor. The rule of poverty did not extend to stripping themselves of books. The opinion of St Thomas Aquinas that the intellectual life needs its means and also its conveniences, surely appears also in Master Jordan's smile when he gave back to a too scrupulous novice the Bible which seemed to him a diabolical luxury and, to put an end to his fear of knowledge as a counsellor of pride, ordered him to read it and to study it.

Another preoccupation, which was certainly his, is shown in the custom inaugurated when he became Master General of sending to the whole Order, after the annual General Chapter, a letter of exhortation which was also undoubtedly a bulletin of information, a 'communiqué'. Only the official narrative of the translation of St Dominic, which he addressed to the whole Order, has come down to us; and it is probably more ceremonious, more dithyrambic in tone than his other messages. Nevertheless these circular letters must have been both numerous and precise. The *Praedicator Camuteus* appealed to one of them as late as the seventeenth century as a source of authentic teaching. By this means of universal correspondence, Jordan evidently wished to put each one of the Friars Preachers abreast of what was going on in the entire Order and to knit together more effectively the fraternal ties between Priory and Priory, Province and Province. To achieve unity and to maintain it, to fortify it against internal divergencies born of ignorance about one another, was one of his major concerns.

This desire for unity appears also, after his generalate, in an effort after liturgical reform. This was the work of Humbert of Romans who effected it about 1254. But between 1228 and 1232, very probably following the decision of a Chapter presided over by Jordan, Hugh of St Cher received a commission to unify the text of the Bibles in use by the Friars Preachers, in accordance with the text of the Bible of St Jacques. It is very likely that this revision of the Bible was accompanied or followed by an effort at revising the liturgical books.[2] Jordan, as we know, loved to chant the psalms and to sing; he liked music. It is not temerarious to suppose that at a time when a certain looseness prevailed in this matter, he had the idea of a fixed and unified liturgy proper to the Friars Preachers; and it would be in remembrance of his advice and recalling his preferences that Humbert of Romans later established a Gregorian plain-chant without grace-notes or modulators, quick and virile, which the sons of St Dominic have always used.

Such seems to have been, in broad outlines, Jordan's legislative action. It has been found to be so well adjusted to the needs and aims of Dominican life that the centuries have respected it. In the atmosphere it created, and under its rule, St Thomas Aquinas and Père Lacordaire would both live and both, six centuries apart, freely develop their genius.

As for the method by which Master Jordan had to ensure the observance of this newborn legislation, it was, as far as we can judge, the faithful carrying on of what had been introduced by the first two Chapters at Bologna. A General Chapter met every year at Pentecost, at Paris and at Bologna alternately. Jordan saw to it that the Chapters met regularly, and that they met in these two University cities. He constrained himself, at the expense of great fatigue, to be present at them every time. Only twice was he prevented by serious illness from being there; but afterwards he went over the decisions passed in his absence and, at least in those which concerned St Agnes, corrected them. He built up for himself an idea, very humble and at the same time very lofty, of the functions of the Master General. He who never gave himself any title but 'worthless servant of the Order of Preachers', he who respected scrupulously the inviolable Constitutions which ensured

---

[2] *Analecta Ord. Pr.* 1897 n. 2. 1917-18, 1925-26. The official work was entrusted in 1245 to four friars (one French, one English, one Lombard, and one Teuton) gathered at Angers. In spite of the approval of the Chapter of Angers and of the Chapter of Metz in 1250, Humbert de Romans seems to have corrected it; hence certain fluctuations.

the duration of the Order, had no hesitation in using his power within the legal limits of the authority with which he was vested, and then he spoke and acted like a master. He raised himself, he who had charge of the whole Order, above the particular views of this or that Provincial or Prior; his sovereign regard was for the general interest; he used his right to command fully and with absolute certitude. His letter to Stephen of Spain is typical in this respect:

'... To consider that I have not the right to dispense (from certain points of the Rule) is to believe that the Order has not given me the office of Master General; there is not one of them, however grave it may be, from which I cannot dispense according as I judge it to be fitting in the light of the needs of persons, times and places. I except the three articles which, following the last Chapter at Paris (1228), are irrevocable. With this exception, I have the general power of giving dispensations, of permitting, for example, either travel on horseback, or the carrying of money on journeys, and to give other permissions, analogous or not, for great things or small. If it were otherwise, would I have dared to arrogate to myself a right which I had never been given?'

He showed the same firmness in the veritable battles which he fought to safeguard the future of the Third Order women of Bologna, to maintain the nuns of St Agnes under Dominican jurisdiction, and, in the province of Germany, to prevent the Friars Preachers from renouncing the direction of monasteries of women. He had assayed these spiritual precious metals and wished their treasure to remain in the Order of Preachers.

Master Jordan was a legislator only because he was a director of souls. It is from his supernatural viewpoint that his practical wisdom proceeds. Undoubtedly his lucidity of mind did not neglect material questions; he was an organizer; to use a modern expression, he had 'business sense'. A person does not found 240 Priories (this is the figure given by Père Mortier) in fifteen years, create four Provinces, and leave after him houses which were to endure whether at Paris or Bologna, Edinburgh or Ragusa, if he has not the talent of managing things as well as consciences.

Yet it was only of souls that Jordan thought; the rest was added on because of souls and for their salvation.

Above all else he was a master of the science of salvation, a spiritual director; and herein he trod a path that he himself had entirely blazed. We can say that before him Christian Europe had great saints, prophetic hermits, contemplative monks, ascetics, heroes of mysticism, but that it did not yet know what spiritual direction was. At any rate it has left to us no vestige of it; so much so that certain historians have affirmed that spiritual direction dates only from the seventeenth century.

But with Master Jordan this profound and subtle art appeared in two forms: collective direction and individual direction. In the internal government of the Order, in the education of Dominican novices, Jordan exercised collective direction. With St Lutgarde, the Benedictine of Treves, with Diana d'Andalo especially, he shows himself exercising individual direction.

Master Jordan applied himself to recruiting novices; then he watched over their vocations. Not only was his preference for young men who were ardent and full of promise, but he devoted himself, as much as the duty of his travels allowed, to their training and he watched over the development of their talents. From the time they entered, he steered those whom he had picked out specially: 'Send him (a certain youth of Cremona named Peregrinus, well versed in logic, and very well equipped) to the best Priory of studies in the Province', he wrote to Stephen of Spain before embarking at Genoa for Montpellier.

Albert of Lawingen, without any doubt, received particular direction from him and advice as to studies. But here he was still, or at least primarily, acting as intellectual director, as a professor. His properly spiritual activity can be gathered through remembered anecdotes which the friars now recalled from their youth and repeated to one another with filial gratitude. They remembered how, wherever he arrived, after he had seen the sick, his first visit was to them; how with them he recited the Office, with them he spent his recreation time, sitting with them on the grass in the orchard; and if he desired them to be zealous in their studies, how he also wished them to be simple and jovial, grown children, children of God who lived in the joy of having forever put aside the burdens of the world and had forever given themselves to the heavenly Father. Perfect joy, a Franciscan theme, was a Dominican theme also, a radiant gift which the mendicant Orders brought to the world, Jordan taught to his recruits. 'When he brought with him (to Genoa, in 1229) a band of novices whom he had received in a city where there was no Priory (Vercelli), he reached the inn where they stayed that night; and while they recited Compline together one of the novices began to laugh, and the others, seeing him laughing, began to laugh more and more. One of the Master's companions tried to reprimand them by signs, but they only laughed the more. At the end of Compline, when the blessing had been given, the Master said to his companion: "Brother, who made you Master of Novices? Why should you correct them?" And then, turning to the novices, he said: "Laugh out, my dears, do not restrain yourselves because of this brother. I give you full permission; you have a right to rejoice and to laugh; haven't you escaped the devil's prison, haven't you broken the strong chain which you have borne for so many years? Laugh then, laugh, my dear ones." '

And among those novices were grown men, university masters. But in breaking their worldly chains, they had found childlikeness of heart again. That was what Master Jordan desired; precisely because the Friars Preachers were vowed to study they must have simplicity of heart, the joyful freedom of humour, to counterbalance the austerity of scientific knowledge.

To live simultaneously the monastic life of prayer and penitence and the intellectual life of a student, was a daring new idea. It was not without its dangers, as Jordan was aware. Either the subtleties of theology, new to them, might at times arouse both intellectual pride and temptations against faith in these young minds over-stimulated with the brilliant play of their own faculties, or a kind of supernatural ambition, born of their progressive ascent towards contemplation, might move them to dream of divine favours and high mystical states.

It was by simplicity, and by its sister virtue humility, that Jordan led them along the right path.

To the anxious Prior, who told him of the aberrations in the soul of a novice who thought he had lost his faith, he replied: 'No, Prior; he has not lost it; tell him from me that he believes as firmly as I do myself, and let him be at peace.' And that was all.

To others he told the story of the friar who had for a long time served the Lord in the Order without ever having felt the consolations and divine sweetnesses of which his teachers sometimes spoke. One night he complained bitterly to God. He then heard a great noise and turning around saw behind him a horrible spectre who struck him a severe blow on the back and felled him to the ground. He could only drag himself along on his hands and knees. They took him to the infirmary. He stayed there three weeks paralysed and giving off a terrible odour. Finally he recovered his strength; he had given himself to meditation and he had cured his presumption. He returned to the very spot where he had been chastised: 'O my God', he said, 'I have sinned. I do not merit the least of your kindnesses, I am not worthy of your favours. In justice you have punished me, in mercy you have cured me.' He prostrated himself face down on the ground, asking pardon for his foolish complaints and for his presumptuous thoughts. And a voice said to him: 'If you would receive the consolations which you seek, you must deem yourself as wretched as an earthworm, as despicable as mud.' Then, at the moment when he was humbly rising to his feet, he was entirely filled with consolation.

But there is still another danger, which seems nothing to be on guard about, namely the monotony of religious life. When the first enthusiasm has died down, the persevering effort which religious life requires day by day wearies the young man who has enjoyed the variety of the world. Then distaste enters into his soul and temptations arise. Master Jordan observed one young man thus tormented. He joined him one day in the cloister, at the time when the young man was forcing himself, with a heavy heart, to recite his Psalter. He quietly fell into step with the young man, and when a significant verse was reached, he raised his voice and gave him the response, pronouncing carefully each one of the syllables which the other was saying absentmindedly: 'Expecta Dominum, viriliter age, confortetur cor tuum et sustinui Dominum.' (Ps. 26, 14.)[3] 'Be brave, my son, you have entered into an Order of strong men. Know how to wait, and bear with a generous heart this waiting for God; he will come.' The young man grasped it; he was carried away with courage and hope; he understood that he could have complete confidence in the Master, and that he would be delivered once and for all from his troubles. It was over; they had already left him; he would be faithful until eternal life, and would later tell his experience to Gerard de Frachet.

Sometimes, however, Jordan had the anxiety of seeing one of his sons return to the world. 'For a brother we have left in the world', he writes to Diana, 'we have received a hundred much better.' The triumphant number of new novices did not console him at all for the loss of the deserter. Jordan followed those who had been unfaithful to the Order even when they had returned to the world. He did not abandon one of those who had been entrusted to him, even for only a few days.

Let us visualize this moving scene told in the Vitae Fratrum. It was at a Provincial Chapter. The Master had asked the assembled brethren to pass a resolution concerning an apostate Friar

---

[3] 'Expect the Lord; do manfully; and let thy heart take courage; and wait thou for the Lord.'

Preacher. One of them resisted and refused to consent to helping this brother who had already caused so much trouble and about whom, in his view, it was no longer necessary to concern themselves. Then said Jordan: 'In truth, Brother, if you had given one drop of your blood for this unfortunate man, as Christ gave all of his for you, you would think it right to have some concern for him still.' And the brother, in confusion, prostrated himself face to the ground and willingly gave his consent.

Mutual charity, zeal for fraternal life, is probably one of the themes on which Master Jordan most insisted in his direction of the Order. The Rule of the Friars Preachers respected personality and treated it carefully, much more so than the monastic rules did. It was one of the Dominican characteristics. Seeing that it was conceived for preachers and missioners and applied to men whose hard studies develop originality, it had to have a breadth of spirit which could include the most diverse personalities.

But the reverse side of the medal could show division, the tendency towards quite personal works and practices and, despite of conventual obedience, the taste for 'walking apart from others'. Jordan foresaw this danger. 'It is impossible for Jesus to appear to those who are separated from common action', he wrote symbolically to the brethren of the Priory of St Jacques in Easter week, 1231. 'St Thomas the Apostle did not merit to see him, for the sole reason that he was outside the cenacle. Would you be holier than the apostle? ... I declare to every man... who loves to walk apart from others that so long as he has not more zeal for charity, he will not enjoy the presence of Jesus. For charity does not seek its own interest, but subordinates it to the general interest; it does not know division; it puts its joy in the enjoyment of the common good; it loves unity above all things. Doubtless such a man could experience at one time or other some consolation as slight as it is rare; but he will not be favoured with the full appearance of the Lord if he is not in the house where the other disciples are.'

Even should it be to give themselves to more ardent prayers, to harsher mortifications, to raise themselves to a more perfect life that the religious and the nun let themselves be drawn to separate themselves from the others, their fault would be nonetheless an injury to charity.

To Diana d'Andalo, whose thirst for heroic penance led to the risk of her being carried beyond the common rule, Jordan recommended that she stay humbly in unity with the rest: 'Let your heart be pure. Keep with your Sisters in the unity of religious practice, in concord and in peace; have an immovable charity, a pious humility, guardian of all the other virtues.'

Elsewhere he recalled to her and to all the Sisters of St Agnes the virtue of prayer in common: 'I have great confidence in your prayers, and especially in those which you address to God when you invoke him with oneness of mind all together in your suffrages.'

The work of God is a collective work; no individualism can enter into it without breaking its deep rhythm; and the choral Office is symbolic of the whole religious life; it is by sacrifices accepted and difficulties overcome in the living of community life that we daily acquire purifying virtues and our faithful love of God is perfected, flowering finally as contemplation in our souls.

It was towards this supreme end of their vocation that Master Jordan firmly directed the nuns of Bologna. At a time when it was generally thought that enough had been done for the religious life of women by giving them the enclosure, manual work in common and vocal prayer, he wished them all to have part in the reading of Holy Writ and in meditation; he showed confidence in their virtues and in their intelligence. Even very young religious (for it seems that the following letter was meant for novices who were going to make profession at St Agnes after the Master had left), he taught that they were the temples of the Holy Spirit and ought never to forget it: 'My daughters', he writes to them, 'are bedecked and adorned, but not like the daughters of the world who have the appearance of being temples but in whom there is nothing holy. For the temple of God is holy, and you are this temple... Rejoice in the presence of your Spouse who is within you.'

Let them enter, then, deliberately 'into the joy of their Master', and he makes it precise—of their Master, that is, for them, the Order of Preachers. This is the way by which the Lord wishes them to come to him. Let them have no doubts, nor hesitations, nor scruples, nor turning back. To these 'little handmaids of God', as to the novice who was tormented, he says willingly, 'Viriliter age'. When the first sweetness of their mystical betrothals comes to be followed by doleful temptations, they must not be upset or distressed. 'This war is waged on behalf of the Lord himself, and he himself is your support. What prince, seeing his little serving-maids fighting in their feebleness against very cruel enemies, for his own cause and his own person, would not immediately rise all-powerful to their aid, provided that they have not taken to flight at the first assault but have turned towards him to invoke his help? Fight then.' We recognize here the tone of the man who, during the troubles in Bologna, replied to the devil himself: 'Well, we shall be tempted!' He desired to communicate to the young nuns this splendid gaiety of the '*pugiles fidei*', which is one of the privileges of Dominican spirituality. Let them be for ever delivered from all anxiety by the total gift of themselves 'and also from anguish of heart'. The celestial Spouse would never leave them. 'I have often told you... if your Spouse hides himself, it is so that you may seek him more ardently; so that when you have found him you will hold to him all the more strongly. Such is the Spouse of the Canticle... Be consoled by the very sweet response which he made to another of his spouses whom Isaias shows us forlorn... Can a mother forget her children? ... and even if it could be so, nevertheless I shall not forget thee; I carry thee written in the palm of my hands. If you had this word often in your minds, whatever be your trials, your anguish, or the continued dryness in your hearts, you would never believe... that the Lord has abandoned you.'

Tenacity, endurance, a lasting serenity of faith, in these we have Jordan's spiritual direction at its most intimate. It is in the counsels addressed to Diana d'Andalo personally that its depth is best revealed; to touch upon it we must make bold to cross the threshold of the friendship which united the Father and the daughter in this world and for eternity.

Jordan's tenderness for Diana, Diana's affection for Jordan, is one of those rare flowers which Christian holiness alone can cause to grow from the depths of the human heart. The ancient world never dreamed of anything like it; and if the modern world has known the love of St Francis of Assisi and St Clare, that of St Francis de Sales and St Jane de Chantal, it can be said that in ardour and in closeness—perhaps because the language of the time lends it a greater simplicity—the friendship of Jordan and Diana seems to have surpassed them.

Dialogue is lacking, however, for all Diana's letters have disappeared; but the extant letters of Jordan suffice us to listen to it. These letters were obviously written without any thought for posterity. There is no 'literature' in them to alter their absolute sincerity. There is nothing in them except what came spontaneously from the tender soul of the father and friend. In their grave and simple use of the intimate 'thou', in the familiarity which, far from being interrupted, is maintained by the Bible texts with which they are adorned, there is born an unplanned lyricism, a wonderful freshness, an indescribably deep vibration which, at seven centuries' distance, grips and moves us still.

Of the fifty letters, eight were addressed to all the community of St Agnes, five were sent to Diana and her Sisters, thirty-seven were written to Diana alone. At Paris, at Oxford, at Rome, on his travels, wherever he was, Jordan took care not to forget his daughter. The most precious things of his spiritual life he gave to her, if only in a few lines. He confided to her also his works and his cares. From her he must often have received comfort; and while he restrained her in the enthusiasm of her asceticism, undoubtedly she communicated to him something of the burning fire of her consecrated heart and her enthusiastic belief in the mission of the Friars Preachers. Thus, directed by Jordan, Diana ran with all generosity in pursuit of the divine Spouse; and she, in her turn, drew him along. Being both vowed to the service of God, both immolated for the salvation of souls ransomed by Christ, it was in God that they were united, in God that they loved one another, and, while sighing for one another when they were separated, it was for God they sighed.

'In him, who is our bond, my heart is always united with thine.' 'Am I not with thee? With thee in work, with thee in rest, with thee when I am present, with thee when I am absent, with thee when thou art praying, with thee when thou dost merit, and with thee, I hope, in the reward?' 'Have no further anxiety about me. If thou persevere in the sedentary life of the cloister, and if I go journeying along many roads, we both do it for one love alone—God—and thou who dost stay corporeally in the cloister, I take with me in spirit.'

Thus death, far from separating them, reunited them for always. 'It is of no importance, dear, whether we write to one another. Who shall lead us to the strong City, where we shall sigh no more, sighing neither after the Most High, nor for one another?'

And when this correspondence of more than fifteen years' duration ended, it was because Diana and Jordan were really united in their blessed rest.

As for the direction which Jordan gave to this soul, chosen above all others, it reveals the character of Jordan, and of Diana herself, but it does not fail to outline, in clearly defined strokes, a method of the ascetic and mystical life.

The fundamental recommendation is 'to live in heaven'. One must live entirely turned to God, take refuge in him by holy desire, by the virtue of hope, seek strength only in him. 'It is for us who wish to reach future immortality to conform ourselves in this present life to the future life, to shelter our hearts in the strength of God, and to work, according to our means, as having placed all our hope in the Lord, and all our confidence, and all our firmness, so that just as God remains always immutable and tranquil in himself, so we also imitate him, as much as we can, in this stability.' This is a magnificent teaching, recalling the interior rhythm of certain pages of St Thomas Aquinas.[4] 'With confidence cast all thy cares into the care of him whose power is invincible, whose wisdom is infallible, whose goodness never wearies.' 'By the loss of the grace of God, alone, are the souls of the saints to be troubled. And if God permit it in thy case, I hope in his mercy that he will soon give back to thee more abundant consolations.' And Jordan quotes St Paul: 'All things work together for good for those who love God and are called by him to sanctification.'

Even in the most severe tribulations the faithful soul keeps serene. Its sovereign calm must be not the work of a fleeting effort but the fruit of a reasonable obedience.

'I implore thee not to let thy heart be troubled nor afraid if thou suffer tribulations for Christ. If we are associated in his Passion, we shall be associated in his joy. But let thine obedience be reasonable so that thou mayest please the Invisible Spouse.' That is the note of originality in this essentially Dominican direction, that reason should play its part in the mystical ardour of union with God. Even the major virtues of the religious life—voluntary poverty, which is richness; humility, which alone can open the intelligence to divine treasures, hidden from the proud and revealed to the little ones; even charity itself, their source and their crown have not their full efficacy except in the balance of right reason. Only 'divine love knows no measure': all that is human has limits; and all exaggeration, even in ascericism, is a vice. Moreover there is a certain false intoxication in the

---

[4] *De Moribus divinis*: opusculum LXII of St Thomas Aquinas.

pursuit of penance, which then becomes an end instead of a means. The humble, sweet acceptance of the griefs sent by Providence is worth much more. That never fails. The joy of 'having entered, like a friend and a dove, into the holes in the rock—and the rock is Christ' does not exempt any soul from suffering. It is by suffering that we buy this blessed future, and here and now interior peace: 'When the soul has drunk the bitter cup of tribulation, it is proof against the wiles of the enemy, and it is repaid by divine consolations from on high. How good, then, and how desirable is this bitterness of tribulation! It brings forth patience, balances the mind... and stores up treasures for eternal life.'

As for the ills themselves, they are transient and should be taken lightly. 'Brief the way and short the labour, and infinite the repose towards which we swiftly move.' This life is an exile, but we shall be recalled from it. This thought puts things in their proper place and gives the soul its rightful importance. 'The heart deprived of Christ is like the chaff from which the grain is gone; it is driven by the wind; when the heart is empty it is carried hither and thither by temptation; but the ear which contains its grain is fixed by its weight; in like manner the heart made firm by the presence of Christ, even though it be shaken by temptation, is not swept hither and thither nor carried away by it.'

Balance, thoughtfulness, prudence, discretion: these words often appear in Jordan's affectionate exhortations to Diana. The danger that he feared for her ardent nature was not negligence, but its opposite: 'I do not wish you to hasten towards your end by excessive mortifications; Those who hurry too much stumble.' She should proceed with regularity and prudence; progress is made by degrees, gradually. She should take care of her health. He wrote to her one day: 'I know that you have hurt your foot; that should warn you to show more prudence in future, both as to your foot and to your whole body.'

Rather than bodily penances he infinitely prefers spiritual

mortifications exercised in the daily correction of faults, the daily acquisition of and perseverance in virtues. In this way prudence is in accord with love and penance leads surely to charity. Constantly he recalls Diana to this path, and when he sees her becoming more moderate and more wise he congratulates her on her progress toward perfection. 'I saw you lately in a dream; it seemed to me that you spoke to me in a way so true and so wise that, in remembering it, I feel the joy again; and you said to me: "The Lord spoke to me these words: 'I, Diana, I, Diana, I, Diana', and he added many times: 'I am good, I am good, I am good'." '

Then Jordan could say: What need have you of me; you have God; 'and he will speak to you more sweetly and more helpfully than Brother Jordan'. 'He alone can and must suffice for souls.' 'Why do I write you poor little letters to try to give consolation to your heart, when you can find very near to you a much better consolation, by reading the book which is always before the eyes of your soul, the book of the immaculate Law... immaculate because it alone takes away stains, it alone is charity, and you find it written with a marvellous beauty when you contemplate Jesus, your Saviour, stretched on the cross like a parchment on which he has written with his bruises and which he has illuminated with his generous blood.'

Here is the final word of spiritual direction which a saint can give to a saint, and a sublime prudence; just as Beatrice drew away and hid her face when Dante reached the bright fields where the river of light flowed, so Master Jordan was silent when the soul of his beloved daughter came into the divine presence.

Moreover his humility prevented him from attributing to himself as director any human authority. 'You believe', he writes to an unknown young Woman—*ad Virginam devotam*—whom he had doubtless seen at Trier or at Cologne, and perhaps later introduced into the convent of St Agnes—'you believe you have received the grace of your conversion by my ministry. For my part, I believe that the Holy Spirit had made your soul fruitful before we met.'

He was not and did not wish to be anything but a docile instrument of grace. Constant and devoted as he was, firm and prudent, he was never authoritarian. As a director of conscience in his breadth and delicacy, Jordan had the Catholic sense of the omnipotent and infinite freedom of God and of the supernatural freedom of souls in relation to God.

In his letters to Diana, Jordan showed himself to be a letter-writer of the first order and, for his times, a remarkably good writer. His Latin is superior to that of his contemporaries; it is more classic, more modulated also; it has more cadenced phrases, happier assonances, and its symbolic imagery, then customarily in use, is less subtle and in better taste.

The religious was served by the scholar; the master of arts, with his great culture, showed through the spiritual director.

The other works attributed to Master Jordan confirm this impression. If the prayer to St Dominic '*Sacerdos Dei sanctissime*' and the letter on the Translation of 1233 are eloquent morsels, the *De Initiis Ordinis*, the early history of the foundation of the Order of Preachers, has the qualities of precision and composition proper to a great work; finally, if they are really his, the writings of the grammarian and still more of the famous mathematician Jordan de Nemore—particularly the *De Ponderibus* which was so long a classic—bear the mark of an elegant and concise style, of powerful thought, which knows how to make play with analysis with an unusual firmness and perception.

In Master Jordan the talent of the litterateur and the savant can introduce us to the art of the preacher. His eloquence, we learn from his contemporaries, was mesmeric; yet it must be admitted that the few texts, probably fragments from some transcriptions of old notes of his sermons, which are offered to us by the *Vitae Fratrum*, by Thomas de Cantimpré and Stephen of Bourbon, are reduced to anecdotes and are of such a nature as to disappoint anyone who expects to discover in them a great orator.

On the other hand it can be said that there were two kinds of eloquence in the thirteenth century: university eloquence and popular eloquence. Doubtless, the sermons to the clergy were in Latin, with many Scriptural quotations, and those to the people in the vernacular. But we cannot prove that it was not the same sermon, or almost the same. The edifying anecdotes credited to Jordan have a touch of heartiness, sometimes a vein of humour raw enough to strike an unlettered audience. For example on the last day and the judgment, there is the story of a great sinner who had never neglected, each night before going to bed, to sign his forehead, lips and heart with the saying: 'Jesus of Nazareth, King of the Jews, have pity on me, O Lord.' One night he died suddenly and was delivered to the demons in horrible darkness. But an angel of light came to him and touched him with his finger, and there on his head, his face and his breast shone out three lights in the form of crosses and made the demons draw back. He went through a sort of frightening tunnel at the end of which the angel appeared to him again and told him that the Lord Jesus had had pity on him because of the devotion which he had showed to his royalty and that he was allowed to return to life to do penance and to make a good death. And so it came to pass.

There is the story, too, of the good woman who believed firmly in the prophecy of the cuckoo's call. This was doubtless a peasant superstition; as often as one heard the call of the cuckoo, when he began to sing in the first days of May after the long winter silence, so many years had one still left to live. She was very old, very shaky, very bent, this good woman, but she had heard the cuckoo five times this spring and rejoiced that she had five more years to live. A few days later she fell sick unto death. Her daughter urged her to confess to the priest; she would not hear of it; she had five years to live! To every exhortation she replied by saying: 'Cuckoo'. And, no longer able to speak, she died while holding up five impenitent fingers!

But is not the tone, the accent, the same in the other anecdotes which were only meant for clerics? Let us judge. This is one of Stephen of Bourbon's stories, the story of a religious who adjured a demon by whom he was presented to tell his name; and the other replied that he was called 'A thousand artifices' because he had a thousand ways, a thousand tricks to seduce men. 'Let me tell you', he said to him, 'that I lead astray great theologians, decretists and lawyers, as well as barons, soldiers, magistrates and merchants'; and he began to mimic the words, gestures and manners of all these, even to the antics of the young chamber-maids who waited on ladies in their rooms, flattering them by idle tattle and wheedling words.

There was the story of a handsome young man who could not decide to embrace poverty and to enter the Order; Jordan advised him to contemplate each day the beauty of his limbs and to think what a pity it was that they should be given over to the fires of hell.

If there is more finesse here, there is also a mischievous observation. The Master was not afraid to use the same language to the Pope, before some Cardinals who were one day reproaching the Friars Preachers, charged with canonical visitations, with going too fast in their work and shortening the procedure too much: 'Holy Father, they have done just what I did when after my travels I wanted to enter a Cistercian abbey. My companions and I found the road which led to the door so long and winding, although the abbey itself was there very close before our eyes, that we cut across the fields.'

Quick symbolism, direct allusions, and unanswerable. It is thus that he was preaching one day at Paris on the gate of hell, that is, sin: 'If someone saw, several days in succession', said he, 'a student sitting at the door of the Priory of the Friars Preachers of St Jacques, wouldn't he naturally think that this student was going to enter the Order? How then not believe that those will enter hell who stay so long seated at its door?'

The imagery has an historical savour, suggested perhaps by a recent clothing ceremony at St Jacques.

Jordan must have improvised a good deal, or better, interpolated improvisations for which he seems to have had a special gift. 'All things to all men', he was sensitive to the feelings of his audience, of the presence perhaps of a single listener whom his piercing gaze could read, and he could throw out remarks which went straight to their goal.

One feast day when, after the sermon, the Friars Preachers were receiving a student, he addressed himself suddenly to the audience: 'If one of you were going alone to a wedding feast, would all his companions be so indifferent that not one would want to go with him? Yet see to what a feast God has invited this man; will you let him go to it alone?'

The story adds that at these words, one of the students leaped into the middle of the assembly, saying: 'Master, here am I; according to your word I will join this banquet, in the name of Jesus Christ.' And Jordan embraced him. Was he, perhaps, expecting exactly that?

These improvisations sometimes took on a less concrete, more spiritual character. One day when he was sick, he was begged by the friars gathered for the Chapter to say a few words to them. He came along and, taking the liturgical text of the day—'They were all filled with the Holy Ghost', he said that only an empty vase could be filled. Let your hearts be emptied of the love of this world and all personal preoccupation, and the Spirit of Truth will fill them.

Here we have the geometrician, the physician, lending his experimental reasoning to the Preacher. It is perhaps not too much to think that what was so original, so new, so precisely 'taking' for the University men in Jordan's eloquence came from its being scientific.

His contemporaries are reported to have said (*Vitae Fratrum*) that 'the grace of the Word which he had received was such that no other could be found like him'.

Youth is the same in all ages; it was to listen to something new, in a new form, no doubt that the crowd of students pressed around Jordan.

Sacred eloquence does not seem to have followed the general movement of the times; to young men in particular it must have seemed out-of-date. The twelfth century had offered the Universities fine discourses, humanist and precious, but to ordinary folk dry explanations of the *Pater* and the *Credo*, good enough for the serfs of abbeys and chapters, but insufficient for citizens with minds awakened.

In the course of the twelfth century, society had evolved very rapidly from a purely feudal regime to a communal regime. In the same period the growing importance of the Quadrivium, the publication of works by the Arabian mathematicians and, through these, the works of Archimedes and Aristotle, were changing the mental outlook of the schools. The notable exception, but one without a sequel, namely the apostolic success of Foulques de Mouilly in raising up the common people and converting the students, had not been renewed. For both something else was needed. Jordan knew this better than anyone else. What masters, what examples of preaching seem to have been his models? Dominic certainly; still more certainly, Reginald and Henry of Cologne, two men of learning who sought less to please than to prove.

The Friars of St Jacques and the students of Paris saw in Jordan, in his first sermons, the successor of Reginald and the providential continuer of his work. Like Reginald, rapid and convincing, he went straight to the heart of things, to the depth of souls.

To the rhetorical fashion of the twelfth century this demonstrator of Euclid and Archimedes, this faithful historian opposed a way of speech doubtless more plain but one more powerfully logical, irrefutably conclusive. The brief and compelling reasoning was based on facts of experience or observation of types which struck the conscience at a vulnerable point.

This simple and progressive argumentation, belonging to science more than to literature, was more convincing than flowery discourses whose charm quickly evaporates. This was probably the secret of the wonderful and effective prestige of Jordan's eloquence in University circles.

He spoke their own language to masters and to students, and he spoke with effect. With him the dialectic of the sciences could lead to the knowledge and the contemplation of God, a novelty which was to make headway; *Reginaldus genuit Jordanum—Jordanus genuit Albertum Magnum—Albertus genuit Thomam Aquinatis.*

Nevertheless, even for intellectuals something else besides pure intelligence is required. The most intimate pages of *De Initiis Ordinis* and the letters to Diana still bring to us a certain human grace, tender, alive and lovable. Jordan has the gift, rare among intellectuals, of perfect naturalness which being without formality frees the sentiments and emotions. It was doubtless by his openheartedness, no less than by the authority of his knowledge, that he remained even in his old age so close to young men, so beloved by them, and so truly their friend.

His contemporaries have told us that he was as eloquent in familiar conversation as in his sermons. Robert Grosseteste, Bishop of Lincoln, writes that he retained an unforgettable memory of the private interviews which the Master granted to him in Oxford. No doubt Jordan was, as we say today, a conversationalist. Not perhaps dazzling; better than that, he was one who could enter into the mind of those who were speaking to him, listen to them, understand them, speak to them in a manner that accorded with their condition, their character and their needs. 'I have endeavoured', he himself said, according to Humbert of Romans, 'to penetrate into the saying of the Apostle: *Omnibus omnia factus sum*—I have made myself all things to all men. I have endeavoured to conform to others without deforming myself, whether it be to knight, to religious, to student, to one who is tempted, in fine to all.'

To have drawn into the Order so many masters and students of the Universities he must have seen much of them in other and closer ways than from the height of his professorial chair. It was in more secret conversations, in the cloister of Bologna or St Jacques, under the shadows of Oxford, perhaps also on the roads which he travelled so much, in the bypaths of the Alps where he met students who were travelling, it was thus that he took hold of their souls and made them read their own vocations there.

For this, sweetness would not have been enough. Something more gripping was needed. Master Jordan exercised a dominating power on mind and will. Walter of Strasbourg, who felt the force of this while resisting Jordan before abandoning himself wholly to him, spoke of him to the students of Vercelli as 'a bewitching power'.

Something more than eloquence properly so-called comes into action in an irresistible attraction of this sort. It emanates from what makes a man to be himself—this man and no other—from his originality and his genius.

Jordan had not the blazing genius of St Dominic; he did not have those illuminations which brought forth imperious decisions, unexpected initiatives, actions of tremendous import. He had not that superabundance of charity which seems to have produced in a few years, like an accidental flowering, a creation such that a whole long life's effort and the concentration of all the faculties of an exceptional man could only have outlined.

His own sphere was not to create but to actualize. A well-balanced personality, at once energetic and gentle, a complete man, a true master, he wished nevertheless to be a man of one preoccupation. It was in order to ensure the recruiting of the Order in the world of learning that he went through Europe in every direction, teaching and directing, preaching and praying. It was in order to guarantee its future and to ensure its traditions that he made himself the historian of its beginnings. It was in order to make possible its fruitful development, in doctrine and in merits, that he first put science at the service of the Faith.

He did not dissipate the multiple talents with which he was endowed. Without mixing with the world he knew how to act upon it. To explain his immense work, his influence on the students, his part in the ending of the Paris University crisis, the mystery of his eloquence, of his personality, we must have recourse to hypothesis.

And yet, Father, Master, friend ever young to those who dedicate themselves to the world of thought, you are not far from us. Has not this century some resemblance to your own? Especially those two ills of the mind, eagerness to find instruction outside the sure ways and ignorance of doctrine even in souls of good will, are these not chronic in poor humanity?

Christian students and professors are not lacking among us. But so many of them have in their souls one closed section, with water-tight compartments, for their personal convictions, and another, equally tight closed, for their professional life.

Against this paradoxical lack of coherence you would set yourself, tolerant and liberal, but strong. You could not suffer anyone to be set out in quest of truth in the sciences without going on to the total truth which is in God alone; you would have understood nothing of our excessive specialization, our arid divisions and sub-divisions between the divers modes of human thought, and you would have been as surprised to have presented to you a great savant without the knowledge of salvation, as you would have been to have an accountant praised as scrupulously honest in his office and outside it a forger and thief.

You have made practical use of this unity of powers of the soul inhabited by grace, which makes of man the most harmonious being in creation if he does but consent not to disturb the balance himself: a magnificent simplification which can still be a lesson to our complexities which have no rule.

Master, you have walked through all our lands, sampled our towns and countrysides; you loved those turbulent students whom you came to teach; and you gathered around you an incomparable band of chosen ones whose talents you strengthened and whose souls you lifted to great heights. Do not abandon your heirs and sons. Do not abandon the young men of the schools. Give them masters who are the friends of God. Obtain for us servants of God who shall be masters.

THE END

www.ingramcontent.com/pod-product-compliance
Lightning Source LLC
Chambersburg PA
CBHW010824070526
44583CB00022B/2929